Paul Devereux is an experienced and respected author and researcher primarily dealing with archaeological themes and ancient lifeways. His work spans the range from academic to popular. He has written or co-written over twenty books since 1979. He has also written a range of peer-reviewed academic papers. Other aspects of his work include the investigation of unusual geophysical phenomena, and consciousness studies: he is a Research Fellow of ICRL (International Consciousness Research Laboratories), Princeton, USA, and collaborates with scientific researchers.

Selected titles by the same author:

HAUNTED LAND

STONE-AGE SOUNDTRACKS

THE SACRED PLACE

THE ILLUSTRATED ENCYCLOPEDIA OF ANCIENT EARTH MYSTERIES

THE LONG TRIP

RE-VISIONING THE EARTH

LINES ON THE LANDSCAPE

EARTH LIGHTS

EARTH LIGHTS REVELATION

THE LEY HUNTER'S COMPANION

LIVING ANCIENT WISDOM

UNDERSTANDING AND USING ITS PRINCIPLES TODAY

PAUL DEVEREUX

RIDER

LONDON · SYDNEY · AUCKLAND · JOHANNESBURG

1 3 5 7 9 10 8 6 4 2

First published in 2002 by Rider,
an imprint of Ebury Press, Random House,
20 Vauxhall Bridge Road, London SW1V 2SA

Random House Australia (Pty) Limited
20 Alfred Street, Milsons Point, Sydney,
New South Wales 2061, Australia

Random House New Zealand Limited
18 Poland Road, Glenfield,
Auckland 10, New Zealand

Random House South Africa (Pty) Limited
Endulini, 5A Jubilee Road,
Parktown 2193, South Africa

The Random House Group Limited Reg. No. 954009

Papers used by Rider are natural, recyclable products made from wood grown in sustainable forests.

Typeset by seagulls
Printed and bound by Mackays of Chatham plc, Kent

A CIP catalogue record for this book
is available from the British Library

ISBN 0-7126-1287-4

To study something of great age until one grows familiar with it and almost to live in its time, is not merely to satisfy a curiosity or to establish aimless truths . . . By the recovery of the Past, stuff and being are added to us; our lives which, lived in the present only, are a film or surface, take on body – are lifted into one dimension more. The soul is fed.

Hilaire Belloc, *The Old Road*

CONTENTS

INTRODUCTION

Recovering Ancient Wisdom

When we visit the sacred monuments and temples of antiquity, or learn of the rituals and religious beliefs of ancient and traditional peoples, we are peering down into the deep well of the human mind and soul. We are encountering the remnants of the world-views and spiritual or psychological insights of our ancestors. These ruins and remnants are sometimes referred to as 'ancient wisdom' or 'lost knowledge'. These are adequate as general terms, as long as we bear in mind that our ancestors were not always wise, and their knowledge is not completely lost. Attempting to discern what is left and of value to us today is somewhat like finding a jigsaw or mosaic with its pieces scattered or missing. Careful sifting is required to find the pieces of ancient wisdom that can add something to our modern perceptions, thinking, or feelings.

We will never again be the ancient people who erected Stonehenge or the pyramids, nor should we be. It is not a question of going 'back to the caves'. But what we can seek to access are the *principles* that underpinned some of the themes of ancient wisdom, and to re-adapt them for our own times and situation. Principles are perennial – they do not age.

How this book works

This book is divided into four parts, each of which focuses on one of the primary themes underpinning the main patterns of ancient thinking. They are not to be confused with what are called 'ancient mysteries' or 'earth mysteries' in today's popular terminology: topics like 'ley lines', 'earth energies', 'ancient astronomy', 'occultism', and suchlike are ***our*** notions and creations, not those of the ancient mind. Although aspects of these kinds of topics are discussed and placed in context where they warrant it, it is the understanding of the actual nature of ancient wisdom itself that is the purpose of this book.

Each of these parts of the book is divided into three main sections:

Overview: an informed, comprehensive description of the theme in general, and its manifestations worldwide. This section is the heart of each part of the book, providing you with a solid foundation for understanding the subject.

Site Examples: a brief sampling of real-world places that express or embody the theme, so demonstrating that we are not just dealing with abstract or invented ideas about the past.

Principles and Practice: a final section where the basic principles underlying the theme are identified and brought into a modern context, followed by a selection of exercises or experiments that draw on those essential principles.

About the exercises

The practical work is not, therefore, intended to turn you into some kind of a cultural throwback, but rather to offer you different, alternative ways of seeing, thinking or feeling. It can extend your experience as a human being if you allow it to and work at it. You are invited to pick and choose among the various exercises and activities described. There is no need to tackle them all, unless you feel so inclined. They range from the (deceptively) simple to the more demanding, requiring time and effort. Try out the ones that most appeal to you. I have tried to write the descriptions of the practical experiments in such a way that I hope you will be able to catch a glimpse of the changes in thought and perception they are about even if you do no more than read them! Whatever your choice, rest assured that the exercises presented in the following pages have all been used in some context or other, and I have personally experienced them, though not necessarily in the neat and tidy way they are presented here for your use. Earlier versions of some of those described here have appeared in other works of mine in different contexts, notably 'ecopsychological' ones, but most of them have never before been presented in an 'ancient wisdom' framework. Indeed, to the best of my knowledge, this is the first practical book of its kind.

There are two fundamental types of exercises included here: one focuses on making psychological and perceptual adjustments, while the other kind indicates various outdoor activities – 'fieldwork', we might say. Both types are safe, but it would simply be common sense to be cautious if you have a marked propensity towards feelings of unreality or dissociation. In the end, the execution of any of the exercises must remain your own responsibility.

The exercises should be used on only a temporary basis, for it is important that you return to the normal everyday perspectives of the world you belong to.

Glancing out of the corners of our eyes

The contents of the following pages can be thought of as an antidote to the ever-encroaching cultural globalisation we are being subjected to at the start of the third millennium. This cultural homogenisation is building on itself at a rate and scale never seen before. With the rocketing speed of communication and travel, and the increasing international nature of media and commerce, a distinct 'monoculture' is beginning to enfold the world. There may be many societies covered by that monoculture, but they all share essentially similar views on reality. It is always difficult for people to think in terms outside those of the cultural system in which they are immersed, and because our modern culture is not bound to a defined region, it poses special problems in this regard, and has great bearing on how we view the world.

The hallmark of Westernised culture is modern science and technology, and this has devised ways to make itself portable, and now acts on the world like no other knowledge system has managed to do before. It is important that we realise this, otherwise we can all too easily lapse into the assumption that there is only one, 'real' way to see the world – our way. It is a seductive assumption for us to make that any other world-view has to be inferior, superstitious. By familiarising ourselves with aspects of ancient wisdom – insights, knowledge, and cognitive tools developed by other cultures long before ours came into existence or, at least, had become dominant – we can catch glimpses of other ways of seeing ourselves and the environment. Even if only momentarily, we can change how the world appears to us by changing our viewpoint. The anthropologist and philosopher Gregory Bateson reminded us that 'two descriptions are better than one'. Two of anything produces what he called 'news of difference', which is *information* – the sum being greater than the parts. What matters is that you allow in enough other views to season your normal perceptions and ways of thinking.

This book is devised to help you do just that, to glance out of the corners of our culture's eyes, so to speak, and fleetingly share the perceptions of people of other times and modes of thought. In order to do this successfully, the exercises in the following chapters require that you temporarily suspend your received understandings about what is real. For just a few moments, let in the light of another world.

1

WORLD CENTRES

Many ancient cultures possessed the concept of a sacred world centre or navel. *This was a symbolic spot situated in the physical world that took many forms. Because we have lost this idea in our culture it can seem strange to us, yet as we look more closely at it in the following pages it will be seen that it had a sound psychological basis, and one we can reinvent for ourselves today.*

OVERVIEW

Of all the themes in ancient wisdom, the concept of a sacred world centre is probably the most fundamental – and the most pervasive. It literally oriented the ancient mind, giving a people their anchor in space and time, and was operative at many scales, as we shall now observe, starting with largest and proceeding to the smallest.

Sky: Pole and Zenith

In numerous nomadic tribal societies, the starry firmament, the great dome of the night sky, was viewed as the roof of a tent. The stars were holes through which the glorious Beyond shone, and the Milky Way was the seam. The north or pole star, Polaris, supported the celestial tent like a tent pole, for the sky seems to rotate around that star. This is because Polaris happens in our era to mark the north celestial pole – overhead at the north pole, and at an angle above the horizon equivalent to the angle of latitude it is viewed from further south. The Lapps (Saami), as well as the Siberian reindeer herder tribes, called Polaris the Nail Star. The Buryat of Siberia refer to it as the Pillar of the World.

In tropical regions north of the equator, Polaris hangs so near the northern horizon that the extreme overhead point in the heavens, the zenith, often took on greater significance for ancient and traditional peoples there. Native American societies in Mesoamerica ceremonially recognised the phenomenon of the zenith passage of the Sun, in which it passes directly overhead at noon on two days in the year, their dates depending on where in the Tropics the location is. This is a dramatic moment, because all shadows briefly disappear. It was understood at a mythic level that these were the moments when the Sun god descended to the Earth. The rising and setting points of the Sun on the days of zenith passage would also have been well known at any given location.

In the southern hemisphere, Polaris is not visible at all, of course, and there is no southern star to mark the pole of the heavens.

The zenith 'Sky Centre' was therefore marked by some societies using other means. In South America, the Indians of the Andes use the Milky Way, that radiant band of diffuse starlight that marks the heart of our galaxy but which appears to us to girdle the night sky. Anthropologist Gary Urton has made a study of Misminay, a village community of Qechua-speaking Indians, descendants of the Incas. The plane of the Milky Way is offset to that of the Earth's rotation, so its rising and set patterns seem to swing wildly. When the course of the Milky Way crosses the zenith, it stretches in an 'inter-cardinal' direction, say north-west to south-east; twelve hours later, when the band of the other hemisphere of the Milky Way passes through the zenith, the axis will run north-east to south-west. So over a twenty-four-hour period, the Milky Way notionally cuts two lines across the sky, dividing it into four quarters. At Misminay, this imagined zenith crossing of the two halves of the Milky Way is called Cruz Calvario, the Cross of Calvary. The layout of the community reflects this celestial configuration in that two inter-cardinal paths cross at a point known as the Crucero (Cross), marked by a small chapel in the centre of the village. The community's irrigation canals similarly mirror this X-shaped pattern. The Calvario and Crucero could be imagined as being connected by an invisible vertical pole, forming an axis.

Land: Sacred Tree, Holy Mountain

In northern Eurasia and Siberia, the World Centre was often envisaged as a World Tree. The Yakuts of north-east Siberia, for instance, believed there was a magical tree growing at the 'golden navel of the Earth', but the most famous northern World Tree is doubtless the Norse Yggdrasil, the mighty, mythic ash tree where the gods met. Its branches formed a canopy over the cosmos, and from them fell the dew. The mighty trunk of Yggdrasil was thought to link the underworld, the central, human, plane of Midgard, and the heavenworld of Asgard. The roots of Yggdrasil grew deep into the underworld. Sometimes four stags – the four winds – are shown in its branches, along with other animals. In Norse myth, the powerful god Odin hung on Yggdrasil for nine nights in order to gain the knowledge of the runes.

Elsewhere in ancient Europe, it is probable that the pagan Celts used a pole as symbol of the World Tree. Navan Fort, for example, in County Armagh, Northern Ireland, was part of a great Iron Age ritual landscape that included sacred pools and earthworks. Around 100 BC a huge timber temple was erected, 125 feet (38 metres) across, containing five concentric rings of oak posts, which may have supported a massive roof. In its centre there had been a great oak post estimated to have stood 36 feet (11 metres) tall. It seems the tree from which it was fashioned was 200 years old at the time it was cut down, prompting Celtic scholar Anne Ross to point out it may have been a sacred tree, traditionally known in Ireland as a *bile*. She further remarks that the giant post would have formed the focal point not only for the temple, but also 'for the entire countryside where it must have acted as a sacred marker, comparable with that of Goloring in Germany or at Pilsdon Pen in Dorset' (Ross, 1986). It is quite likely that aspects of the Christmas tree and the European maypole (the German *Maibaum*) are late reflections of sacred trees and the ceremonial poles that developed from them (Plate 1).

Such versions of the *axis mundi* figured in several Native American traditions. Different nations of the Plains Indians of North America, for instance, had varying versions of a sacred tree that probably emerged from a single source. According to a beautiful Omaha myth, a council was being held in order to devise a way of keeping the various bands of the tribe together, thus saving the Omaha from extinction. While this was going on, a young Omaha brave out hunting alone got lost in the forest. As night came on, he slumped down exhausted, and waited to see if he could spy the 'motionless star', Polaris, in order to get his bearings. He suddenly saw a light glinting in the distance, through the trees. As he approached it he was amazed to find that it was a tree with its trunk, branches and leaves all shining as if it was alight, yet it did not consume itself nor give off heat. At daybreak the light of the gleaming tree faded until it looked like any normal tree. Perplexed and mesmerised, the young man waited until nightfall again, and as the daylight faded so the tree began to glow again. Finding his way home, the youth told his father with great excitement of the wondrous thing he had found, and the two of them went to the place where the tree was. It was still glowing. The father noticed that four well-beaten animal tracks led to it, as if the tree had drawn together the creatures of the Four Directions. Seeing this as symbolic of the tribal problem, the older man informed the council and it was agreed that the magical tree was a gift from *Wakonda*, and it was cut down with great ceremony and hewn so it could be carried to the village. The tree was trimmed to its trunk, painted, and then the pole was rested at an angle on a specially made forked stick.

In the actual, historical Sacred Pole ceremony of the Omaha (the *He'dewachi* ceremony), the pole represented life and tribal unity, and the ceremony that centred on it involved the distribution of gifts among other activities – such as the skewering of the flesh with willow twigs if someone such as an elder had died – but the full range of the ancient form of the ceremony is not clearly known. It was the practice to set up the pole on the south side of the village leaning northwards at an angle of about 45°. E. C. Krupp, Director of the Griffith Observatory in Los Angeles, has noted that because Omaha territory fell at the latitude of around 45° North, this would mean that the Sacred Pole pointed roughly towards Polaris. This would fit in with the part of the legend in which the young man lost in the forest was waiting for the appearance of the 'motionless star'.

It is interesting to further note that some neighbouring tribes to the Omaha associated the north star with chieftainship; the chief of the Nebraskan Pawnee, for instance, was thought to be the earthly manifestation of the-star-that-does-not-move. The connection was sometimes made by association – the tree trunk used in the bear-sacrifice ceremony of certain Algonquian tribes formed the centre post of a building that was regarded as the projection on Earth of the Great Bear constellation (Ursa Major – the Plough or Big Dipper). The skin of the sacrificed bear represented the Sky Bear, and was hung on the centre post, which was imagined to project upwards to the heavens.

(Yellow Smoke was the last Omaha elder to know and 'possess' the legend of the Sacred Pole, and in 1888 he took the decision to pass it on to Joseph La Flesche, because he knew that the ancient ways were coming to an end. He warned La Flesche that he would have to take on responsibility for receiving the knowledge. The interview lasted three days, at the end of which La Flesche took suddenly ill, and within two weeks he was dead. The Sacred Pole itself, one of the sacred objects of the Omaha, was handed over to the Peabody Museum in the same year. It was given back to the present-day Omaha in 1989.)

There were various other pole legends and ceremonies among the Plains Indians, but the best known today is probably the Sun Pole of the Lakota Sioux, erected on the third day of their Sun Dance. As with the Omaha, a scouting party finds a suitable tree. Then a party of young warriors charge towards it as if to battle. Telling of his prowess in war, one man strikes the tree with an axe on its eastern side, and this is followed by others who similarly strike it on the south, west, and north sides. They are then succeed by a young woman in a robe of white antelope skin who makes the final cuts to fell the tree. It is then taken to the village, and stripped into the form of a pole. When it is erected at the dance ground, sage, sweet grass, and buffalo hair are placed in a fork left at the pole's top. In the course of the Sun Dance, braves are attached to the pole by thongs that are affixed by skewers to their chests. Dancing, blowing a bone whistle, and looking at the Sun, they try to pull themselves free. If they faint, they are revived. (A white American performance artist who repeated this practice in modern times found himself going into a trance which culminated in a profound out-of-body experience.)

For many other cultures, the *axis mundi* was manifested not by a sacred tree but by the equally deep-rooted landscape image of a Cosmic Mountain. Hindu and Buddhist cosmologies see the mythic Mount Meru or Sumeru as standing at the centre of the world, with the pole star shining above it. The physical counterpart of this magic mountain is understood as being Mount Kailas in the Himalayas. This motif of the central mountain can be traced throughout Asia. The Chinese considered their country to be at the centre of a rectangular world, with a sacred mountain on each of the four horizons. Thai cosmology conceived the world as being a quadrangle with Mount Meru in the centre (see Angkor Wat, below). The pagan Celtic version of the Cosmic Mountain in Ireland was a hill, Uisneach, situated nowadays in Westmeath, formerly called Mide, at the centre of four (surviving) provinces, Ulster, Munster, Leinster and Connacht. On its slopes is a large natural boulder called Aill na Mireann, the Stone of Divisions (Plate 2). An ancient text tells how the god Fintan referred to this stone as 'the navel of Uisneach'.

City: Centre Place

The Etruscans of pre-Roman north-west Italy ritually dug a pit, circular trench, or shaft that the Romans tell us was called the ***mundus*** (world) at the centre of a city. From this point, where the two main streets crossed, quartering the town, the usually gridiron street plan was laid out. This shaft was mythically supposed to run directly to the underworld, and was capped by a large stone the Romans referred to as 'the stone of souls' which was lifted on special days, when the dead were allowed to ascend the shaft and mingle with the living, or when the first fruits were cast into the pit as a harvest offering. The division of the street plan reflected the Etruscan view of the heavens. They believed the sky was divided into quarters, each of which had esoteric significance. The Romans respected many traditions from the older Etruscan culture, and legend has it that Romulus brought in Etruscan augurs, or diviners, at the foundation of Rome. Throughout their empire, the Romans always put the equivalent of a ***mundus*** at the centre of their towns, and even their military camps. The layout of the street grid would commence from this point, where the north–south (***cardo***) and east–west (***decumanus***) roads crossed (***cardo*** gives us the ***card***inal points of the compass). In Roman-founded British market towns, the *mundus* evolved into the 'Cross' or 'High Cross'.

The classic Old World example of a city as a sacred World Navel surely has to be Jerusalem, revered as it was and is by Judaism, Islam and Christianity alike (see below), and the form of a city, town or village could also be seen as an image of the Sacred World Centre in other cultures and religious philosophies. In Hindu towns the central temple represented Mount Meru – eighteenth-century Jaipur was built to this traditional model – and the city related to the form of a mandala or yantra. (A mandala is a visual meditation device used in India or Tibet whose basic form is a circle or square with a central dot, while a yantra is a visually complex symmetrical diagram believed to be able to focus mystical force.) This symbolism was deep, intricate and *experienced* – lived by a city's inhabitants – as Robert Levy has shown in his massive study of the ancient Hindu city of Bhaktapur, in the Kathmandu Valley of Nepal (Levy, 1990), which has evolved its own Hindu identity out of early Himalayan, Tibetan and Burmese elements, remaining effectively free of outside influences. This relatively unspoiled archaic city today has 40,000 inhabitants, and its layout is idealised as a yantra within a mandala, and is drawn as such by the priests of the city, containing nine mother-goddesses. Bhaktapur's outer circular 'mandalic' boundary separated the organised sacred space of the city within from the wild, dangerous but generative space of the countryside outside, both literally and symbolically. The boundary was protected by eight Tantric mother-goddesses (*matrkas*), each visualised as being situated on one of the eight compass points (the four cardinal plus the four inter-cardinal directions). Each also protected one of the eight mandalic divisions of the city. The ninth goddess was located in the centre of the yantra. In the actual geography of the city, the goddesses had their shrines around the periphery and in the centre, but not in the symmetrical, diagrammatic order of the yantra. Levy found that this disparity between actual and symbolic space did not bother the inhabitants, who could move around in either, or both at the same time, quite comfortably. The goddesses have open shrines in their symbolic city

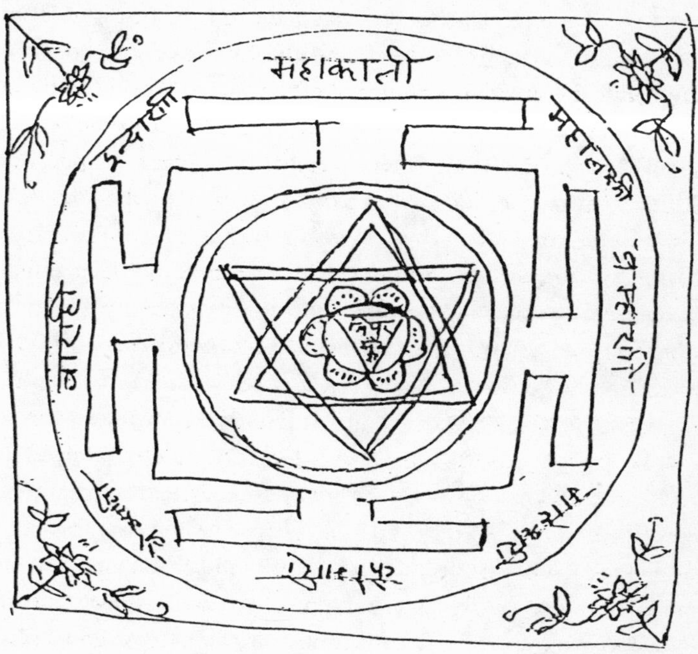

Figure 1: A drawing by a Brahman priest of Bhaktapur showing the city's groundplan in idealised form as a yantra. The name of eight of the mandalic goddesses are written in the eight compass point positions, with the ninth at the centre. (*Courtesy of Richard P. Werbner; Werbner 1989*)

positions, and also a 'god house' in each city segment, where the portable image of each goddess is kept when not being paraded during certain festivals.

This symbolic, spatial and social ordering within the yantra of the city is held together by annual solar and lunar festival cycles, some of which can last for days. There are some seventy-nine festivals in all, but the major ones involve the whole population, and many of these follow a processional route that passes through the major divisions of the city so that the people experience 'the city's symbolic world rotating around them, engaging them in contemplation and action', as Levy puts it. The nine-day solar new year festival focuses on the two halves of the city, upper and lower, expressing the struggles and antagonisms between them, but finally brings unification when a giant pole is erected on the dividing line between the two halves. This pole is fashioned from a tree that may be as much as 40 feet (12 metres) high. It represents a god, Yasi, and the top branches are left to represent the god's hair, and a short pole is fixed crosswise to represent his arms.

So it is that the city represents an ancient model of the universe, of which it is the centre. Its inhabitants live out this model in ceremonial time and symbolic space throughout their lives.

The 'city' form of the World Centre motif is also to be found in the Americas. In *Maya Cosmos*, David Freidel describes how he first became aware of Mayan concepts of the World Navel. While travelling through highland Chiapas, his Mayan guide pointed out *mixik' balamil* – the navel of the world. The Indian was indicating a curious little hill on the skyline. Freidel was puzzled why the 'belly button of the world' should be represented by such a nondescript eminence when there were towering mountains visible in all directions. Years later, when surveying the ancient Mayan city of Cerros in Belize, he found that the smallest and least impressive of the pyramids there was the pivotal structure anchoring the whole groundplan of the city. He excavated the little pyramid, and discovered an earlier temple buried within. 'That small mound turned out to be the heart of the town,' Freidel writes, 'dating from its most ancient beginnings as a royal capital. Like the *mixik' balamil* of Zinacantán, it was a small, unimpressive bump off to one side of the sacred landscape.' He had a similar experience later, when working on the Maya site of Yaxuna in Yucatán. He was seeking the axes of the ruined city, and standing on the east–west axis, he sought a north–south line of sight. He found it a little to the west of the main acropolis. As he stuck the long metal survey pin into the ground at that spot, he saw he was standing next to a large black spider with bright orange markings on its eight legs which were so arranged as to be pointing to the Four Directions. A Mayan helper told him they called the creature an *am*, which is also the Mayan word for a divining stone. Freidel's survey revealed that the spot he had selected was just a few feet from what turned out to be the true centre point of ancient Yaxuna. It was marked by a small pyramid.

The Pueblo of the American south-west have a basic cosmological belief that they emerged from a previous existence beneath the present surface of the Earth. The First People then wandered searching for the Middle, or Centre Place. Spider Grandmother, the Earth Mother figure of the Hopi, persuaded the First People to climb a ladder out of the underworld, and to find *Itiwanna*, Centre Place. She then lay down, and stretched her limbs in the Four Directions so her heart could mark Centre Place. The Zuni have a similar myth that gives Zuni Pueblo, in New Mexico near the state line with Arizona, the status of the Middle, of World Centre. The Tewa of New Mexico consider each of their village centres as 'Earth Mother, Earth Navel, Middle Place'. A ring of stones on the south plaza marks this sacred spot, which is maintained by regular dances and other activities. The concept of Centre, the Four or Six Directions (the compass points plus up and down), is fundamental to Pueblo thought, affecting both religion and daily life which, like so many traditional cultures, are deeply interwined. Indeed, as Hamilton Tyler has observed, 'the importance of direction is so ingrained in the Pueblos that it has become almost instinctive; the whole community orients itself around a center with a rigidity we would call compulsive if it were a question of individual behaviour' (Tyler, 1964).

The Four Directions were notionally related to key stations of the Sun through the year, specifically the sunrise and sunset points on the horizon at the summer and winter solstices. The cardinal directions were computed from these points. The directions of up and down also notionally related to the Sun in that it is seen overhead in the day and at night goes beneath the horizon and shines on the underworld.

Temple: Heart of the World

In Greece and the eastern Mediterranean area, temples often had dedicated 'navel stones' or *omphaloi* (*omphalos* is Greek for navel, synonymous with the Latin *umbilicus*). In their classic form, these stones were usually cone-shaped or domed stones a few feet high, looking rather like upright half-eggs, but they sometimes took other forms.

The World Centre was expressed in many Native American holy places, too. The kiva was the Pueblo Indian 'temple'. This was a subterranean or semi-subterranean ceremonial chamber, used for 'smoke talk', for the conducting of certain ritual chants, dances and displays, for initiation, and for visionary work, often using mind-altering plant hallucinogens such as jimson weed (thorn apple) or the peyote cactus. The largest surviving kivas, 'Great Kivas', were built by ancient peoples such as the Anasazi. We have already noted that the Pueblo peoples of the American south-west emerged from the Earth, according to their cosmology. This point of emergence is symbolised in a kiva by a hole in the ground known as the *sipapu*, Earth navel, which is also the point of spiritual access to the underworld (Plate 3). The Earth navel is given a further spin in Tewa tradition. Their world is bounded by four sacred mountains, one in each of the Four Directions. The long axis of the second plaza at the San Juan pueblo or village orients on Truchas Peak, known to the Tewa as Ku Sehn Pin ('Stone Man Mountain'), their sacred peak of the east. The Tewa consider that at the top of each of the four sacred mountains is a *nan sipu,* Earth navel, in which dwell the *T'owa é*, spirits who led the First People out of the primordial underworld.

Much further south, an Aztec omphalic temple existed on Mount Tláloc in the Valley of Mexico. Probably far older than the Aztec culture itself, it consists of a platform area on the 13,130 foot (4,000 metre) summit, approached by a straight processional way sunk between drystone embankments 10 feet (3 metres) high. Similar banks surround the quadrangular platform. No trace remains of the buildings or sculptures that existed within the quadrangle, but basalt boulders project out of the platform. These clusters of rock happen to rise at the inter-cardinal (north-east–south-west, south-east–north-west) points. This inter-cardinal quartering was a recurring feature in some Mesoamerican cultures, and was a feature of the layout of other Aztec cities and ritual sites, as well as of some of the pages of Aztec painted manuscripts known today as codices. Another rock cluster stands to the east, and another in the centre of the quadrangle. These rocks undoubtedly figured in the rainmaking rituals that took place at this site. The *Codex Borgia* shows the Tláloc ritual, with four Tláloc figures at each corner and a fifth in the centre. It seems that the Tláloc Temple echoed this layout, this sacred geography, forming a microcosm of Mount Tláloc and its surrounding peaks. There is a shaft on the east side of the quadrangular platform that was cut 30 feet (9 metres) into the bedrock, forming a 'navel'.

Dwelling: Hearth of the World

The World Navel was also symbolised at the level of the humble dwelling in many old cultures. At this level, the motif crosses to the more intimate scale of the human being. The central tent post is, or was, to be found in the structure of many tribal dwellings, including those of the Ainu of the north Japanese islands of Hokkaido and Sakhalin, many Native American peoples, and the Khasi of north-east India (Assam). Everywhere it was common practice to place offerings at the foot of the post.

The domestic fire, too, was considered to be the omphalos of dwellings in many traditional societies. In the ancient Roman household the hearth was the seat of the goddess Vestia, and a table containing ritual items would be placed before it. In traditional Irish households the hearthstone was usually in the middle of the floor, and was associated with the Christianised pagan goddess Brigit. There was an old Celtic ritual known as Blessing the Kindling, conducted before retiring for the night. In this, the embers were carefully spread in a circle around the hearthstone, then divided into three equal sections with sods of peat. This 'mandala' was then covered with ash, and the woman of the house would intone a prayer for protection to Mary 'on top of the house' and St Brigit 'in its centre'.

In the New World, the traditional Navajo dwelling, the *hooghan* or *hogan* ('place home'), is a particularly well-preserved version of the dwelling as model of the cosmos. It is basically a circular structure, representing the circuit of the horizon, built from logs over a shallow pit. Gaps in the log walls are filled with mud. Upright posts mark north, west, and south, and the door faces east, the starting point of the sunwise (clockwise) ceremonial directional order. The fire is located in the centre of the floor, and symbolises the pole star. The hearth is in a way symbiotic with the *hooghan* as a whole, for a home in which the death of a young person has occurred can be referred to as a 'no fireplace home'. Navajo chants highlight and emphasise the cosmological significance of the *hooghan* structure.

Body: The Microcosm

If the sky and land are the macrocosm, and the city and temple the mesocosm, then the human body is the microcosm – and such it has always been regarded by esoteric scholars. The motif of the Sacred World Centre reaches its deepest (and primary) context with the human body, which forms an axis between head and feet – above, sky; below, earth – at the hub of the four bodily directions of front, back, left, right. Extended, these become the Four Directions; they are projected on the outer world as the cardinal directions. In other words, World Centre symbolism is in part the projection of the experience of the body's spatial properties; it has a physiological basis, and that is why it is cross-cultural and so occurs in ancient cultures throughout the world.

Each human being has its navel, the point from which it grew in the womb. Its origin point. At birth, this point is at the centre of the child's form, but in the course of maturation its position moves up the body. The canonical (ideal) drawings of the human form by masters such as Leonardo da Vinci and Albrecht Dürer give the navel a *phi* (ϕ) or Golden Section relationship in the

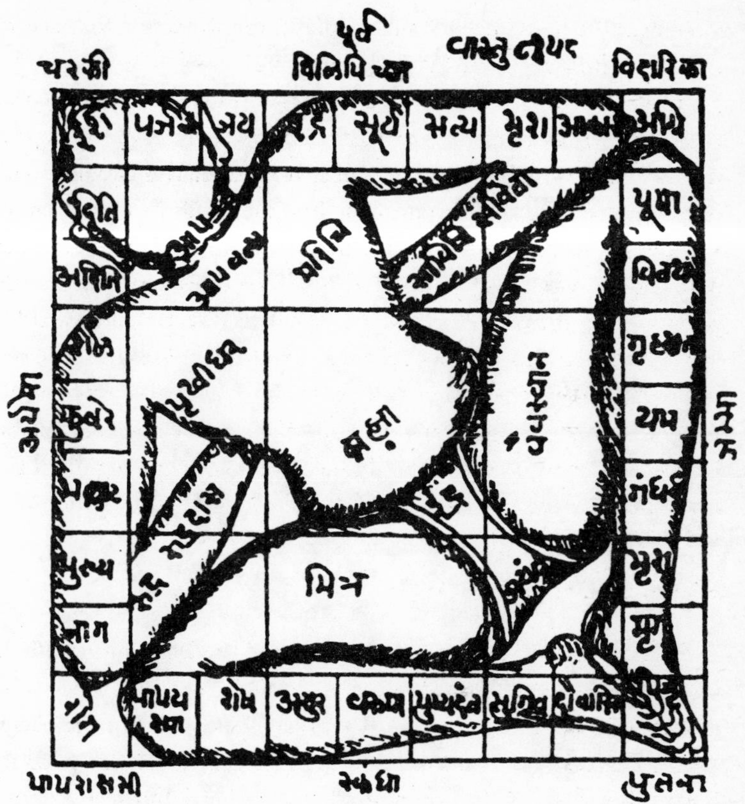

Figure 2: Purusha, the Cosmic Man, shown on a Hindu temple plan.

proportions of the ideal body. The Golden Proportion is one of the geometric motors that drive organic growth, and this is expressed in the form of a growth spiral that can be found in nature in numerous forms, most famously, perhaps, in the conch shell. Robert Lawlor observes that in ancient Egyptian, Greek, and Japanese traditional canonical systems the navel is similarly associated with the *phi* division of the body.

It was Heraclitus who said, 'Man is the measure of all things,' the idea being that the human form contains the proportions inherent in the universe, and that there is a reciprocity between the human archetype and the cosmos. There have been any number of depictions through the centuries of 'Man the Microcosm'. This idea was used by the temple architects of old, because the basic function of a temple was, of course, to link man with the cosmos. So, for instance, the proportions of the *Vastu-purusha Mandala* represent the Cosmic Man, Purusha, the seed image of Brahma. The Hindu temple is what architect and geometer Keith Critchlow calls a 'geometric formalisation' of this undefined entity or essence. A similar idea was expressed by the architects of the cathedrals of the medieval Christian world. In abstract Christian dogma, the Church is the Body of Christ, and the groundplans of physical churches literalised this idea by schematically representing the body of Christ – another anthropocosmic image. The crossing of the nave by the transepts represents the heart and umbilicus area of the Christ figure, whose head is at the altar and feet at the door.

The physiological basis or correlate of the Four Directions and thus the World Navel image may be expressed not only in conceptual projections but also in a bodily fashion by the use of ritual. Anthropologists have long discussed what actually constitutes ritual, what its basic foundation is. David Parkin has suggested that it be seen as always being concerned with movement, directionality, and spatial orientation, remarking that what interests him is the use made in ritual of 'axes, cardinal points, concentric zones' (Parkin, 1992). We can see this in examples such as the Native American ritualist offering prayers and incense to the Four Directions. In burial ritual, the Giriama of Kenya, to take just one example, bury their dead on the right side, with the feet pointing to the west and the eyes facing a legendary point of migratory origin to the north.

Mind: The Shaman's Journey

We have traced the World Centre motif through successive scales from the sky to the human body, but its roots reach into the human mind. This is revealed by shamanism, that most ancient of religious expressions belonging to tribal societies through the ages and

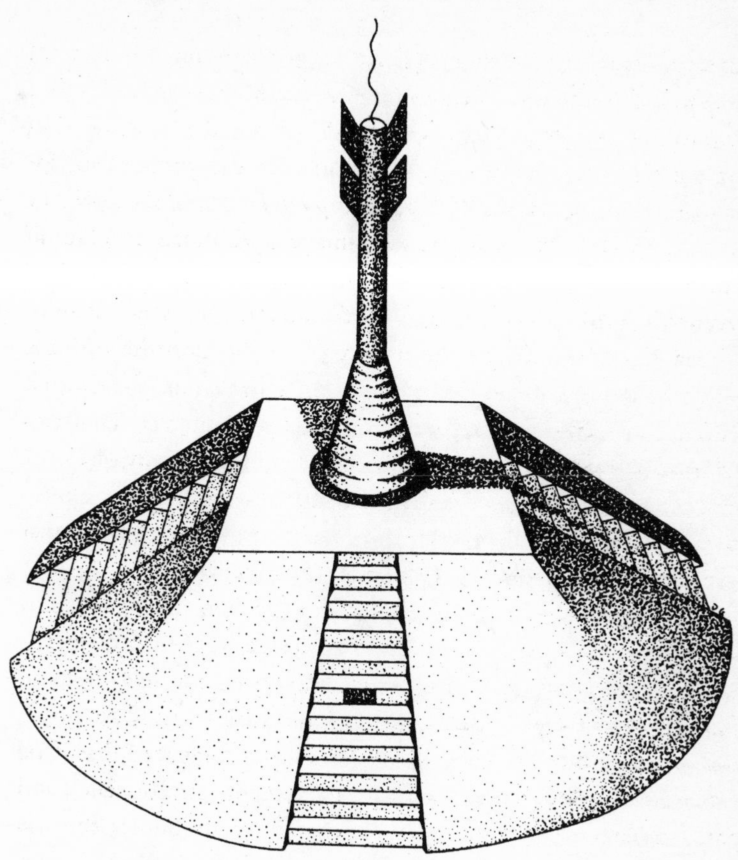

Figure 3: Cosmogram of the Dogon of Mali, Africa. In their scheme, the *axis mundi* is an arrow penetrating the base of an upturned granary basket. A string runs from the arrow up to heaven. The four sides of the basket face the cardinal directions. (*Donna Gordon after Griaule, 1965, in* Brain, Symbol, and Experience, *Laughlin et al., 1992*)

around the globe, in which the practicant enters a trance and goes on an ecstatic ('out-of-body') journey to the spirit worlds on behalf of the tribe. The basic cosmological model of shamanism is of three worlds connected by a 'vertical' axis: the underworld, the middle world of human existence, and the upperworld of the gods – as was noted earlier in the image of Yggdrasil. In some societies this model has developed into more complex forms, but this is the basic template. Depending on the culture, the vertical axis was imaged as a World Tree, a Cosmic Mountain, a pole, a spindle, and many other things. In trance, the shaman used this *axis mundi* to access the upper and lower worlds. In Siberia, the frame of a shaman's drum was said to have been fashioned from a branch of the World Tree, and sometimes the drum skin would carry an image of the primordial tree, or it was emblazoned on the shaman's ceremonial robe. The Siberian Chukchee saw the pole star as a hole in the sky through which the otherworld could be accessed. The spirit of the entranced Siberian shaman was thought to rise with the smoke of the central fire through the smokehole of the yurt, or else the shaman would cut notches in a pole, perhaps the central tent pole, and climb it during his seance to symbolise his ascent of the World Tree. This happened not only in Eurasia but around the world, and in some cases shamans actually made flapping motions with their arms at the top of a pole to indicate spirit flight.

The 'axis' connecting the three worlds was a concept to express the idea of a passage between the worlds. It was a way of describing profound experiences in altered states of consciousness, for it is these mental realities that form the esoteric core of the whole Sacred World Centre image.

SITE EXAMPLES

Jerusalem

The site was occupied as far back as the fourth millennium BC, and the sacred core of Jerusalem became what is known as Temple Mount. It was the site of the legendary Temple of Solomon, originally conceived by David to house the Ark of the Covenant. A series of temples were reconstructed on the spot after various sackings of Jerusalem, the most notable being the so-called Second Temple built by Herod, in the course of which Temple Mount was augmented by a massive platform. The Romans destroyed this temple in AD 70, and a temple to Jupiter

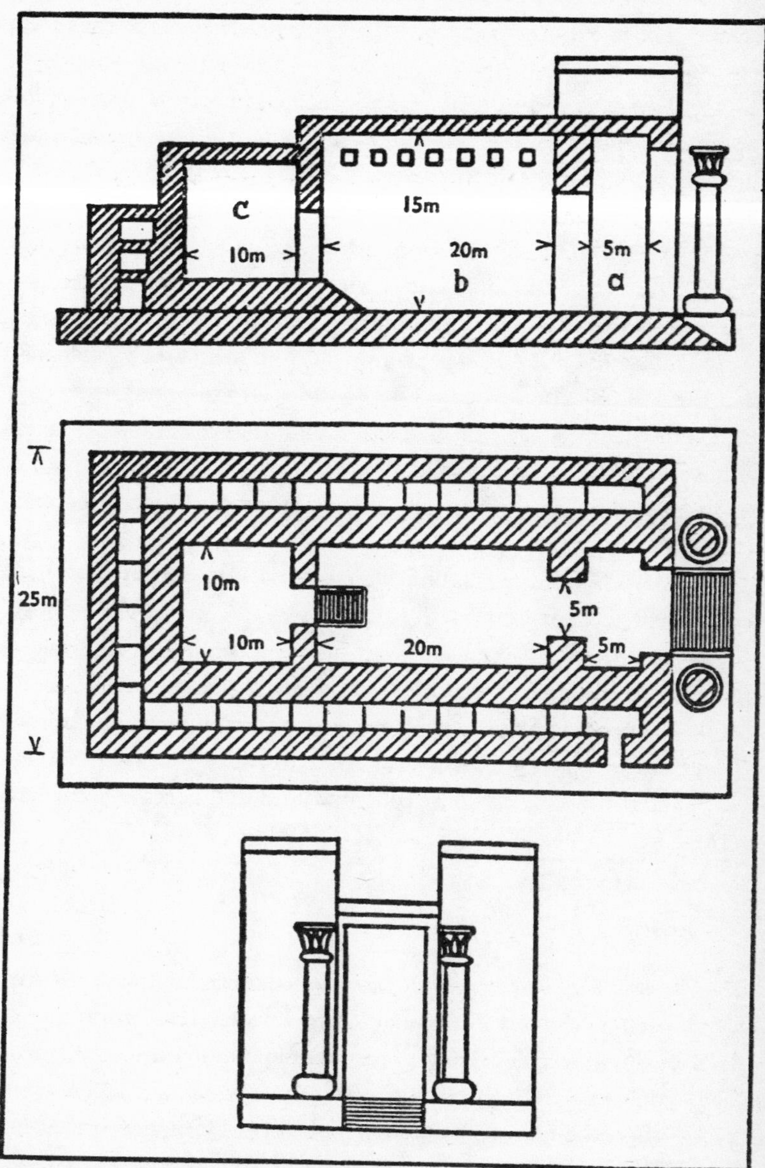

Figure 4: Suggested plan and elevations of the Temple of Solomon. (*From C. Watzinger,* Denkmäler Palästinas, *1933–5*)

was erected on the site. After AD 325, Jerusalem experienced three centuries of Christian domination. Then the Muslims conquered the city, building a mosque, the Dome of the Rock, on Temple Mount.

The Jewish perception of Jerusalem is conveyed in Hershon's *Talmudic Miscellany*: 'The land of Israel is situated in the centre of the world, and Jerusalem in the centre of the land of Israel, and the Temple in the centre of Jerusalem, and the Holy of Holies in the centre of the Temple, and the foundation-stone on which the world was founded is situated in front of the ark.' Christianity marked its claim on Jerusalem as World Navel at both a local level and at a global, conceptual level. Locally, the navel point for the Christians was the Hill of Golgotha, the site of the crucifixion and resurrection. On this hill, the Christians built the Martyrium basilica and Anastasis (Resurrection) rotunda, today known as the Church of the Holy Sepulchre. Pilgrims of old called a stone in the choir of this church 'the Compass of the Lord'.

The World Navel perception of Jerusalem was portrayed at the conceptual level by medieval Christians in their *mappae mundi* (maps of the world), which were essentially religious diagrams showing Jerusalem in the centre. The Ebstorf map of 1235 is one of these schematic maps, with Christ's head in the east (which was always at the top on medieval ecclesiastical maps), the hands at the north and south sides of the circular border, and the feet at the west. Jerusalem is specifically located at Christ's navel.

Delphi

The classic ancient site expressing the 'sacred centre' theme has to be Delphi, a moody and atmospheric Greek oracle temple complex dramatically situated on the lower slopes of Mount Parnassos above the northern shore of the Gulf of Corinth. It was active as a sacred place early in the first millennium BC, said to have been dedicated to Gaia, the ancient Greek Earth goddess, and the abode of the she-serpent, Python. There are two founding legends. One tells of a herdsman, Koretas, who happened across a chasm issuing fumes that caused him to fall into a trance in which he saw visions of the future. The other says that Zeus released his two eagles (or swans or ravens) from the eastern and western ends of the Earth respectively, and where they flew past each other was considered the centre, the navel, of the world, and was marked with a stone. The pseudo-history of the place then records that the shamanic god Apollo came along and put down Python, the serpentine symbol of the Earth. This is probably the folk memory of the usurpation of a Bronze Age goddess shrine by a later Apollo cult. Today's ruins of the Temple of Apollo at Delphi date from c. 400 BC. The prophetesses of the Apollo cult were known as Pythia, in remembrance of the original serpent. Delphi was active for over a thousand years: it was the major oracle of its age and carried considerable influence. Kings and military leaders were among those who consulted it.

Figure 5: Drawing of a fifth-century BC relief from Sparta showing Apollo (left) with Artemis. An omphalos stone stands between them, along with two birds facing opposite directions. (*W. H. Roscher*)

Within the steep sacred precinct at Delphi are the ruins of various shrines and temples, an amphitheatre, a stadium, and other features, with a Sacred Way winding up through them. There are two surviving world navel stones or *omphaloi* in the complex. One is a plain grey rock shot through with veins of quartz, shaped like the nose cone of a missile and now standing alongside the Sacred Way. The second is a larger domed object, its surface carved with a curious lattice pattern or net, and said to be a Roman copy of an earlier version (Plate 4). This sandy-coloured stone was found by the south wall of the Temple of Apollo, but now stands in the small museum at the site. (We will look at the oracular characteristics of Delphi in Part Four, when considering the theme of divination.)

Many temples of this period in the eastern Mediterranean region had their own navel stones. The omphalos at Delos, another Greek oracle temple, was carved with an encircling serpent, as was that at Pergamum, a Greek temple in Turkey. The serpent represented the seething forces of the Earth, held down by the umbilical stone, with perhaps reference towards Python of Delphi. Some other depictions of *omphaloi* on early coins and relief carvings show a domed stone flanked on either side by a bird, their heads turned away in opposite directions – presumably a reference to the founding myth of Delphi involving the birds of Zeus.

Angkor Wat

Angkor Wat is part of a huge sacred complex in Cambodia (Kampuchea) over twice the size of Manhattan, containing more than seventy monuments. Its full extent was not realised until air photographs were taken after World War II. The complex was commenced in AD c. 900, though Angkor Wat itself dates from the twelfth century, built by Suryarvaman II as his sepulchre (Plate 5). Massive architecture covered in finely detailed carvings and reliefs give an almost cathedral-like quality to the vast structure. The five central towers of Angkor Wat represent the peaks of Mount Meru, the cosmic mountain. The outer wall around the temple represents the mountains at the edge of the world, and the moat beyond represents the cosmic ocean in which the world floats. This view of a World Centre or axis, at the heart of the Four Quarters, surrounded by a cosmic ocean was, we have noted, the main cosmological blueprint for much of ancient Asia. Elsewhere in the Angkor complex, other temples rose out of large constructed areas of water or reservoirs (*barays*), symbolising the same cosmological image. The architecture is replete with symbolism, so bridges are rainbows (rainbow snakes), and it has been claimed that measurements of parts of the structures give numerical equivalents of the years in the great ages of Hindu cosmology.

Cahokia

This Mississippian Indian urban and ceremonial complex in southern Illinois flourished between AD 700 and 1500. It contains the terraced Monks Mound, at 100 feet (30.5 metres) the tallest prehistoric mound in North America (Plate 6). It was the navel of the complex, as noted by Joseph Campbell: 'Since it is in the middle of the site, its symbolic function, as representing the axial height joining earth and sky, is evident' (Campbell, 1988). Monks Mound is surrounded by the remains of many smaller mounds, certain of which were distinctively ridge-shaped, and these marked out the compass points, the Four Directions, relative to Monks Mound. It is thought that on its summit platform the king's or chieftain's palace once stood. In front of this there was erected a massive post which reached tens of feet into the air.

PRINCIPLES AND PRACTICE

Principles

We have seen that the mysterious *axis mundi* was the focal point of shamanic cosmology, being the passage between this and other worlds or states of consciousness. The World Centre at the intersection of the Four Directions is the crack between the worlds, the place where communication with the spirits and gods is possible. Projected outwards beyond mind and body, it is the reference point for ordering the Earth and the heavens, and thus space and time, for it did not only involve the symbolic centre point on Earth from where the division of the four cardinal directions (and eightfold and sixteenfold subdivisions) could be made, it also represented the intersection of sky and land. If the primary directions on Earth provided orientation and thus ordered space, then the division of the horizon marked the cycles of heaven, ordering time. In short, it gave a people their territorial bearings as well as locating them in symbolic space. It placed them in both calendrical and mythic time, and it also helped to map their inner space.

World Centre imagery and cosmology is at base a physiological and mental reflex. It is the experience of being 'here' writ large, and 'here' is portable while never moving. This is literally the crux of the primordial instinct of the World Centre, and why it could exist anywhere, in any culture. 'Here' is always the centre; all human beings are at the centres of their worlds. The depth to which the perceptual and bodily Four Directions are ingrained within us is indicated in C. G. Jung's identification of an archetype of quaternity. He commented on 'the centring process and a radial arrangement'. That is the deep, subconscious blueprint of the World Centre. It is the legacy of the ancient child within us, born anew with each human being: the pioneering experimental psychologist Jean Piaget claimed that children have what he referred to as an 'egocentric' outlook, by which he meant that, perceptually, a child feels himself to be at the centre with objects receding from him in all directions. In Piaget's view, it takes the more abstract cognitive processes which develop in later years to become conscious of perspective and to be able to mentally model positions in space different to one's own.

A similar development can be seen in a culture-wide context with regard to modern society. In former times, the cycles of heaven were perceived from a geocentric viewpoint – the universe surrounded a central Earth, and it was the heavens that moved, not our planet. But with Copernicus, and the subsequent age of thinking we call scientific, the Earth lost its central position in the universe, and became merely a speck in a boundless cosmic space – a cosmos without periphery or centre. This development has not remained simply a matter of astronomy, it has been the foundation for today's cosmology and has thus had deep cultural repercussions, profoundly affecting the way each member of the modern world literally perceives his or her place in it.

Our modern culture is truly eccentric, a word which derives from the Greek *ekkentros*, meaning 'out of centre'. We cannot naturally live in any world other than the eccentric one we have been born into, and it might even prove dangerous and unproductive were we to do so, but we can moderate it, and it is healthy to give ourselves quite literally other viewpoints from time to time. In this case, that means finding ways to give ourselves a sense, a taste, of the 'world centre'. In that way, we might find a measure of psychological healing, relief from an ailment most of us have not even diagnosed that causes us to have a low-key, underlying feeling of being lost, lonely, and restless. We can then better judge the actions of our culture, and get a better perspective on how it behaves in the world. But we first have to open our eyes in order to change our own perspectives. The following exercises are to help you do just that, to subtly alter your perceptual and psychological vantage point for a brief time.

Practice

Becoming Less Eccentric

A simple yet instructive experiment to start with. Get away into an open space, with no one immediately around you. It could be a beach, a moorland, a desert, a mountain peak – even the top of a tall building. Anywhere with open views all around. Stand still, and take a few deep, calming breaths. Realise that in our actual day-to-day experience each of us is at the centre of our world, whatever else we 'know'. Slowly and smoothly, begin to turn completely around. Observe and *sense* the horizon encompassing you. Move your head up and down, and note that the skyline is also your eyeline: it always moves up or down with you. Then consider the sky. We all feel that it seems to arch like a dome over our heads – especially on a starry night. (A planetarium has a domed ceiling to create just that illusion.) But why should the sky seem like a vault, a dome, when it is actually just an unstructured space, a cosmic gap? Well, the heavens are modelled in our perceptions like the dome of our cranium. The sky is what is above our eyeline, the skyline; what is below it is the body (or the land, the body of the Earth).

Watch for a bird, a plane – even a shooting star – to cross your field of view. Permit yourself the feeling that it is flying not only in the vault of the heavens, but also through the dome of your skull. This may seem like a strange thought to have, but, then, you are trying to be less eccentric than usual.

Eyeline/skyline; heavenly vault/cranium dome. Front, back, sides/north, south, east and west. Become consciously aware how the model of your body that you carry in your mind also shapes your perception of the world around you.

Don't worry about anyone catching you performing this exercise – they won't have a clue what you are up to. True, if they do they might think you slightly eccentric, but you will know that precisely the contrary is true. You will also now know that you cannot be lost again, for you are always *here*, at the centre of things.

You have been found.

Round in Circles

Make a circle, so modelling the circuit of the horizon. Be like those megalith builders of old who constructed the stone circles (only you can be a little less ambitious than were the creators of Stonehenge). Find an open spot in a natural setting – fields, moorland, mountains, desert, or even a deserted beach. If not, then a quiet corner of a local park or even your own lawn – but raw wilderness is by far the best if you can possibly manage it. Bring with you a few yards of cord with one end tied to a short stake, tent peg, or similar, and a sharp stick, skewer, or suchlike attached to the other, along with a mallet, a compass, and anything else you feel would be useful after you have read the description of this exercise. Be alone for this exercise.

Select the precise spot where you want to construct your circle. Take your time about this, and operate on intuition. Select a spot that *feels* right to you, or seems the best of what is available to you. Move, stand still, look around, be conscious of standing where you are at, then move on to another spot and repeat, until you settle on a location. The Greeks had the phrase *oikeios topos*, which means 'favourable place'; the word *oikeios* shares a root with the modern word 'ecology'. So be a good ecologist.

When you have decided on the right location for you, fix the stake or tent peg firmly into the ground. Unwind a length of the cord – not too long, perhaps 3–4 feet (90–120 centimetres), or else select a symbolic measure, such as a length equivalent to your own height. Pull the cord reasonably taut and with the sharp tool at the other end inscribe a circle. This can be executed fairly roughly, as long as you get a working idea of the circle's circumference. (It's a good idea to keep the cord extended while you go on to define the circle in case you need to recheck parts of the circumference position.)

How to mark out the edge of your circle? Any way that comes to hand that doesn't permanently damage the surroundings. If you are on a beach or soft ground then it is easy, of course, as your inscribing tool – sharp stick, skewer or whatever – will make a clear, strong mark. Otherwise, you might place small rocks or pebbles at reasonably close intervals to define the circumference. If none are available, then use twigs and other bits of natural debris that may be lying around, or lumps of soil. You might possibly have brought a small bag of sand with you so you could sprinkle that along the circle's rim. You can also be creative and subtle, like the British land artist Richard Long. He has made circles in nature in all kind of ways. He selected a place in the Sahara that was covered in loose shale and small rock debris. He defined his circle by *removing* the rocks, leaving a cleared space (*Hoggar Circle*, 1988). In Anatolia, Turkey, he simply walked the form of a ring into dusty ground (*Walking a Circle In Dust*, 1989). In one of his most beautiful creations, he walked in a precise circular fashion in a Scottish mist, leaving a dark ring in the moisture-laden grass (*Walking a Circle in Mist*, 1986). You will find your way to define your circle.

When completed, remove the peg and cord, stand back and contemplate your circle. The creation of a circle in nature is a primal act of consciousness, well expressed in that drawing by William Blake of God creating the universe by wielding a pair of dividers. Next, enter your circle – slowly, consciously, deliberately. By being sensitive and alert, you will notice a distinctly different feeling being inside the circle from when you were outside. Even though there is nothing of any substance between you and the outside, you will feel curiously secure, even cosy. The circumference of your circle, of any circle, is a *temenos* – a boundary signifying a break between sacred and mundane space. Inside this boundary is what religious historian Mircea Eliade referred to as 'a qualitatively different space'. By an act of consciousness you have created a kind of sanctuary for yourself; it is literally a sanctified place, because both sanctity and sanctuary share the same etymological root, the Latin *sanctus*. By moving into the circle, you move into a different space inside your head.

You can now make your circle into your omphalos point or World Navel. Staying inside the circle, take out your compass and find north. From that, mark off the cardinal directions by placing a stick, larger rock or other marker at the appropriate points on the circle rim. Then with smaller markers indicate the midpoints between these. This will of course divide your circle's circumference into eight parts. Now we get really weird – truly non-eccentric: turn around in your circle, stopping to face each of the eight directions and asking yourself how you *feel* each time. You will really have to dig down into your subtle sensing abilities, but they are there if you try to find them – DNA will not let you down if you give it half a chance. Does one particular direction make you feel happier, more hopeful, comfortable or calmer than any of the others? On the other hand, does another direction make you feel depressed, fearful, or dismal in some way? Identify your 'best' and 'worst' directions. Remember what you learn – it is yours to keep. (If you discover your 'good' direction, you might use it at some future point when you are fearful, lonely, depressed, or when you are in the midst of an argument – who cares if you look odd by suddenly turning to face a corner of the room in the middle of a shouting match?) If after trying this you nevertheless have difficulty identifying a specific feeling with any direction, do not worry – what is more important is that you have made the effort to find the unfamiliar link between direction and feeling. The effort alone can have a healing effect on your normal, habitual mental programming. Remember that you are trying to avoid being eccentric.

Cardinal Virtue

Do you know where the cardinal points, the Four Directions, are when you are in your home? When you face the wall with a picture of Grandma hanging on it, do you happen to also know you are facing north-west? It is startling how few of us are oriented in our own homes – at least, in anything other than in the most general terms. Traditional people would always know their orientation with considerable accuracy – we have already noted that Pueblo Indians are almost obsessive about directionality, and similar observations have been made about Australian Aborigines. One early European settler in Australia reported that he was struck how in major intertribal gatherings, Aboriginal groups would take up a place in the encampment 'precisely in the position from each other their country lies according to the compass (of which they have a perfect notion)'. Again, researcher David Lewis noted while in the Simpson and Western deserts that his Aboriginal guides were very accurate when asked to point out the direction of distant locations – especially when they were standing at sacred spots. This was partly because they knew the network of dream journey routes ('songlines') which helped them to orient, and also, as one of Lewis's Aboriginal informants tried to explain to him, because 'North, south, east and west are like this in my head' – he was able to draw a cross in the sand to accurately represent the compass directions, even though the terrain was featureless to Lewis's eyes.

Never mind a desert, just get your home sorted out. Use a compass to establish the cardinal directions. Is your home aligned to these or not? Use some marker – an image or an object significant to you – to mark a specific cardinal point (even if it is a corner of a room or corridor) so you can always orient yourself. In our culture, you would probably wish to indicate north, but east would also be a highly appropriate choice, as the word 'orientation' comes from the Latin verb to rise, particularly with reference to the Sun or Moon. The term 'the Orient' was applied by Europeans to the lands of the east because, of course, that is where the Sun, or virtually any heavenly body, rises. Words like 'original' and 'aboriginal' have the same roots. So go on – be original.

Many cultures ascribed colours to the Four Directions, and you could develop this into your whole scheme of interior decoration. But there is no specific need to go into another culture's symbolism – it is what affects your thinking that counts in this context. You could base the directional colours on solar symbolism, so that, for instance, north could be black or blue (no Sun, cold), east, yellow (rising Sun), south, orange (heat of the day), and west, red (sunset). Or whatever you feel is right for you – it could be purely intuitive. This colour symbolism can be subtle – there is no need to paint whole walls in vibrant colours, unless you want to. A small object or picture with the selected colour as dominant would work equally as well. If you have no walls that are oriented on the cardinal directions, then you will need to develop a colour scheme for the inter-cardinal directions, or find ingenious ways to place cardinal colours in corners – flowers of a particular colour in a vase, for instance.

Your directionality can be expressed in other sensory ways, too. So, for instance, you can use smell as an additional way of marking the Four Directions. Use your own intuition to select a specific scent for each direction. Each day, by means of incense or an essential oil burner, choose one direction and burn the fragrance you have decided to be appropriate to that direction. Linked with colours and objects, this will become a profoundly powerful way of orienting your domestic space.

It is fun and it's relevant to do this in your home, because it reminds you of the Four Directions and so promotes refreshingly ancient systems of awareness, provides subtle psychological orientation, and conceptually links you to the wider universe.

Welcome home.

Getting Into Focus

One of my pet moans is about the decreasing presence of real fires, true hearths, in modern homes. While central heating and gas or electric fires may be more convenient and efficient, something is truly being lost. The warmth and natural flicker of flames are an attractive focal point for our attention, and promote a reflective state of mind, a very useful mental condition for exploring memory, for seeing aspects of one's life with greater calmness and clarity, and sometimes for problem solving in a variety of contexts. Furthermore, the pattern of glowing embers can conjure scenes in the mind's eye, such as the twinkling lights of magical cities, or mysterious lanterns in the night – the slowly shifting, luminous lineaments of archetypes that invite our subconscious minds to come out to play. The sense of well-being a fire can encourage, and the primordial sensations that the scent of burning wood can evoke, are sensuous signals that can connect us to deep transpersonal memories haunting our cells. A fire can help us recollect ourselves; it can centre us, for the English word 'hearth' is at heart but 'heart' with an added 'h', is it not? Not for nothing do we use the Latin word for hearth, *focus*, to mean to attend to, or centre on something. Our modern homes are losing their hearts, and we are breaking ours. We are slipping out of focus.

If you have a fireplace in your home, use it. Use it as a tool for meditation, for exploring your mind and your psyche. Never mind the banal function of warming the room – the fire is for mind as well as body. The next time you stare into a fire, pretend that you have never seen such a phenomenon before. Marvel at it. Go back to your roots and rediscover fire, the gift of the lightning bolt, of the gods. But what if you do not have a fire, a hearth, in your home? Arson is not to be recommended – what you need to replace the absent hearth is some sort of other *focus*. This could be a personal altar, on which you place objects and images that provoke your *recollection* in deep and satisfying ways. A better option is to create something natural that can provide a *focus point* in the artificiality of your home environment. One example might be a large bowl filled with sand or white gravel into which you trace broad, sweeping lines like eddies in water, with a few carefully, intuitively, placed pieces of rock, so the whole arrangement becomes reminiscent of the sea washing around islets. As a meditation device, this could act something like a Zen monastery garden. Again, you might buy and tend a bonsai tree, to similar effect. Or even create a rockery in a large bowl or built onto a tea-tray as a base.

To be truly elemental, why not create a feature that utilises trickling water? Tiny electric pumps, container bowls, and other basic components are readily available nowadays in garden centres for you to build your own design, or you can purchase one already built (Plate 7). The advantage of this type of *focus* is that it offers not only an additional element, but also a natural sound – and the sound of gushing or trickling water can act on the brain in a similar fashion to the flicker of firelight. You could put candles in association with the water feature so you get soft flickering light to accompany the burbling of the water. Allow yourself at least one or two evenings a week when you can take half an hour or so, switch off the lights, and let the candle flames and water use their elemental powers to unwind your stressed-out mind, body, and soul. Conduct a meditation or enter a reverie by staring into the glinting reflections caused by the candlelight in the spilling water. Make it a habit.

Sometimes a focus can be created in an almost ridiculously simple way. I even made one by accident. I was replacing a figurine of the Buddha that had been on a windowsill for ages with a tall pot plant. As the figurine and plant sat briefly next to one another, I suddenly realised that it looked like a tableau of the Buddha sitting beneath the Bodhi tree, where he obtained his enlightenment. I have ever since left them together to silently remind me of that marvellous moment in spiritual history. Now, occasionally, I catch sight of the 'tableau' and for a few fleeting moments my spirit is lifted by thoughts of higher things than the morning mail, doing the washing up, or the rest of the deluge of domestic trivia and daily concerns that so readily swamps all our lives. There is something about the unexpected moment of catching sight of the plant–figurine set-up that allows its message to jolt the awareness in ways out of proportion to its modest nature. It ambushes the soul.

Contemplating Your (National) Navel

Many ancient lands had an acknowledged territorial omphalos, and most countries have an optimum geographical centre point – a national navel which may or may not coincide with the symbolic national omphalos. In some places today, especially relatively newly defined nation states, this will not be commented on, or even known, and you will have to figure out the optimum point. Because a country's boundaries tend to be irregular, there are usually several locations jockeying for the honour of being the national territorial centre. In the United States, for instance, one candidate for being the centre of the contiguous states is taken to be a point close to Lebanon, Kansas, where a stone plinth fitted with a plaque supports a flag-pole flying the Stars and Stripes. An associated 'Hub Club' has apparently been formed there, according to John Michell (*At the Centre of the World*, 1994). Rival locations claiming the distinction include Junction City and Fort Riley. If Alaska is considered, then the centre is posited as being at

Castle Rock, South Dakota. With the inclusion of Hawaii, the point is said to be six miles further west, though this is presumably a rather abstract calculation, considering that Hawaii is far out in the Pacific Ocean.

Australians made their formal effort to identify their territorial centre in 1988, during the country's bicentenary as a modern nation. By plotting thousands of coastal points, a geometry was created that allowed calculation of the centre of the landmass, which was found by a 'Centre Safari' to be on the land of Lilla Creek Station near the southern boundary of Northern Territory. A replica of the flagpole at Parliament House, Canberra, was erected on the spot. This didn't settle the matter for everyone, though, as other experts variously thought that other systems of calculation should have been used. In any case, the people of relatively nearby Alice Springs had always considered their town to be at the centre of the country, while the Aborigines for untold generations had seen the dramatic natural feature of Uluru (Ayers Rock), also in the general vicinity, as being at the heart of the land.

In Europe, there are various claimants to being the centre of France. The ones most contested are villages in the vicinity of Bourges, which takes its name from the Bituriges, a Celtic tribe who lived in the region. The place most people accept as the navel of France is Châteaumeillant (Middle Castle), which does indeed sit close to the geographical centre of France. Another contender, though, is Chartres, located further to the north. Now famous for its magnificent Gothic cathedral, Chartres was once an important place of assembly for the pagan Celtic tribe the Carnutes: Caesar noted that they considered their territory to be the 'centre of all Gaul'. Michell observes that Chartres does indeed sit at the centre of a circle that encompasses the whole of ancient Gaul (as opposed to modern France). It was the custom of the pagan Celts generally to situate the chief judicial and sacred assembly points in the middle of their territories.

The English omphalos is likewise a confused matter, with various fairly centrally placed locales coming into contention. The Venerable Bede, the English monk-historian active during the seventh and eighth centuries, identified Lichfield in Staffordshire as Angli Mediterranei, the Middle of England. The site of this navel is said to be now occupied by the present cathedral. However, the place more often touted nowadays as the geographical centre of England is the unremarkable village of Meriden,

Warwickshire, where the village cross and local pub vie for the honour of marking the supposed exact spot. The notion that Meriden was at the middle of England does not come from any specific, authoritative source, but seems to have emerged from local folklore. Oxford, the city of the dreaming spires, is yet another candidate. In the ancient Welsh text the *Mabinogion*, the strange story of 'Lludd and Llefelys' tells that the Celtic king Lludd was advised by his brother, Llefelys, to measure the length and breadth of the island of Britain in order to determine its centre, and there to dig a pit and bury in it a tub of the best mead with its top covered with a piece of silk. This was to be used in an ingenious fashion to trap two dragons fighting there who were making a terrible shrieking noise that filled the land. Llud had the island of Britain measured, and its 'point of centre' was found to be Oxford.

The Roman surveyors identified the centre of Britain (along an axis running from the south coast to as far north as Hadrian's Wall) as Venonae, now referred to as High Cross, where they placed the crossing point of two of their great roads, Watling Street and the Fosse Way. This is today a somewhat isolated point on the Warwickshire–Leicestershire border, a few miles from Hinckley. Four parishes meet here, and because of its elevated position the crossroads was used as a beacon site. A pillar was erected in remembrance of Venonae in 1711, but today only its plinth survives (Plate 8).

Other candidates for being the English, and sometimes even the British, omphalos include the site of the Midland Oak at Lillington, close to Leamington Spa, and the central junction in Dunstable, marking the crossing of Watling Street and another Roman road, Icknield Way (the four streets at the junction here are named after the cardinal directions), among others.

My personal preference is for yet another site, Croft Hill in Leicestershire. In this I follow a local historian, T. L. Walker, who wrote in 1879 about this remarkably symmetrical and atmospheric hill a few miles south-west of the city of Leicester:

> Every early nation appeared to have had its Sacred Hill or Omphalos. In Ancient Gaul there was said to have been a Mesomphalos in the centre of the country, on the River Legre or Loire, where the Druids met periodically for special ceremonies and councils. This

> Mesomphalos was an isolated hill in the midst of a plain . . . The idea of such a Mesomphalos was said to have been borrowed from Britain. Now, as no Druidical temple had yet been described in Britain at all corresponding with the description of the Gallic Mesomphalos, and as Croft Hill did, as it was an isolated hill in the midst of a plain, nearly in the centre of the country, on the banks of the River Leire or Soar, and having still traces of a ditch around its base, it seemed quite possible that this hill might have been the Mesomphalos of the British Druids.

There is supportive evidence for this idea in that not only does Croft Hill stand virtually on the River Soar, it is a bare four miles from the village of Leir. This place name has been traced to the word 'Legra', meaning Loire (which was called Ligeris in ancient Gaul). Croft Hill was also clearly an important spot in past times: in AD 836, King Wiglaf of Mercia held a council there attended by important dignitaries of the day, including the Archbishop of Canterbury and eleven bishops. Other records also suggest that Croft Hill may have been an open-air court, as well as the site of an annual fair or rural gathering. Although Croft Hill is but a modest eminence, it is nevertheless prominent in the flat landscape surrounding it (Plate 9), and extensive views are to be had from its summit (Plate 10). It sits almost exactly at the midpoint of a line connecting the Norfolk coast in the east with the Welsh coast in the west, and is situated less than three miles from the north–south axis of the Roman survey (and only five miles from High Cross). So it is geographically very central. The ancient name of Croft Hill was Crebre, a Celtic word comprised of two elements, *bre*, 'hill', and *cre*, which may derive from *craeft*, '(rotating) machine' (such as a mill – and mills have certain symbolic associations with the *axis mundi* in some ancient European traditions). In the nearby village of Croft there is an Arbor Road, and 'arbor' also refers to the axis around which a wheel turns. Taken together, these clues strongly hint at a hub or fulcrum symbolism being associated with the hill in former times. Croft Hill gets my vote as being the pre-Roman navel point of Britain, or at the very least of the southern half of the British Isles. The long-forgotten heart of Albion.

There are clearly different ways to assess a national centre – geographical, symbolic, notional. Having decided which one to opt for, take time out to visit it, so as to have the physical sense of standing at the centre of the land that you live in, and so to complete the inner and outer symbolism of the sacred centre. As you stand there, turning to the Four Directions, you might silently recall the lines from a song the Lakota sang at the foot of the central pole in the Sun Dance ceremony:

At the centre of the Earth
Stand looking around you
Recognising the tribe
Stand looking around you.

2

PILGRIMAGE

Pilgrimage is commonly thought of as being a pious, dutiful, or petitionary journey to a holy place, often one associated with miraculous healings. The nature of pilgrimage is, however, both broader and deeper than this, for though the purpose of pilgrimage may be to arrive at a sacred destination, in our era of rapid transit we can overlook another, equally important aspect – the actual process of it, the act of the journey itself. The deepest Latin roots of the term 'pilgrimage' give a basic meaning of 'to walk through the fields'. We can therefore look at pilgrimage in its richer context of 'sacred journeying'. Pilgrimage is a deep human instinct that has never left us, and we can rekindle its broader principles today, whether or not we go on a traditional pilgrimage – as we shall discover.

OVERVIEW

In its purest form, pilgrimage is a spiritual quest or meditation packaged as a geographical journey; outer, physical travel with an inner destination. There are also broader effects of a pilgrimage, especially one that involves a journey outside the pilgrim's own region or country. It enhances the pilgrim's cultural identity on the one hand, yet can be an agent for change as well, for the pilgrim brings back new ideas and fresh perceptions along with the souvenirs and tokens obtained at the pilgrimage destination.

Pilgrimage can additionally be a kind of vacation – a release from normal duties and constrictions, a refreshing of the mind, body, and soul. This aspect of traditional pilgrimage has survived in modern tourism; indeed, the very term 'holiday' derives from 'holy day'.

Going on a Holy Day

The earliest form of tourism as we might recognise it today was initiated by the ancient Greeks, who called it *theoria*. The Greek traveller would journey to special places, and try to get a fully rounded sense of a site, not only by studying and exploring it, but also by finding out about the legends and local knowledge concerning it. Many locations would have special guides known as *periegetes* who were versed in the local lore. In eighteenth-century Britain and northern Europe, well-heeled young men would round out their education by making the 'Grand Tour' to Italy and other Mediterranean lands, visiting the ruins of classical antiquity. The original culture vultures, they would bring back objects and relics, thus helping to found many a private collection – this contributed in turn to the concept of museums. Then, in the nineteenth century, along came Thomas Cook, the Baptist minister and social reformer who hit on the idea of organising tours to promote moral improvement.

Key destinations for many of today's tourists remain ancient temples, ruins and exotic sacred sites of many kinds. Although tourists visit such places nowadays without investing in specific belief systems associated with the monuments, the locations can nevertheless still induce a sense of the sacred, of things outside of mundane concerns, and can provoke contemplation and deeper thoughts than usual in the visitor. Just like the pilgrims of old, modern tourists will bring back pictures of the monuments they have visited, and perhaps gift shop souvenirs, not only to help them remember a place, but also to prove to others that they were there. And, perhaps, to attempt to capture a fragment of sanctity.

Other immensely popular destinations for visitors today are museums – especially the great and famous ones. This too can be seen as an echo of traditional pilgrimage:

> Many museums (at least in the Anglo-Saxon world, for instance the British Museum) are traditionally designed as if they were Greek temples, imbued with a classical rather than Christian sanctity, a holiness vested in the distant past . . . The glass museum case is a kind of reliquary; the museum room (labelled 'Egyptian', 'the Angerstein Collection' or 'herbivorous Quadrupeds') is equivalent to the private chapel . . .
>
> The final stop in a trip to a museum (and often also its starting point) is frequently the museum shop. The tokens one purchases – postcards, replicas, books – are a way of bringing home something of the charisma of a special location. (Coleman and Elsner, 1995)

The Nature of Pilgrimage Places

Pilgrimage by definition celebrates a special place – one goes to a sacred destination, and returns from it. Many places are initially made holy because a vision of the Virgin appeared there, or because a god dwelled there, or because the miracle-working bones of a holy person are held there. Pilgrimage places endorse belief systems in a concrete fashion. Some sacred places, though, are not built or designed by man, or associated solely with one religious faith;

rather, they have a spiritual power, a thrill of natural sanctity, a numinosity all their own. Such sites can take forms such as a distinctive mountain or hill, a remarkable rock outcrop, a waterfall or spring, a venerable old tree, or a cave. These types of place are often adopted and re-adopted by succeeding faiths, religions, or sects, and so have to be able 'to absorb varieties of interpretation . . . capable of accommodating diverse meanings and practices' (Walter, 1988). But whether a holy place is natural or artificial, or both (such as when a temple is built at a natural site of sacred significance), the end result for the pilgrim is essentially the same. 'The religious program of a sacred place engages or disengages the senses, edifies the mind, and leads the soul back to the world of the spirit,' the scholar E. V. Walter points out. In the Hindu tradition, a holy place is a *tirtha*, a ford or crossing point, offering the pilgrim the opportunity of a passage from the secular to the sacred, from this world to the spiritual realm. By visiting a place as a pilgrim, one reinforces its sanctity. It eventually becomes holy as much for the fact that it is the focus of a pilgrimage as for the original reason that it was created or selected.

The power of a pilgrimage location was usually projected well beyond its geographical location. Pilgrimage through the ages has occasioned considerable industry involved with the manufacture of tokens such as little lead images of saints, stone, ceramic, or metal plaques displaying holy images associated with a site, boxes, bottles, and other containers made of wood, clay, metal, or glass, holding oil, water, earth, or dust from a pilgrimage destination. Sometimes it could be a piece of stone or wood as an actual relic of the place. These objects acted not only as sacred mementos for the pilgrim, but as advertising on behalf of the pilgrimage location. This is perfectly exemplified in the great European pilgrimage tradition associated with Santiago de Compostela (St James of Compostela), Spain, where scallop shells, actual and manufactured, became the symbol of that pilgrimage shrine. In some cases, pilgrimage tokens were pressed into ritual use back at the pilgrim's home region, as if they had their own intrinsic power. Sometimes, a token or relic from one place would be taken and deposited at another shrine, thus creating subtle networks of sacred significance.

This diffusion of the power of a pilgrimage place could be further facilitated by a circuit of associated sacred places in the vicinity, or by shrines and communities developing along the routes leading to and from the main destination. As art historian Michael Dames points out, 'every satiated pilgrim is eventually happy to disperse the intensity of the peak experience along the ordinary roads that lead from it' (Dames, 1992). This leads us to a defining characteristic of pilgrimage – it is literally a moving experience.

Sacred Movement

Pilgrimage is essentially about a holy journey. Dames writes about 'mythological walks' that 'show us who we are and where we are going' (Dames, 1992). Pilgrimage involves movement through symbolically charged landscapes, and a pilgrimage route often provided a choreographed experience – though more so in the past than nowadays. A pilgrim would stop at a shrine here and there, pass by locations associated with miracles and visions, stay at wayside hostelries for pilgrims and there share stories and beliefs with others on the same journey, and when finally nearing the desired destination, he or she would be granted beckoning glimpses of the pilgrimage's goal, be it a holy peak, cathedral spire, or gleaming temple dome.

The ancient and traditional form of pilgrimage could be considered as sacred walking. In 1962, Satish Kumar, editor of *Resurgence* magazine and a former Jain monk, conducted a 'peace pilgrimage' from India to the then four nuclear nations of the world. Apart from the crossings of the English Channel and the Atlantic, he travelled entirely on foot. He found that walking long distances, sometimes with little food, and often surrounded by landscape vistas and deep wilderness, primed the mind for spiritual revelation. 'Walking in itself was an end, a form of meditation, a way of being,' he has written (Kumar, 1992). The outer, physical journey became 'a trigger for the inner journey'. The Indian pilgrimage scholar Rana P. B. Singh has argued that pilgrimage ideally expresses 'the human quest for a divine connection between man and the environment' (Singh, 1991). Philip O'Connor, an articulate vagrant, wrote movingly of his 'wayfaring' experiences. He noted that his ego progressively merged with the environment, and experienced 'an incomparable feeling of being at home in the outside, as though one were a prayer winding along a road' (O'Connor, 1963).

When the pilgrim reaches the goal of the pilgrimage, sacred movement scales down into ritualised actions. He or she has to observe the proper sequences, forms, and movements at the location, such as circumambulation. In fact, the architecture and procedural rules at shrine sites subject the pilgrim to controlled movements – very similar to the way modern tourists are ushered into an organised tour of an ancient monument or a museum.

The Mystique of the Margin

Pilgrimage has two subtle, less commonly considered aspects that are nevertheless fundamental to it. The anthropologist Victor Turner identified them as 'liminality' and *communitas.*

He took liminality from an earlier scholar, Arnold van Gennep, who spoke of the 'liminal phase' of *rites de passage.* The word 'liminal' derives from the Latin *limen*, boundary, from where we get 'limit' in English. The Romans had household gods, and Limentinus was the deity of the doorway, the god of the threshold. Liminality is a 'betwixt and between' stage and can occur in many contexts – temporal, spatial, social, and psychological. So we have the 'witching hour' of midnight as a liminal point in time. Similarly, New Year's Eve is liminal, as is Hallowe'en. Strange things happen at these cracks in time – spells can be made and broken, spirits walk, the dead return. Twilight ('between lights') is also a liminal time: not fully light, not quite dark, when the forms of things can loom and seemingly shift their boundaries. Places, too, can be liminal. Territorial borders and boundaries are classic examples, and empty stretches of ground between identifiable blocks of territory are typically referred to as no-man's-land. A threshold is liminal – neither inside nor outside, used for both entry and exit. Similarly, cave mouths are liminal locations, which is why they were favoured in some societies as places for initiatory activities. Forests and woods are liminal places, with obscuring foliage creating a soft green gloaming. Outlaws are liminal people – so Robin Hood is the legendary liminal figure dwelling in the greenwood. The moments before falling asleep, or on awakening, like other 'twilight' mental states, are psychologically liminal: half in, half out of a dream.

Turner likened pilgrimage to initiation, and identified phases in both that were liminal. The pilgrim, like the initiate, is detached from the normal daily routine, and exists outside the security of the community, and while on the pilgrimage has not yet reached the secure context of the sacred destination. 'During the intervening "liminal" period, the characteristics of the ritual subject . . . are ambiguous; he passes through a cultural realm that has few or none of the attributes of the past or coming state' (Turner, 1969). The pilgrim, or the initiate, is temporarily in the outer shadows of normal society, on its margins. While on a pilgrimage a person is literally neither here nor there.

Then there is *communitas*. Being outside the normal social structure, Turner argued, pilgrims could strike up friendships with one another across social class. A sense of camaraderie in a shared physical and spiritual adventure developed peculiar to both types of temporary outcast – pilgrim and initiate. Pilgrimages could take days, weeks, months, even years, and would in many cases be the peak experience of a person's life. The thrust of perception and expectation was different to that in mundane life; pilgrimage was a physical act that moved the person out of the routine levels of consciousness to conditions that exposed the mind to new sensibilities.

First Steps

We can be sure that sacred walks were taken in the early morning of human history, and though we cannot now directly see those pilgrimages in action, evidence of them survives. In the prehistoric rock art of southern Scandinavia and the Iberian peninsula, there are actually carvings of footprints; in the Scandinavian instance, they seem to indicate connections between certain places in the immediate vicinity. In rural areas of northern Portugal, local peasantry still make pilgrimages at certain times of the year to rocks marked with prehistoric engravings (see Part Three). Similarly, we have archaeological evidence of ceremonial ways in Neolithic Europe, such as the earthen Avenue leading to Stonehenge, or at Avebury, where we have the Kennet Avenue marked out by two lines of stones. From the same general era of prehistory in Britain, there are particular kinds of henge (circular ditch and bank enclosures) which have double entrances opposite one another (many other types of henge have just one entrance). In studying these features, archaeologist Roy Loveday has come up with the curious finding that their axes share similar orientations with local stretches of Roman roads. Loveday pondered whether or not this relationship could be simply a bizarre coincidence, for there obviously could not be a direct connection between the Neolithic builders of the henges and the Roman road-makers over two thousand years later. Yet the relationship between such orientations occurred too frequently and was too widespread to be due to mere chance. On the back of considerable deduction and research, Loveday has come to the conclusion that, essentially, the double-entrance henges were pilgrimage sites on pilgrimage routes. His theory posits that the cultural significance attached to this system eventually declined, the henges fell into disuse and all but disappeared from view, but the general courses of the routes were found useful to later societies and so they survived in different contexts, the Roman roads being just one of the later ones. Loveday observes: 'as our green lanes and footpaths testify, once a route has been established it is likely to endure . . . whatever its change of status.' (Loveday, 1998).

Perhaps the best-known examples of archaic sacred journeys are those of the Australian Aborigines. Popularly known among non-Aborigines as 'songlines', these Dreamtime journey routes mapped out an invisible sacred geography across the face of the vast Australian continent, but only a few remnants of the practice now survive. In Aboriginal cosmology, the Earth was featureless and uninhabited in the 'time before time', the *tjukuba*. During this Dreamtime, giant totemic beings appeared and walked the country, and created the topography that now exists by leaving behind their tracks and campsites, and the places where they defecated, fought, copulated, or carried out rituals. When these world-creating beings left, they turned into rocks or entered the ground. Aborigines, for unknown generations, have traced the journeys of these Dreamtime ancestors. The Yolngu of Arnhemland refer to them as *djalkiri*, 'footprints of the ancestors'. Some of these dreaming tracks are, or were, followed by whole tribes, often as part of their seasonal, nomadic circuits over the Outback, but they can also be followed individually by tribal members, creating the 'Walkabout', so misunderstood by non-Aborigines. Australian author James Cowan points out that with these dream journeys 'we are not just dealing with an unending journey back and forth across tribal territory solely in pursuit of food. Instead we are looking at a sacred journey in which . . . the land is transformed into a metaphysical landscape saturated with significations . . .' (Cowan, 1989). The course of a dream journey route would link together natural sacred places, each of which would have a story, song and ritual dedicated to it, and sometimes it would have ancient rock paintings which would be refurbished during each journey.

Other traditional peoples also retain memories of ancient sacred journey routes. In New Guinea, inland forest tribes still pass on the knowledge of ways through the jungle that lead to the 'land of the ancestors'. In appropriate seasons, or times of personal distress, native peoples in southern Africa go on sacred journeys to distant cult centres and land shrines up in the central highlands of Botswana and Zimbabwe. They speak of this as 'going to Mwali' (*Mwali* = 'God Above'). This pilgrimage pattern has been extant for some centuries, and quite probably echoes similar journeys made by many of Africa's peoples from beyond the dawn of history.

Hindu Pilgrimage

Hinduism has evolved over five millennia and has many gods. It supports a great tradition of pilgrimage, and India boasts nearly 200 major centres that collectively draw about 20 million pilgrims annually, in addition to unnumbered smaller shrine sites. The act of travelling to or between pilgrimage sites is considered sacred in its own right. The *Vedas* indicate the benefits of sacred journeying thus:

> Flower-like the heels of the wanderer,
> His body groweth and is fruitful;
> All his sins disappear,
> Slain by the toil of his journeying.

An Indian (Sanskrit) term for pilgrimage is *tirthayatra*; *yatra* relates to travelling, while *tirtha* means 'ford', a word that can also be applied to saints and ascetics, holy texts, and, as we have noted elsewhere, to sacred places. The reason the word can have such a wide range of meanings is because of its essential sense, which can be expressed as 'crossing over'. This can relate to the physical act of fording a river, or, by metaphor, to passing from the mundane, secular world to the sacred realms. India's sacred rivers – the Ganges, Yamuna, Godavari, Narmada, among others – can be thought of as '*tirtha* waters' (Eck, 1981), in that on their banks are some of the holiest 'crossings', combining in many cases both the physical and metaphorical sense of *tirtha*. The great pilgrimage centre of Varanasi (Benares) is the classic example of one of these. Other examples of *tirthas* can include high sanctuaries in the Himalayas, sought by countless pilgrims in the summer months; isolated hilltops crowned with temples; coastal locations like Puri in the east or Dvaraka on the west coast; forest retreats, such as in the Naimisaranya in north India; cities such as Mathura, birthplace of Lord Krishna; and Hardvar, where the Ganges enters the Indian plains from the mountains.

> The recognition of India as sacred landscape, woven together north and south, east and west, by the paths of pilgrims, has created a powerful sense of India as *Bharat Mata* – Mother India. Pilgrims have circumambulated the whole of India, visiting hundreds of *tirthas* along the way, bringing water from the Ganga [Ganges] in the north to sprinkle the *linga* at Ramesvaram in the far south and returning north with sands from Ramesvaram to deposit in the riverbed of the Ganga. (Eck, 1981)

As well as sacred space, Hindus are also cognisant of sacred time: some periods are thought to be more suitable for pilgrimage than others, and sacred journeys and processions are often synchronised with favourable astrological conjunctions and events.

A pilgrim's acts of devotion, *puja*, will include offerings to the deity of substances relating to the various bodily senses, such as food, flowers or perfume, bells, and so forth. In the same vein, the pilgrim will wish to take away from a sacred location physical substances – such as ash, water, or flowers – considered to be imbued with the immaterial essence of the god of the place. While at the site, a key way the pilgrim seeks spiritual or material benefit is by obtaining *darshan* – the sight, however brief, of the holy image. Temple architecture is generally aimed at allowing this form of contact between devotee and icon, with the eyes of the effigy in its sanctuary often being directed at where the pilgrim enters – but to reach the image, the devotee has to circumambulate in ever-decreasing circles (Coleman and Elsner, 1995).

Even the briefest sampling of Hindu sacred journey destinations has to mention Varanasi, which can be considered as the Jerusalem or Mecca of Indian pilgrimage. In some parts of India, initiation ceremonies for young men often require the candidates to take seven symbolic steps in the direction of Varanasi. This great pilgrimage centre is especially sacred to Shiva, and is situated on the banks of the Ganges, 'the flowing ladder of heaven'. Elderly pilgrims often go to Varanasi in order to die by the sacred river – a very good death to have. The holy city has over seventy *ghats*, riverside shrines consisting of platforms and stairs rising up to 50 feet (15 metres) from the water. There are five specific ghats which form a pilgrimage sequence, and pilgrims bathe at them in order. The sacred territory of Varanasi is bounded by a major pilgrimage route, the Panchakroshi Yatra, but, in all, Varanasi has fifty-six pilgrimage circuits, forming a sacred geography (see Part Three).

Buddhist Pilgrimage

After the Buddha's death in the fifth century BC, the religion that arose from his teachings spread out from its original heartland in northern India throughout the subcontinent. Over the subsequent centuries it spread as far as Syria in the west, northwards to Tibet, and eastwards through south-east Asia to China, and, ultimately, Japan. In many areas of its westwards expansion it was later to retreat before Islam, and before Hinduism in India itself, but, as we know, it has remained a major religious influence in many parts of Asia. According to tradition, in his last days the Buddha himself urged pilgrimage to the four places associated with key moments in his life – his birth at Lumbini, Nepal; Bodhgaya in Bihar, India, where he attained enlightenment; the deer park at Sarnath, near Varanasi, where he first preached; and Kushinagar, where he died. The sight of these places, he said, would arouse a sense of spiritual urgency in pilgrims. Eventually, other sites associated with the life of Buddha also came to be venerated and therefore became targets for pilgrims, as did sites associated with the lives of the Buddha's main disciples and later Buddhist saints.

Buddhists in India continued an earlier tradition of the religious use of caves. Probably the best-known Indian Buddhist cave shrine is Ajanta – richly painted rock-hewn temples and monasteries in a spectacular setting in a bend of the Waghora River in the Deccan. They were hewn out between 200 BC and AD 650. Although no formal religious observance is made at this site any longer, pilgrims do still come to leave flowers and incense. Another cave pilgrimage complex in the Deccan is Kanheri, near Bombay, which was like Ajanta, but continued as an active centre for longer. Over 300 caves were cut out of the rock at this site between the first and tenth centuries AD, and natural caverns were enlarged. They contained steps, rooms, carvings, and stupas, and archaeologists have uncovered inscriptions left by pilgrims.

Relics related to the Buddha or Buddhist saints became part of the pilgrimage scene, and in Sri Lanka some notable pilgrimage sites developed around Buddhist relics. At Anuradhapura, a cutting said to be from the Bodhi Tree (*Sri Maha Bodhi*), under which Buddha sat when he experienced his great enlightenment (Part One), grew into a tree that was attracting pilgrims even in the time of Christ. The remarkably aged tree now at the site is supported by iron pillars and is surrounded by a wall and railings. Other shrines contain, variously, what are said to be the Buddha's alms bowl, hairs from his head, and even fragments of bone. The most famous relic shrine, though, is the Dalada Maligawa Temple, situated beside an artificial lake in the heart of Kandy. Secured there, inside seven golden boxes, each smaller than the next, is the Buddha's tooth. Each year there is the week-long pageant of the *Perahera*, Procession of the Tooth, in the course of which a bull elephant carries the golden reliquary.

Buddhism reached China, probably by way of traders' routes, in the first century of the present era. This kindling process was augmented and completed by individual scholar-pilgrims who came from China to visit the Buddhist holy places in India between the fifth and seventh centuries – notably the fifth-century monk Fa-Hien. They wrote about the Indian shrines and their pilgrimages to them, and translated the Indian Buddhist texts into Chinese. One of the great Buddhist pilgrimage destinations in China became Wu T'ai Shan, in the north of the country. A holy place of earlier traditions, in Buddhism it was associated with Wenshu (Manjushri), the Bodhisattva of Wisdom. The five-peaked mountain attracted devotees as a place of miraculous happenings. Even in quite modern times, strange light phenomena have been witnessed there, and there are caves exhibiting bizarre curiosities such as shallow pools of water that can never be emptied despite having apparently no water source issuing into them. It was thought to be exceedingly beneficial to go to Wu T'ai Shan, for there one would find the truth about oneself, and at that place alone did one stand a chance of seeing the Bodhisattva. It is said that many pilgrims never left Wu T'ai Shan, staying to have the visions and dreams that the place is supposed to encourage.

Like the Indians, Chinese Buddhists also liked to use caves for their religious activities, a dramatic example being the Caves of the Thousand Buddhas (the Magao Grottoes) in Gansu Province. They were in use for a thousand years from the fourth century AD. The site lies on the ancient Silk Route – one of the ways Buddhism entered China – and comprises 500 surviving rock-hewn caves, containing a total of 2,000 statues and 45,000 wall paintings. Western adventurers at the beginning of the twentieth century relieved the guardian monk there of thousands of valuable manuscripts, some of which had been brought back from India for translation by the seventh-century pilgrim-monk Xuan Zhang. Colourfully painted figures made of plastered terracotta depicting the Buddha and other Buddhist personages emerge from the walls of the caves, while the murals show scenes from the life – and past lives – of the Buddha, the paradise of Amitabha full of pavilions and palaces, as well as sweeping landscapes and scenes from daily life.

In Japan, mountain pilgrimage emerged out of the fusion of indigenous Shinto and folk religious beliefs with the incoming Chinese influences of Taoism and Buddhism. In the eighth century, Buddhism developed the 'Nature Wisdom School', in which enlightenment was sought by being close to nature. The indigenous shamans and healers who had developed their powers by mountain asceticism became loosely associated with this, and there emerged *Shugen-do*, the Order of Mountain Ascetics. The Shinto *kami* or spirits of the mountains were subtly transformed into manifestations of Buddhist divinities. During the eleventh and twelfth centuries mountain pilgrimage started to become very popular, and pilgrims were conducted in their ascents by experienced mountain ascetics.

In Tibet probably more than anywhere else, the incoming

Buddhist influence fused with the existing indigenous religion, which in the case of Tibet was shamanic. Most scholars have tended to tease out what they see as 'Buddhist' elements from what are 'shamanic' or 'indigenous' in Tibetan pilgrimage practice. In fact, these elements are all so melded together that any such separation is really an academic exercise. Tibetans refer to a sacred place as *gnas* or *gnas-pa*, which they use more like a verb than a noun to mean a location that is pervaded by the existing presence of a spirit, a god, a Buddha, or other supernatural force – an active residence of spiritual powers where one can have an 'encounter' (*mjal-ba*). Such a place may even have the appearance of the entity that inhabits it (see Part Three). Tibetans commonly use the term *gnas-skor* to refer to a pilgrimage centre, meaning 'going around a *gnas*', because a Tibetan pilgrimage is usually a circular journey. The circumambulation can take place in either direction, clockwise or counterclockwise: it is sometimes glibly stated that only the former way is used by Buddhists, but this seems to be shot through with exceptions. Women, for instance, tend to do half a circuit in each direction. A well-known characteristic of traditional Tibetan pilgrimage is the performance of full-length body prostrations (*phyag'tshal*) to accomplish a circumambulation of a sacred place. In this way, the body makes full contact with the sacred ground, which means with the spirit powers residing there. This is seen as having both a purifying and empowering effect.

A peculiar strand of Tibetan Buddhist pilgrimage is the *terma* tradition. '*Terma*' means 'hidden treasure', specifically in regard to sacred objects and texts, and *terma* pilgrimage can be seen as a kind of spiritual treasure hunt. The tradition states that these hidden items were secreted by Padmasambhava, who spread the Buddhist doctrine in Tibet in the ninth century. *Terma* were said to be hidden in rocks, trees, temples, effigies, and directly in the ground. The exoteric reason for such concealment is that the items were to be available to help keep the doctrine pure should it become adulterated over the centuries, but *terma* also have an esoteric or metaphorical function, as indicated by other parts of the tradition which state that they can be concealed in the sky, and even in the human mind, where they can be revealed by dreaming, in meditation, or spontaneously. Subtle aspects of the tradition indicate that *terma* are not physically present in their place of concealment until they are found, at which precise point they become materially manifest, and only an appropriate person (*terton*) able to read the appropriate signs can access them. This aspect of the tradition further indicates that *terma* can bestow blessings on human beings and enhance their spiritual progress, as well as encouraging faith by providing proof that there had been great *yogis* in Tibet who had been able to transmit the primordial wisdom to disciples across the centuries through the agency of the objects.

In September 1986, Span Hanna was able to witness a *terma* pilgrimage in action (Hanna, 1994). He and two companions were allowed to tag on to a group of pilgrims at Nyingchi, on the main highway from Sichuan Province to Lhasa. They were led by a middle-aged woman called Khandro Khachi Wangmo, and her brother. Khandro was a 'Powerful Lady' of the Tibetan Bonpo religion, empowered to locate *terma*. (Bonpo is older than Buddhism in Tibet, but was able to accept the new influence because it considered the Buddha to be an incarnation of the Bonpo sage, Tonpa Shenrab.) The party headed off for Bonri, a nearby mountain sacred to both Bonpo and Buddhism. The circumambulatory pilgrimage path or *khora* around Bonri could be covered in less than two days, but Hanna's pilgrimage party took five days due to various stops and encounters along the way. They were on the final leg of the pilgrimage circuit when they cleared a ridge near a natural monolith called 'Samantabhadra's Heart'. Khandro stopped next to a large boulder, gazing around at the sky and surroundings. It transpired that the previous night she had learnt through whatever secret means that *terma* were concealed in an elephant-shaped boulder resembling the Buddhist sacred mountain of Emei Shan, in Sichuan Province. She felt that the boulder she was now standing by fitted the description. A shrine was assembled roughly 50 yards (45 metres) from the boulder, offerings were laid out on a large cloth, and a scripture was recited. The ritual went on for about two hours, in which time sleet and hail fell, and vultures began wheeling overhead (this was taken as an auspicious sign). The weather then cleared, and Khandro stripped to the waist before lightly striking the great boulder. Immediately afterwards, Hanna heard 'the delicate but arresting sound of a clear, small bell'. This was soft, and quickly faded. (He later learned that one of his companions also heard the ringing sound, *but slightly earlier*. Hanna realised he couldn't determine just where the sound had emanated from.) With support from a helper, Khandro climbed part of the way up the rock, and struck it again. She located and removed several slabs of stone nestling on the boulder, then reached into a cavity beneath where they had lain. She removed a figurine a few inches long of the seated figure of Amitayus, the Buddha of Long Life, and a *dorje* ('thunderbolt sceptre') of a similar size, along with some powder (*sindhur*, 'dakini dust'). As the crowd pressed forward to study the objects, Khandro's brother opened a pack of blessing papers which blew off on the wind. Offerings of scarves and valuables were collected from the crowd, and these were stuffed back into the cavity and the slabs replaced. Khandro carried the *terma* away, and Hanna was informed that other *terma* had been transmitted into the rock by some great lama of the past, but it was not the time for these to manifest.

Pilgrimage in Non-Buddhist China and Japan

As with Tibet, both China and Japan had indigenous religions that preceded the arrival of Buddhism, and coexisted with it thereafter. In China, there were the ethical and mystical philosophical systems of, respectively, Confucianism and Taoism, and there was a tradition of nature pilgrimage. This particularly related to Taoism, which is famed for its core image of the universe as existing because of the interplay of yin and yang, the feminine and masculine principles of creation, a concept that has insinuated itself into much traditional Chinese thinking. The best-known text associated with Taoism is probably the *Tao-te Ching*, dating to the third century BC. This is often ascribed to Lao Tzu, said to have been the founder of Taoism. Taoism has essentially animist and shamanistic roots, and this explains its strong nature-worship aspects. To Taoists, the Tao is the Way of Nature.

There was a vaguely similar indigenous religion in Japan, in the form of what came to be called *Shinto*, the Way of the Gods. This also is animist in nature, recognising the existence of nature spirits – *kami*. The physical feature that is a hallmark of Shinto is the *torii*, a sacred gateway formed from timber uprights joined at the top by two gently curved crossbeams. *Torii* are found giving symbolic access not only to formal shrines dedicated to *kami*, but also to natural places considered to be holy, such as certain mountain approaches, woodland groves, and viewing points for waterfalls. There are thousands of Shinto shrines throughout Japan, though most are in Honshu, on the northern coast of which is the Izumo Taisha Shrine, the oldest continuously used Shinto shrine in Japan. Dating from at least the seventh century, it is dedicated to Okuninushi, the deity who introduced medicine, silkworms, and agriculture to the world. The shrine is a pilgrimage destination, used mainly as a divinatory site concerning romance, and a popular place for weddings. After donning white robes and washing hands in running water, the pilgrim claps twice to summon the god. Forty-five yen is thrown into the collection box (in Japanese, 'forty-five yen' is *shiju-goen*, which phonetically also happens to mean 'constant chances for romance').

The foremost Shinto shrine, however, is the Ise complex, in southern Honshu. Its inner shrine is inhabited by the spirit of Amaterasu, the Sun goddess, with other spirits residing elsewhere in Ise's 200 buildings and shrines. Ise has over a hundred priests in attendance, and although the shrine complex as a site is ancient, its actual antiquity is not known because its thatched wooden structures are entirely rebuilt every twenty years in exactly the same way using unpainted and unvarnished cypress wood and traditional means of construction. Pilgrimage to Ise was a major lifetime event for many people in centuries past, and devout followers of Shinto are expected to make a pilgrimage to Ise at least once in their lives. Over 8 million people still visit it every year.

Natural sites also continue to attract pilgrims. Mount Fuji, as a prime example, is sacred to both Shinto and Buddhist devotees. It is dedicated by the Buddhists to the Bodhisattva of Wisdom, and in the Shinto religion to Konohana Sakuya Hime, goddess of flowering trees. A pilgrimage route up the mountain was established by the fourteenth century. Various cults formed in the following centuries based on visions experienced by mountain ascetics. The mountain was a key holy place, and after the restoration of imperial rule in the nineteenth century it also became tied to nationalism. Although the Japanese defeat in World War II caused the religious adherence to Fuji to suffer, the mountain remains a focus of pilgrimage, with up to 400,000 people making the ascent during the key period of July and August. Straw models of the mountain are burned as part of a fire ritual, an association with the volcanic nature of the mountain, and a lacquered model weighing over a ton is carried to the summit. The pilgrimage route has ten stations, at each of which a character is branded into the pilgrim's walking staff. At the top, ideally reached at dawn, the pilgrim circumambulates the crater rim.

Islamic Pilgrimage

The world's greatest annual pilgrimage is the *hajj*, the Muslim sacred journey to Mecca, Saudi Arabia, usually seen in the light of being a *return* rather than an outward journey, as is so often the sense of a Christian pilgrimage. The hajj has a central role in Muslim life, being included as one of the five pillars of faith. It is required that every able-bodied adult Muslim with sufficient means makes at least one pilgrimage to Mecca, the birthplace of the Prophet Muhammad. Mecca provides the cardinal direction in the compass of faith for Muslims: prayer has to be conducted facing the direction of Mecca from wherever one is situated, and this sacred direction, the *qibla*, also governs the orientation of mosques. Before the institution of Islam by Muhammad in the seventh century, Mecca was a station on the 'incense route' between the Orient and the Mediterranean, and was already an ancient centre of pilgrimage built around the sacred well Zemzem.

The Koran states that Abraham, the Father of Israel, started the custom, and it is said that his son, Ishmael, Father of the Arabs, laid the green serpentine platform that supports the Ka'ba, the prime focus of the hajj and the sacred centre of the Islamic world. The Ka'ba is a cuboid structure 43 feet (13 metres) high of grey-green granite blocks. It was a sanctuary used in pre-Islamic rites, with statues of various gods placed inside it and around it. It was restored by Muhammad and his followers, and the Prophet placed a sacred black stone, a meteorite, into its eastern corner a few feet from the ground. Previously, this rock, probably viewed as being a *betyl* stone embodying a deity, was carried around by the nomadic Bedouin, so its fixing at the Ka'ba by Muhammad was a symbolic act of religious dominance. The present Ka'ba is a restoration of the seventh-century building, and it is draped with a black curtain, the *kiswa*, which is emblazoned with Arabic lettering embroidered in gold and silver thread. It stands within the vast precinct of al-Harram Mosque, the largest open-air temple in the world.

During the period of the hajj every year, 1–2 million Muslims from all over the world descend on Mecca. Before entering the sacred area of the Holy City, pilgrims – who must be Muslim – have to enter *ihram*, a state of purity effected in part by abstaining from indulgence of the physical senses, and men must don a special garment made of two pieces of seamless white material, and have hair and nails cut. After removing sandals and crossing the threshold of al-Harram Mosque at the Gate of Peace with right foot first, pilgrims start off their rituals by circumambulating the Ka'ba seven times counterclockwise, a procedure known as the *tawaf*. There can be ten or twenty circling lines of pilgrims, calling out specific prayers at each corner of the Ka'ba. A special prayer is said at the Black Stone, which the pilgrim tries to touch and kiss; if the numbers of people make this impossible, then a gesture is made towards it. Following the *tawaf*, pilgrims make for a causeway linking two small hills adjacent to the precinct, al-Safwa and al-Marwa, and run back and forth on it seven times. Later, the pilgrim travels to Mina, 5 miles (8 kilometres) away in the desert, and then on to the Mount of Mercy at Arafat, about 10 miles (16 kilometres) further east. The day is spent there saying prayers and listening to sermons. The following day, returning towards Mecca, the pilgrim stops at Mina, and over the course of three days throws forty-one stones at three stone pillars. (This curious ritual seems to stem from a popular tradition that Abraham threw stones at the Devil, who was tempting him to disobey God's command to kill his son.) Finally, the pilgrim returns to Mecca from Mina by foot, and then performs another *tawaf*.

The second most important pilgrimage destination in the Islamic world is Medina, where the Prophet is buried, and from where he launched his military campaign to establish the Islamic faith. Jerusalem is for many Muslims their third most sacred city.

Jerusalem and Multi-Faith Pilgrimage

For Muslims, the key place in Jerusalem is the Rock of Ascent, the slab of rock on Temple Mount (Mount Moriah) that dominated the platform King Herod constructed there for his temple. Their tradition has it that this rock is where Muhammad came on his winged steed during his Night Journey from Mecca, and from where he ascended by a ladder of light to heaven during his great vision in which he received the Five Commands of Islam from Allah. The Dome of the Rock encloses a bare surface of the sacred Rock, which has two depressions said to be the footprints left by the Prophet as he started his climb to heaven. A reliquary placed within the Dome is said to hold hairs from Muhammad's beard.

To Jews, the Rock was the centre of the world, as we noted in Part One, and Jerusalem was the capital of the Hebrew kingdom c. 1000 BC. They built temples on the Mount that were successively destroyed by the Babylonians and Romans, and from the seventh century AD the spot has been occupied by the Dome of the Rock. After one of the Roman demolitions of the Jewish Temple in AD 70,

Figure 6: From an old Hebrew manuscript, showing the Messiah led by the prophet Elijah (blowing a shofar) entering Jerusalem by the Golden Gate.

the first signs of a Jewish pilgrimage to what was believed to be the Western Wall of the ruined temple commenced. This hardened into a formal ritual after the fall of Rome, and visiting the Western (Wailing) Wall of course continues to this day.

Jerusalem came under Christian authority between 325 and 638. Although the Persians destroyed much of Christian Jerusalem in 614, up until that point churches were being continually added to the sacred cityscape. Scholar Wendy Pullan has argued that the Christians were projecting an image of the Heavenly Jerusalem onto the physical city (Pullan, 1993), and they built 326 churches plus three Constantine basilicas – the Church of the Nativity in nearby Bethlehem, the Eleona Church on the Mount of Olives, where Jesus taught the Mysteries to his disciples, and the Church of the Holy Sepulchre on the Hill of Golgotha in central Jerusalem, the site of the crucifixion and resurrection. The various sites were conceptually linked in the form of the Jerusalem Liturgy, developed by Cyril, the Bishop of Jerusalem between 349 and 386. This involved movement from one church to another, with scriptural readings and prayers relating to the New Testament significance of each site being recited at that place at the appropriate time of day, week, or year. So at Easter, for example, all the places involved in the events – the Last Supper, Jesus' arrest, the interview with Pilate, the scourging, and the final Passion – were linked in sequence by processions. People would have thronged the streets, the sound of songs and lamentations rising amidst the flicker of candlelight and the smell of incense. Most pilgrims spent far longer than one day traversing the sacred course through the city, and some stayed years in order to fully experience the Liturgy. Pilgrims saw and touched the places where they believed Christ had been present, and sometimes this became more than merely a journey of the devoted imagination: for instance, St Paula, who came from Rome, reportedly saw visions of Christ at the appropriate locations, and St Helena, mother of Constantine, had a vision on Golgotha which revealed where the True Cross, the cross of the Crucifixion, had been buried, and it is said she authenticated it by raising a dead person there by her touch. Later, various pilgrims claimed that when the True Cross was brought out for them to kiss, a mysterious star would appear in the sky overhead.

Jerusalem became the ultimate destination of Christian pilgrimage, with nobles and commoners mixing together side by side – *communitas* in action. The arduous and dangerous journey to and from the Holy Land became an integral part of the pilgrimage experience, a holy activity in its own right. In the Holy Land, the sacred sites were tended to by specialist priests and monks who acted as guides and interpreters for the pilgrims. The experience created was for the pilgrim like a form of religious text, using real geography and architecture instead of pages. Pilgrims brought home flasks of oil sanctified by contact with the wood of the True Cross, and lead or clay containers filled with Jordan water or earth from a venerated tomb. These souvenirs were often used back in the pilgrims' homelands as charms for blessings or healing.

Jerusalem fell under Arab control in the seventh century. This was a great shock to Christendom. Though the Muslims were fairly tolerant towards Christian pilgrims, Islamic places began to take dominance, and the goal of Jerusalem gradually became increasingly unattainable for the Christian pilgrim. Christianity itself went through changes, with a split and rivalry emerging between the Greek, Eastern (Orthodox), and Western, Latin (Catholic) forms of the faith, and it became more militaristic. Eventually, at the end of the eleventh century, the first of a series of Crusades was launched by the Christian leaders of Europe, aimed at regaining the control of the Holy Land. These military adventures, which were framed as pilgrimages, emerged out of an unholy, conflicting mix of ambitions and instincts – from piety and chivalry at one extreme, to opportunism, greed, bellicosity, and political expediency at the other. By the end of the twelfth century, a truce was signed with the Arabs, who agreed to allow Christian pilgrims access to Jerusalem. But the holy wars, the militancy on all sides, and the barely interrupted rulership of the Holy Land by the Muslims had inevitably taken their toll on Christian pilgrimage to the region. Although various Christian pilgrimage sites had existed in Europe for many centuries, medieval Christians of western Europe began to look to the greater hallowing of their own native landscapes.

Christian Pilgrimage in Continental Europe

In western Europe, Rome became a major pilgrimage centre for Catholic Christians, boasting, along with its great antiquity and the presence of the Pope, the tombs of SS Peter and Paul, and a fragment of the True Cross. Loreto, also in Italy, was noted for the presence of the Holy House, the home of the Virgin Mary. This had supposedly been preserved in Nazareth because St Helena had had a basilica built around it. Legend states it had been brought to Europe by the agency of four angels in 1291 – though old documents reveal that the Holy House was moved from Nazareth to Loreto after the Crusades by the Degli Angeli family, and show the structure being transported by ship. Other sacred nodal points gained in importance as an increasingly organised and busy network of pilgrimage routes developed across western Europe.

The greatest was Santiago de Compostela in Galicia, north-west Spain, containing the tomb of St James (see below). This had been venerated since the ninth century, and came to be the pre-eminent pilgrimage destination for western Europe, with routes leading to it from all over the Continent. Some of these started in France, at Tours, Vezelay, Le Puy, and Arles and Avignon in the south. A pilgrimage route from Cologne in Germany linked to Vezelay, and another from Worms (which was also on a route to Rome from northern Europe and even Iceland) connected with Avignon. All routes came together at Puenta la Reina, in north-east Spain, where the Camino de Santiago commenced, running from east to west across northern Spain. Holy places on these routes were themselves either already established pilgrimage sites, or became so because of their positions on or near main through routes to Compostela. Cologne, for instance, had an original ninth-century cathedral built on a site that had housed a Christian community in the fourth century, but a great new Gothic structure was commenced in 1248 after the reputed relics of the Magi were brought to Cologne from Milan, where they had been deposited after being transferred from the Holy Land by way of Constantinople. Cologne also has the Church of St Ursula, containing the bones of the martyred British saint and two of her virgin disciples.

Sites associated with the Virgin Mary were very popular with European pilgrims – even today, of an estimated 6,000 active pilgrimage shrines in Europe, two-thirds are devoted to the Virgin. Because of the belief in the Assumption – the Virgin's physical ascent into heaven – there could be no bones of the Virgin available for use as relics, but various items of her clothing were reputedly found in the Holy Land by Christian pilgrims such as St Helena, and taken to Constantinople, from whence they were dispersed to other European centres over time. So, for example, a piece of silk 16 feet (4.9 metres) long said to be the Virgin's tunic became a prized possession of Chartres Cathedral in the Middle Ages. Due to the general paucity of claimable relics, though, other more mystical manifestations were conjured. These could range from artefacts, like a feather said to have fallen from the wings of Gabriel at the Annunciation, to places sanctified because visions of the Virgin were reported there. There were also many locations holding phials of what was supposed to be Mary's Milk. This fad derived from a legend which told that when the Virgin was suckling the infant Jesus in a cave, some of her milk fell onto the stones and turned them white. Pilgrims to the Holy Land found that there were caves beneath Bethlehem and Nazareth, and one came to be designated as the Milk Grotto, in the Church of the Nativity. By the seventh century, limestone dust from these sites was being collected, mixed with water, and presented as Mary's Milk, suitable for all female complaints.

The most mysterious of the Virgin artefacts, though, are the so-called Black Madonnas. There are said to be over 400 surviving examples of these in cathedrals, churches, and shrines – and now also museums and private collections – throughout Europe. These images show the Virgin's face and hands coloured black, in some cases they were painted that way, while others are black, it is said, because of their age, due, perhaps, to centuries of exposure to the smoke from candles and incense. Many people do not accept this explanation, though, pointing out that other colours in such effigies have not darkened in the same way, and suggest that there was a secret cult of the Virgin in medieval times identified by these blackened images. Some have even hinted that it is essentially a pagan survival clothed in Christian iconography. Black Madonnas are usually in the form of statues, but they can also appear as paintings and icons, the most famous example of the latter being the Black Madonna of Czestochowa, Poland. Even now hundreds of thousands of pilgrims come to venerate this image every year on the Feast of the Assumption. The original icon is said to have been brought to Constantinople by, yet again, St Helena, before eventually finding its way to Poland. The existing image, though, is an early fifteenth-century restoration in the Byzantine style. The National Shrine of Switzerland, in the abbey church of the Benedictines at Einsiedeln, has a statue 40 inches (1 metre) tall known as the Madonna of the Dark Wood, which has been venerated by pilgrims since the fourteenth century. Chartres Cathedral also was famed for its wooden Black Madonna, destroyed in the French Revolution. A replacement sculpture now stands in the crypt. Chartres was earlier a pagan Celtic sacred site, and it has been proposed by the French author Louis Charpentier that the original *Notre Dame de Sous-Terre* had been the representation of a Celtic goddess. Intriguingly, a stained-glass window in the cathedral dating to the twelfth century shows St Anne, the mother of the Virgin, as having a black face.

The medieval pilgrim in Europe tended to be recognisable by specific apparel – a wide-brimmed hat, a staff, and a scrip (a kind of satchel). Many pilgrims were dignitaries and well-to-do people, but there were great numbers of ordinary, common folk taking part as well. People would be given a blessing by their local church, and would be released from any legal or social obligations while they were away on their pilgrimage. There were organisations that arranged pilgrimage tours. Pilgrimage routes also encouraged the development of long-distance commerce and communications, as well as the creation of 'service industries' such as inns, hostels, shops, food processing, transport, the provision of guides and interpreters, the production of souvenirs, and so forth, along them. There were even matchmaking enterprises – the medieval prototypes of today's dating agencies – as pilgrimage allowed more scope for people to meet and court one another than did their routine daily lives. The exact scale of the pilgrimage business in medieval times and the high Middle Ages is not known, but some records survive that may give an idea of the situation in the fourteenth and fifteenth centuries: up to 40,000 pilgrims arrived daily in Rome, and as many were at Aachen on a single day in 1496; 60,000 passed through the city gates of Munich in one week in 1392, while it is thought that between 500,000 and 2 million pilgrims came to Santiago de Compostela each year. Even smaller pilgrimage destinations like Wilsnack in northern Germany received about 100,000 pilgrims annually. All these people, coming and going across the face of Europe. And not only by land: the shipping of pilgrims to and from Venice en route to their destinations provided the foundations of its port, and a fifteenth-century traveller counted eighty pilgrim ships lying in the harbour of Corunna on a single day. As scholar Peter Yeoman has written, the 'first concept of a common Europe was expressed through pilgrimage' (Yeoman, 1999).

Pilgrimage also meant big business for the Church, of course, with the proliferation of shrines and churches and cathedrals, and with all the money changing hands for souvenirs (or 'blessings' as they were often called) and on-site services. Further, it consolidated the power of the Church in many ways, not only by increasing income, but by wielding the influence of favoured pilgrimage sites, and having the opportunity to reinforce the Christian doctrine in the minds of countless pilgrims, and the millions more they came back home to. There was also another, more subtle advantage for the Church in the pilgrimage phenomenon – the energetic building of new churches and shrines allowed it to quietly Christianise old pagan sites such as holy wells, hills and caves, which still retained their attraction for local people (Stopford, 1994). This allowed the Church to more or less eradicate lingering pockets of paganism.

The Hallowing of Britain

British Christians joined in merrily with the traffic of pilgrims on the Continent, but they were also busy hallowing their own lands, from the Orkney Islands off Scotland's north coast to the southern tip of England, as even a brief glance at some examples can testify.

One of the northernmost – and oldest – of great British pilgrimage centres is Iona, a tiny island off the western coast of the Scottish Highlands. St Columba came here as a refugee from troubles in Ireland in the sixth century with a small group of followers. Columba was high born of Irish royal stock, and though Christian, he seems to have retained an aura of ancient Druidic magic, as he was credited with powers to control the elements, and with various miracles. Iona was probably already considered a holy isle when Columba set up his monastic settlement there in self-imposed exile, or 'white martyrdom'. Iona was the saint's base, from where he struck out to convert the pagan peoples of Scotland, who were composed of four main groups, the Scots from Ireland being only one of them. He would return from his missionary sorties (which involved challenging the power of Pictish Druid priests, and, it is said, a confrontation with the Loch Ness monster) and take up the same duties as his monks, tilling the land, fishing, praying, meditating, studying, and copying manuscripts – it is thought that the Book of Kells was produced on Iona. In 574 Columba chose and anointed Aiden, a new king of Dalriada, the Scots territory centred on modern-day Argyll, and returned briefly and triumphantly to Ireland to successfully negotiate the independence of the Dalriada Scots from their Irish overlords.

When this great Celtic Christian saint, seer, and magician died in 597, the fame of Iona had spread far and wide. Though subsequent centuries of Viking raids, with a massacre of monks on an Ionian beach in 986, caused its influence to diminish, it continued to be considered sacred, and in the famous burial ground of Reilig Odhrain, Scottish, Norse, and Irish kings were buried between the eighth and eleventh centuries. A Benedictine abbey was built c. 1200 over the remains of earlier churches, and a tiny cell shrine by the west end of the abbey probably marks the position of Columba's grave.

There were many other important pilgrimage sites in Scotland, including those at Dunkeld, Scone, St Andrews, Isle of May, Glasgow, and Edinburgh, among many more. Glasgow's medieval St Kentigern Cathedral is so well preserved that the modern visitor can replicate the experience of the medieval pilgrim in tracing the carefully crafted route to be taken from the west door to the shrine holding the relics of the saint. Kentigern died in Glasgow in 612, and his burial place soon became a focus of pilgrimage, but it was the deliberate cultivation of a cult of Kentigern by Bishop Jocelin for political reasons in the late twelfth century that led to the surviving cathedral shrine. In Edinburgh, the remains of the reliquary chapel of St Triduana has not fared so well, being hemmed in by housing estates on the east side of the city. The legend of Triduana tells that

Figure 7: An old print of the lower part of St Triduana's well-shrine.

she rebuffed the advances of a Pictish chieftain very effectively by plucking out her eyes and presenting them to him skewered on thorns. Her cult became associated with various holy wells throughout Scotland, even as far as Papa Westray in the Orkneys – an example of the Christianisation of pagan places. The wells were noted for the healing of eye complaints, and this aided the saint's popularity, as blindness was rife as a consequence of the vitamin-deficient diet common at that period in Scotland. Her chapel in Edinburgh resulted from the heightened interest in pilgrimage in the later medieval period. The upper part of the two-storey hexagonal chapel has gone, but the lower part had a well-shrine.

Holy wells were popular places of pilgrimage in all Celtic lands, and saints were used to Christianise and so legitimise these much older patterns of veneration. Wales had many such places, so it is no surprise that two of its better-known pilgrimage sites were associated with wells. One is St Winefride's Well in north Wales (see below), and the other at St David's in the extreme south-west. St David (*Dewi Sant*) is the patron saint of Wales, and not much is known for certain about his life. He was a native Welshman who lived in the sixth century; a great missionary, he established churches and founded monasteries in England and Wales, including St David's, of course, where the saint finally based himself and where he died. It is said David passed away in a state of ecstasy, and at the moment of his death, St Kentigern, elsewhere in Wales at the time, saw a vision of him. David has many ancient churches dedicated to him not only in Wales, but also in Devon, Cornwall, and Brittany. His mother is said to have been St Non. Legend has it that at his baptism, a fountain of crystalline water burst forth from the ground – this is now St Non's Well (Plate 11), overlooking the sea and about a mile from St David's Cathedral in St David's, a village that is also a cathedral city, known to the Welsh as Tyddewi, 'House of David'. The present cathedral stands on the site of St David's original monastery in the Vale of Roses, and is said to be at least the third cathedral to have stood on the spot. In the twelfth century, King Henry II is said to have visited St David's dressed as a pilgrim.

England was as deeply hallowed in Christian times as it had been during pagan ages. The names are known of over 300 Anglo-Saxon saints. Though the Norman Conquest in the eleventh century caused many of these to fall from popular memory, all was not lost, for with the rise in pilgrimage fervour through the medieval period some of the ancient saints saw their cults revived and their relics enshrined in the new cathedrals and other ecclesiastical structures. Some of these still survive, and continue to provide a destination for pilgrims, while others have fallen into obscurity. There is space here to only very briefly pick out a few examples that express this range and the magical nature of the hallowing of England.

English Pilgrimage Destinations

Off the Northumbrian coast is the small island of Lindisfarne, approachable by foot at low tide. Considered the birthplace of

English Christianity, this became 'Holy Island' from the early seventh century onwards, when the Celtic saint Aidan (a product of the ecclesiastical community of Iona) set up his monastic base there in 635, to set about Christianising the Angles of the region at the request of King Oswald. The island became noted as a centre of learning. St Cuthbert came to lead the monks of Lindisfarne in 664. As a shepherd boy, he had seen 'a globe of fire' in the sky which he took to be the soul of St Aidan, and it was this that set him on the road of Christian ministry. He spent his last years in contemplation on the even more remote Farne Islands, but when he died he was buried on Lindisfarne. His body was found to be still preserved when it was later moved ('translated' is the proper term) to a new shrine on the island, and by the end of the seventh century a cult had developed around the saint. When the Vikings threatened Lindisfarne in 875, the monks took the body inland in a carved casket. It was rested at different locations until a final home was found at Durham in 995, where a vision showed the spot for it to be laid. A Saxon church was built for the saint's body, but no trace of it survives today. The building of a cathedral at the site commenced in 1093, and it remains probably the finest Norman building in Europe. Cuthbert's body, which became known as the *cor-saint*, 'holy body', because of its apparent freedom from corruption, was placed in a shrine behind the high altar in 1104. It attracted throngs of pilgrims, and miracles and wonders were reported.

One of St Aidan's pupils was St Cedd, who founded a monastery in a remote spot on the edge of the wild Yorkshire moors at what is today Lastingham. St Cedd was among the last generation of the Celtic saints, for he attended the crucial Synod of Whitby in 664, where the Roman strand of Christianity introduced into Britain by St Augustine asserted its authority over the native Celtic Christianity. Cedd retired to Lastingham that same year, where he died of plague after tending the sick. He began to be venerated and attracted pilgrims. His monastery was razed by the Vikings in the ninth century, but in 1078 Abbot Stephen of Whitby built a crypt as Cedd's shrine. This crypt is in effect a whole little church under the ground, and is well preserved to this day and is profoundly atmospheric. There are holy wells nearby dedicated to Cedd and to St Chad.

Among eastern England's pilgrimage sites is Ely Cathedral, a magnificent Norman edifice on a low island in the East Anglian fens. Before these were drained in recent centuries, access to the Isle of Ely had to be by boat or causeway. The site of the later cathedral was found in the seventh century by Etheldreda, a beautiful princess. She vowed herself to virginity, and though married twice, apparently she was able to maintain her intent. She persuaded her second husband to release her, and she went to the Convent of Coldingham, but the fellow decided he had to have her back and pursued her. She fled to the Isle of Ely, which had been part of the dowry of her first marriage, and where it is said various miracles took place that prevented the husband from continuing his pursuit. Etheldreda founded a Christian community at Ely, and six years later, in 679, she died. Sixteen years after her burial, Etheldreda's body was found, like that of St Cuthbert, to be free from decay, and it was enshrined. Etheldreda became the most loved and venerated of Old England's female saints, and thousands of pilgrims came to her shrine. When the Norman cathedral was built, the shrine was positioned (rather unusually) in front of the high altar. The relics of SS Oswald, Withburgh, and Botolph (his head) were also venerated at Ely, as were the remains of numerous other saints, including Etheldreda's sister, St Saxburgh, and St Erminhild, whose grave was said to issue a sweet perfume when she was laid to rest. Etheldreda's shrine was destroyed in 1541. Parts of her body were taken to a chapel dedicated to her in Ely Place, Holborn, London, while her left hand can be venerated at the small Roman Catholic church in Ely to this day. Another key pilgrimage place on the eastern side of England is Walsingham, Norfolk, the site of a vision of the Madonna in 1061, but more is said about this below.

Two great pilgrimage centres to the west and south-west of the country are Hereford and Glastonbury. The original church on the site of Hereford Cathedral (Plate 12) has long since disappeared, but legend says it was built by Geraint, cousin of King Arthur. This may in fact be a folk-memory of a Celtic Christian centre, active before St Augustine brought his Roman Christianity to English shores. In 825, King Offa of Mercia built a church on the site to house the shrine of St Ethelbert, King of East Anglia. Offa and his wife had murdered Ethelbert in order to annex his territory, but repented when he was acclaimed a saint and miracles began to be attributed to him. This attracted so many pilgrims that a larger building was erected, but the whole structure was destroyed by Welsh marauders in 1056. The cathedral we now see was begun c. 1079, and building continued for some centuries. It contains many treasures and curiosities, including the shrine of the thirteenth-century St Thomas (Thomas Cantelupe), which for reasons unknown survived the Reformation.

Glastonbury, once an island in a shallow sea that is now the Somerset Levels, was another great centre of Celtic Christianity, and doubtless of pagan sanctity long before that. It is considered by many to be the 'holyest earthe' in England. Legend states that the young Jesus walked here, accompanying his tin-merchant uncle, Joseph of Arimathea, who returned after the crucifixion bringing the Holy Grail and founding a simple wattle church on the site now occupied by the Abbey ruins. Certainly it was an early Christian settlement, and the Abbey, nestling beneath the weird conical hill known as the Tor (last refuge of the king of the fairies and entrance to the Celtic Otherworld), may have been founded as early as the fifth century. The place attracted early saints such as St David. St Dunstan, monk, musician, and scholar, was the famous Abbot of Glastonbury in the tenth century; when he died his body became the focus of a major cult there. But the sanctity of Glastonbury was such that it held the relics of at least another six saints – it was a major pilgrimage centre, and a rival to Canterbury. It still attracts organised Christian pilgrimage to this day, quite apart from New Age pilgrims.

In the extreme south-west reaches of England, in Devon and Cornwall, Celtic Christianity lingered longer. Pilgrimage sites tended to be holy wells and small chapels, and Cornwall in particular had many saints of its own.

Travelling eastwards across the southern portion of England, we can pause at the great university town of Oxford. Its patron saint is Frideswide, who lived and died in Saxon times before the 'dreaming spires' were built. Frideswide was the daughter of a Christian nobleman and although she was considered to be the 'flower of all those parts' she had set her heart and soul on becoming a nun. Unfortunately, a Mercian prince called Algar pursued Frideswide with such vigour and intensity that she felt obliged to flee to the oak woods of Binsey, on the outskirts of the modern city. She kept a low profile there for three years. Legend has it that Algar was struck blind by a bolt of lightning. When Frideswide heard of this, she miraculously cured his condition by bathing his sightless eyes with water from a well she caused to appear in the Binsey woods by praying to St Margaret of Antioch. The well can still be found close to a small church, both sites dedicated to St Margaret, in what little remains of the fields and woods of Binsey – a curiously quiet and remote oasis of antiquity surrounded by high-tension power lines and drear urban sprawl. The present church has twelfth-century origins, and was built on the site of an earlier Saxon chapel associated with the well, which was a place of pilgrimage for many centuries. It is said that 'the very pavement was worn away by the knees of the pilgrims', and the chapel was hung with the crutches of cripples who were cured at the sacred waters. The well is referred to as a 'treacle well' in Lewis Carroll's *Alice's Adventures in Wonderland* ('treacle' meant a healing fluid in medieval times). Frideswide went on to found a priory in Oxford. She died in 735, and a cult gradually grew around her shrine. After the priory was destroyed by King Ethelred the Unready in 1002, a new church was built to house the shrine. Miracles were reported there, including many involving mysterious light phenomena – light was sometimes seen emanating from the church tower, and on one occasion a golden column of light issued from her tomb. In the course of various developments over the centuries, Christ Church Cathedral and college arose at the location. Frideswide's shrine was destroyed in the sixteenth century, but fragments of its stonework were found in the nineteenth century and these have been reconstructed, and stand in the Lady Chapel in the Cathedral. There are small thirteenth-century carvings on the shrine showing a face peeping out of foliage (Plate 13), probably representing Frideswide's time of refuge in the oak woods of Binsey.

Further east is St Albans, site of the Roman settlement of Verulamium. This is where England's supposed first Christian martyr met his fate in the third century, beheaded for shielding a priest during the period of Roman persecution of Christianity. Miracles were reported as Alban was taken to his execution. His bones were much argued over through the succeeding centuries and became lost, but nevertheless a rich shrine of Purbeck marble was erected in the Norman cathedral at St Albans. Destroyed during the Reformation, many of its fragments were ultimately rediscovered and its reconstructed version stands in the Cathedral to this day. It is noteworthy, though, that archaeological investigation has failed to find any evidence of Christianity in Verulamium in the third century. But the head of a young man was uncovered: he had been killed by a blow to the head, decapitated, scalped, and defleshed. This is reminiscent of some of the Iron Age Celtic bodies recovered from bogs in western Europe, and scholars have suggested that the St Alban legend is in fact a Christianised folk memory of the pagan sacrifice. It seems the site of present-day St Albans occupies what may have been an important pagan religious centre.

In Kent, in the south-east, we come to the greatest English pilgrimage destination of them all – Canterbury. In medieval times, it stood with Rome and Santiago de Compostela as one of the main pilgrimage places of western Europe, but its roots are older, for the pagan Iron Age people settled the site of Canterbury before the Romans. In 597, St Augustine arrived on his mission of promoting Roman Christianity. The original cathedral was built by him on the site of an earlier church, but nothing of this survives, nor does it of subsequent pre-Norman structures. Immediately after the Norman Conquest the existing cathedral was razed by fire; the oldest part of the present cathedral is the crypt, dating to

1100. The magnificent structure we see today is the result of some centuries of work in the medieval period with subsequent rebuilding and restorations (Plate 14).

The cathedral provided the scene for the murder of St Thomas à Becket in 1170, so the Canterbury shrine and pilgrimage was a truly medieval affair in origin, unlike the more ancient ones we have looked at so far in our lightning tour. Thomas was an old friend – as we might say, a buddy – of King Henry II. When he became Archbishop of Canterbury in 1162 (which he did with some reluctance, apparently), the relationship began to change, and Thomas found reason to criticise the fiery king on various occasions, and a power struggle ensued between them. Henry found this to be somewhat wearing, and in a throwaway comment he wondered aloud if no one would rid him of 'this turbulent priest'. Four of Henry's knights took him at his word, and went to Canterbury and entered the cathedral, where they cut Thomas down. Thomas was immediately recognised as a martyr; so immediately, in fact, that contemporary records state that townsfolk came that very night, while Thomas's body still lay in the cathedral, collecting spilled blood and cutting off shreds of his clothing which were then dipped in the blood. Miracles began to be reported at once – a paralysed woman who was smeared with a piece of bloody cloth from Thomas's body was healed on the night of the murder, and twenty more cures were reported in the following three weeks. Within a year, pilgrims were flocking to Canterbury, and in 1173 Thomas was canonised.

Henry II came as a penitent to Canterbury, perhaps out of remorse and certainly to quell public outrage, and was scourged at the shrine. Miracle cures continued to be claimed, and there was a good trade in phials of 'Canterbury Water', in which minuscule drops of the martyr's blood were supposedly dissolved. The shrine, gold-plated and bedecked with jewels, was so glorious that even nobles arriving from abroad admitted to having their breath taken away by it. Uncounted thousands of pilgrims came from all parts of Europe and the British Isles, where pilgrims' paths specifically to Canterbury became recognised. At the cathedral, pilgrims were marshalled into groups by the monks, and conducted on a specific route through the building, stopping at various 'stations', such as the spot where the saint had been killed, the high altar where the body had been laid out shortly after the deed had been committed. When they reached the shrine, pilgrims circumambulated it in bare feet or on their knees, and some even paid the monks to flog them as penance for their sins.

During the Reformation, Henry VIII had everything removed or destroyed, considering Thomas to have been a traitor, and cautious of the power base that had built up at Canterbury. Today, there is an empty space where the shrine once stood, and a modern monument marks where the saint was martyred. But the worn steps eloquently testify to the numbers of pilgrims that came in medieval times.

An Toras – The Sacred Journey in Ireland

The tradition of Christian pilgrimage – the *toras* or pilgrimage circuit – is deeply rooted in Ireland, and fragmentary records referring to it date back to the seventh century. The idea of making a sacred journey to a holy place almost certainly goes back to pagan Celtic times in Ireland. There are Iron Age ritual centres such as Navan Fort in County Armagh, or Dun Ailinne in County Kildare, which seem to have been used at only seasonal times, and so may have been the focus of pagan pilgrimage at those times. They were surrounded by ritualised sacred landscapes through which there may have been a pilgrimage circuit. Various types of evidence indicate that Navan, for instance, continued the importance of the site from the Bronze Age, and perhaps even from the earlier Neolithic era.

An example of an early Christian pilgrimage route with possible pagan antecedents is that to Mount Brandon on the Dingle Peninsula in south-west Ireland. Archaeologist Peter Harbison remarks upon the 'extreme likelihood of the mountain having been the focus of an ancient *Lughnasa* festival during the prehistoric Iron Age' (Harbison, 1994). Folklore indicates that Mount Brandon was sacred to Lug, the pagan Celtic god of light, whose festival took place at the start of the harvest season – the end of July and the beginning of August. The later naming of the peak after the fifth-century St Brendan simply Christianised an existing observance. The remnants of a path known as the Saint's Road lead up towards the peak from the south coast of the peninsula, and form one of two pilgrimage routes ascending the mountain. On the way are features which give an insight into aspects of the pilgrimage. These include occasional stone pillars and natural rocks carved with ogham script and crosses shaped in the characteristic Celtic pilgrim fashion. One of the ogham scripts says simply 'Colman the pilgrim'. Next to the marked boulders are small hollowed-out stones known as *bullauns*. The rainwater which collected in them would have been considered holy, and pilgrims would have collected it for healing purposes. Also on the Saint's Road is the now-ruined twelfth-century church at Kilmalkedar, in the grounds of which is a stone carved with markings which have been interpreted as a sundial for telling pilgrims the hours of the day for their prayers. The church was dedicated to Maolcethair, a saint with a local cult that is known to have preceded that of St Brendan. Also at this site there is a drystone oratory, a most ancient design of monk's cell reminiscent in shape of the hull of an upturned boat. A similar but better-preserved feature, the remarkable Gallarus Oratory, is also to be found on this pilgrimage route.

A more famous example of an Irish mountain pilgrimage is that to Croagh Patrick, on the west coast of Ireland above Clew Bay near Westport, County Mayo. Viewed from the inland plains of Mayo, especially when silhouetted against the late sunset glow, the mountain appears as a huge, solitary pyramid. 'The power that draws us toward it from the distant plains of Mayo is loric . . . We are alone at Croagh Patrick, at the very westernmost edge of the world, in a liminal position held there by the invitation to transcendence,' scholar Walter L. Brenneman poetically observes (Brenneman, 1993). Indeed, it must always have appeared as special and sacred to those who saw it, and to have attracted pilgrims long before Christianity came. This is indicated by the fact that the surviving pilgrimage, in which around 50,000 people, some barefoot, climb the mountain to the summit, takes place in late July – or *Lughnasa*. Up until the mid-nineteenth century only women were allowed to the summit during the pilgrimage, and childless women would sleep on the summit during *Lughnasa* eve in the hope of encouraging fertility.

Though now a Catholic pilgrimage with a documented record going back only to the twelfth century, its origins must surely lie in a pagan past, as seems to be the case with the Mount Brandon pilgrimage. Another indication of this is the legend of the mountain, which says that St Patrick spent the forty days of Lent fasting and praying on its summit in 441, securing an angelic promise that the Christian faith would remain in Ireland until the Second Coming of Christ, and creating such a din with his great bell that he drove out all the demons (pagan spirits) and all the serpents in Ireland – it is a curious fact that there are no snakes in Ireland. This legend is a clear mythic record of the Christianisation of a place that had pagan significance. Today, pilgrims ascend the mountain along the well-worn pathway, stopping at various 'stations' en route. At the summit, where Mass is said continuously during the pilgrimage, pilgrims circumambulate a white chapel fifteen times reciting their prayers awhile, then circle St Patrick's Bed, a small stony hollow said to be where the saint slept, seven times. The final ritual is to say more prayers while walking round three stone mounds called Roilig Mhuire, Mary's Resting-Place, on the west slope of the mountain.

Another surviving Irish pilgrimage is that to St Patrick's Purgatory at Lough Derg in south-east County Donegal. It contains vestiges of the true hardships of medieval pilgrimages. The Lough sits in the midst of wild countryside that itself may have been a sacred geography in prehistoric times, containing as it does prehistoric monuments, indicative place names, and chairlike natural rocks that are now associated with saints, the Christianised pagan goddess St Brigit being one of them. The goal of the pilgrim is Station Island, on which is a basilica and other buildings. (Brenneman recalls that the island in the lake is one of the mythic images of the Celtic Otherworld.) First documented in the twelfth century, the Lough

Derg pilgrimage was famous throughout Europe; nowadays, it is little known outside of Ireland. In today's version of the pilgrimage, which can be taken between the middle of June and the middle of August, the pilgrim is ferried across to Station Island, and there takes part in a three-day ritual. The pilgrim goes barefoot, drinks only black tea or coffee, eats oatcake once a day, makes an all-night vigil in the church, and recites specific patterns of prayers while circumambulating the so-called 'saints' beds' (low-walled circles of stone), standing or kneeling at various points. This is a reduced version of the original practice, which lasted nine days. The modern vigil in the church replaces what had been the core of the old pilgrimage, namely entering a cave or pit which legend says had been revealed to St Patrick. This was closed centuries ago, and descriptions of it vary; medieval accounts of those who spent time in the 'purgatory' cave describe powerful visionary experiences in which both heaven and hell were glimpsed – demons, fantastic landscapes and buildings, nightmarish horrors, and terrifying journeys. While these are couched in Christian terminology, and may be somewhat embroidered, it is highly likely that they do essentially record altered states of consciousness caused by fasting, physical and mental stress, sensory deprivation, and lack of sleep. The pilgrimage possibly marks an earlier anchorite tradition at the lough, and the 'saints' beds' are probably the remains of huts used by the holy hermits.

Pilgrimage to holy wells is also a main feature of Irish tradition, and this practice goes back into the mists of time. It has also been noted that many churches in Ireland were founded on the borders of ancient kingdoms. Archaeologist Nancy Edwards observes that pagan religious sanctuaries occupied similar positions. 'Some important churches were undoubtedly founded in places which had formerly been of pagan significance, and in certain cases pagan rites seem to have continued in a Christianized context,' she writes (Edwards, 1990).

New World Pilgrimage

That pilgrimage was not simply an Old World impulse, much less one indulged in only by the great world religions, is confirmed by its existence in the ancient Americas before Europeans arrived. We can arrive at this conclusion by various lines of evidence supplied by archaeology, ethnology, and the writings of the first Spanish chroniclers of New World traditions.

In North America, there must have been many pilgrimage routes and destinations that are now completely lost to us, but enigmatic evidence of a huge tradition still lies faintly emblazoned on the landscapes of the south-west. This is the network of mysterious roads that crisscross the great San Juan Basin, which occupies what modern Americans call the Four Corners area, where New Mexico, Colorado, Utah, and Arizona meet. A major religious centre in this region was Chaco Canyon, south of Farmington, New Mexico, belonging to the Anasazi, a lost people whose culture blossomed between c. AD 900 and c. 1200. This sandstone rift in arid high desert country has the ruins of 'Great Houses' (thought to have been ceremonial rather than domestic buildings) scattered along its floor, structural evidence of ancient astronomical knowledge, and numerous Great Kivas or semi-subterranean circular chambers for ceremonial and ritual activities. What indicates that Chaco was a pilgrimage centre is the great system of roads that converge on it: these features, visible now mainly by mean of aerial photography or high-tech imaging systems developed by NASA, are up to 30 feet (9 metres) across and are engineered structures, and in some cases lengths of these wide roads ran in parallel. The interesting fact is that the Anasazi did not have wheeled vehicles or beasts of burden – so why did they need such wide roads? The answer has to be that they served some important ritual or ceremonial purpose. Quite recent archaeological investigation is showing that the road system extended into Utah, Colorado, and Arizona, and the latest thinking suggests that the roads were ceremonial ways that linked the Great Kivas in various centres across the San Juan Basin. One piece of

Anasazi rock art situated near one of the great roadways actually shows a line of people walking in single file, and this may be the earliest glimpse we have of pre-Columbian pilgrims.

Because of early Spanish documentation, in addition to a long train of archaeological evidence, we have a sharper picture of pilgrimage in pre-Columbian Mexico. The Aztecs – who were the dominant culture when the Spanish arrived – tended to make pilgrimages to places that were ancient even in their own time. In particular, the great ceremonial city complex of Teotihuacán, built by an unknown people almost 2,000 years ago, was viewed by the Aztecs as their spiritual home, and the 'birthplace of the gods'. They considered pilgrimage to the ruins of the place to be an important act of veneration, and would leave items of pottery there in broken, votive form. The Aztec king Motecuhzoma II is said to have walked to Teotihuacán on a regular basis to worship there. Another key Aztec pilgrimage site was the now greatly ruined religious centre of Cholula (Plate 15), also in the Valley of Mexico. This had been founded by the people of Teotihuacán and developed further by the later Mixteca-Puebla culture. The Aztecs made it the pilgrimage centre of their Quetzalcóatl cult, as they believed the plumed serpent took refuge there. Mount Tláloc near present-day Mexico City formed the destination for an annual pilgrimage made by the Aztec kings of Tenochtitlán, Tetzcoco, Tlacopan and Xochimilco. It took place in April or May at the height of the dry season and its purpose was to call forth rain from within the mountain. The richly attired kings proceeded in procession up the high-walled processional route leading to the temple precinct on the summit of the mountain. This contained stone idols that were dressed by the kings. Sacrificial offerings were made to these representations of the mountain gods, including fabulous dishes of food and the blood of a male child. Other mountain shrines were also honoured by Aztec pilgrimages.

The ancient Mayan culture, in southern Mexico, also had its pilgrimage traditions. When the Spanish first arrived, they noted that the key Maya pilgrimage centres were the shrine of the oracle goddess Ixchel on Cozumel (see Part Four), and the sacred *cenote* (sinkhole) at Chichén-Itzá. One Spanish chronicler, Landa, wrote that the Maya held these places 'in the same veneration as we have for pilgrimages to Jerusalem and Rome'. There is archaeological evidence that the ancient Mayan ceremonial city of La Milpa in Belize was used by the later Maya as a pilgrimage site to venerate and implore the ancestors who dwelled there for help (Hammond and Bobo, 1994). In times of pestilence, pilgrimages would be made to shrines of the god Kinich Kakmo, an aspect of the Sun. In general, there were many local and minor pilgrimage shrines within Maya territory, as well as major longer-distance ones.

Mexico also provides a living pilgrimage tradition, whose origins are lost in antiquity. For unnumbered generations the Huichol Indians have made an annual pilgrimage of hundreds of miles from their mountain homeland to a high plateau region called Wirikuta, considered to be their sacred land of origin. They are mythically retracing the steps of the First People, and they perform various actions attributed to those mythic ancestors at specific locations. At Wirikuta, a hunt for and ritual consumption of the hallucinogenic peyote cactus takes place. The cactus is referred to as a 'deer', and some anthropologists think this whole ritual may hark back to Palaeo-Indian times and traditions of the Great Hunt brought over the Beringia land bridge from Siberia. If so, then this pilgrimage contains vestiges of awesome antiquity. The peyote deer-hunt is the climax of the pilgrimage and is the peak experience in the religious life of the Huichol. Baskets of cacti are gathered and taken back as sacramental hallucinogens for use in religious activities over the coming year.

As in North America, there must be many unknown pilgrimage shrines throughout the vastness of South American rainforests and deserts, but the best known examples are in the Andes, where several ancient cities and temples were pilgrimage centres. In Peru, the two-and-a-half-millennia-old temple of Chavín de Huántar was the main centre for a major cult that used plant hallucinogens. Pilgrims bearing offerings and wishing to consult the oracle at Chavín came from throughout the vast territory influenced by the cult. Further south along the Peruvian Andes is Cahuachi, near Nazca. Dating to between 1,500 and 2,000 years ago, Cahuachi comprised a now almost destroyed temple building, mounds, and pyramids, six of which were giant natural mounds which had adobe facings placed on their slopes. Some archaeologists think that certain of the nearby Nazca lines (long straight markings scoured on the desert surface) were used by pilgrims as ritual ways approaching Cahuachi. Of the ceremonial Andean cities, we can cite Pachacamac on the central coast of Peru, which had a large community catering to the needs of pilgrims, or Tiahuanaco, situated at over 12,000 feet (3,600 metres) in the Andes, next to Lake Titicaca. This place flourished for almost 1,000 years from c. AD 200. It was a holy city, with the architecture of its central core designed for public ceremony. Its main shrine was the Akapana, a huge artificial terraced hill faced in stone. At its height, the city's resident population may have numbered some 40,000, and this would have been increased at times of pilgrimage. Tiahuanaco scholar Alan Kolata has commented: 'Tiahuanaco became the ultimate centre of pilgrimage, an Andean Mecca, the first truly cosmopolitan city of the ancient Andean world' (Kolata, 1996). But as Andean scholars Adriana von Hagen and Craig Morris observe:

> In a sense, all Andean cities were ceremonial centers, some almost exclusively so – meccas for pilgrims who came from afar with tribute . . . In many cases, these pilgrimage centers retained their religious allure long after their influence had ebbed, and people continued to bury their dead there and leave offerings. (von Hagan and Morris, 1998)

To this day, the Ayamara people of the Andes make pilgrimages to mountain shrines to plead to the mountain gods for rain and good crops.

SITE EXAMPLES

Santiago de Compostela

The most famous and important of medieval pilgrimages within Europe after that to Rome was to Santiago de Compostela in Galicia, north-west Spain – at a western extremity of the known Old World. At the height of the pilgrimage's popularity, multitudes were drawn to Santiago de Compostela because of the claims of miracles associated with the body of the Apostle St James the Greater, believed to be lodged there. After the saint's martyrdom in Jerusalem in AD 44, the body was supposedly miraculously transported to Galicia, where it was unearthed in the ninth century by a farmer or hermit who was led to it by a strange star.

Puente la Reina was and is the starting point of the Camino de Santiago, the pilgrims' way that cuts east–west across northern Spain through Burgos, León, and Astorga. This arduous route is hundreds of miles long, crossing two mountain ranges and an arid plain, but there were hospices spaced along it, each a day's walk apart, administered by monastic or military orders. Places where religious personages had been born or died, or where relics were kept, along with monasteries and convents, caves used by anchorites, and sites of miracles and wonders all developed into shrines along the pilgrims' road. Guidebooks and phrasebooks were published to aid pilgrims in their journeying. Papal decree ensured that pilgrims to Santiago would receive a remission of a third of their sins, and if they timed their journey to arrive on the main feast day, 25 July, they would receive additional boons. At their destination, pilgrims bought scallop-shell badges, to prove that they had made the sacred journey.

In the ninth century, there was a stone tomb at Santiago said to contain the saint's relics, and a cathedral was built in the early tenth century to house it. This structure was destroyed by Muslims later that century. A cathedral of ambitious design started to be built in 1077, and over the centuries there were further additions and

1: A May tree (*Maibaum*) temporarily erected for May Day in Aachen, Germany. See Part One.

2: The ancient Celtic navel stone of Ireland, Aill na Mireann, or the Stone of Divisions, on the hill of Uisneach, Westmeath. See Part One.

3: A rock-hewn Anasazi *kiva* at Mesa Verde, Colorado. The *sipapu* symbolising the Point of Emergence is the smaller hole on the kiva floor. See Part One.

4: One of the two surviving *omphaloi* stones at Delphi. See Part One.

5: The main temple of the Angkor Wat group, Cambodia. See Part One. (*Fortean Picture Library*)

6: Monks Mound, Cahokia, the largest prehistoric mound in the United States. See Part One.

7: An indoor water fountain like this can make an ideal meditative focus. See 'Principles and Practice' in Part One.

8: Remains of the eighteenth-century pillar marking Venonae, the Roman centre of Britain. See Part One.

9: Croft Hill, Leicestershire, probably the pre-Roman central sacred hill of Britain. The forgotten heart of Albion? See Part One.

10: Extensive views can be had from the rocky summit of Croft Hill. See Part One.

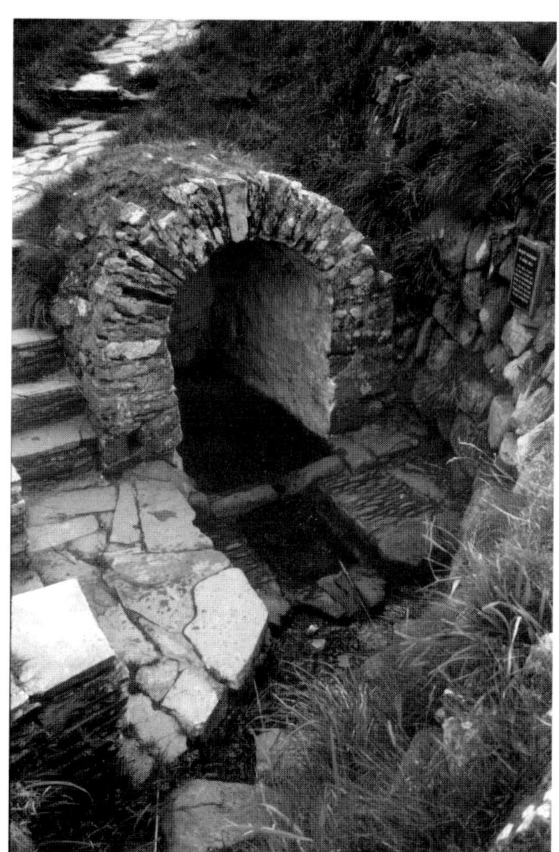

11: St Non's Well near St David's, Wales. See Part Two.

12: Hereford Cathedral, probably on the site of a powerful early Celtic Christian centre, and containing the ancient shrine of St Thomas among other treasures. See Part Two.

13: St Frideswide's face peers out from among foliage on this thirteenth-century fragment of her shrine in Christ Church Cathedral, Oxford. See Part Two.

14: Canterbury Cathedral. See Part Two.

15: Part of the mysterious ruins of Cholula, Mexico, the Aztec pilgrimage centre dedicated to the plumed serpent god, Quetzalcóatl. See Part Two.

16: Known as the 'Lonely Arch', this is virtually all that remains of the medieval priory at Walsingham, the great Marian pilgrimage centre in Norfolk, England. See Part Two.

17: The Slipper Chapel alongside the pilgrims' road near Walsingham. See Part Two.

18: Pilgrims circumambulating Mount Kailas in the Himalayas by means of prostrations. See Part Two. (*William Eddy*)

rebuilding. In the seventeenth and eighteenth centuries the cathedral was covered with an ornate Baroque façade, though the interior was left alone. Entrance for pilgrims to the cathedral was by the magnificent Romanesque west doorway, the Portico de la Gloria, dating to 1168. Then as now, they touched the central pillar of the doorway, worn by countless such gestures. At the high altar, made from alabaster, on which is the magnificent statue shrine of St James, encrusted with silver and diamonds, the pilgrim climbs up steps to reach through an open space and kiss the effigy's neck. A casket supposedly containing the saint's relics is on view in the crypt.

The war between England and Spain in the late sixteenth century brought an end to the heyday of the pilgrimage. The relics were hidden for safety, then lost, and the numbers of pilgrims to Santiago dropped drastically. In the nineteenth century, when the relics were apparently recovered and authenticated, the pilgrimage was revived. Today, tens of thousands of people arrive at Santiago annually. Many travel by vehicle, but some – an average of 20,000 per year – still walk the Pilgrims' Way, getting their pilgrimage card stamped at the appropriate points along the route. Most are devout believers, but many more – scholars, academics, wanderers, spiritual seekers, writers, musicians, artists – simply want to experience the pilgrimage out of curiosity, for cultural reasons, or to find out something about themselves in the journeying.

Walsingham

This is the great Marian shrine of England. It is in the village of Little Walsingham, Norfolk, and came into being as a Christian site in the eleventh century, when Lady Richeldis de Faverches, the widow of the lord of the manor, said she had a vision of the Virgin. The apparition showed the widow an image of the Holy House in Nazareth where Gabriel announced the coming of Jesus, and where the Holy Child dwelled, and instructed her to build an exact replica. Two springs of water burbled into existence at the place where the Virgin had appeared (the reported vision was, in fact, probably a

Christianising of an existing pagan well site). The wealthy lady duly had a simple wooden copy of the Holy House constructed; the legend tells that it was then moved into its precise location by angels under the Virgin's instructions. Here was England's Nazareth.

The wooden structure was later surrounded by a stone building with a thatched roof, and that was followed by a priory later in the eleventh century, and then another in the thirteenth century, from which the monks could provide hospitality to the increasing number of pilgrims to the Holy House and the attendant holy and wishing wells (Plate 16). During this same century, royal pilgrimages began, making the shrine even more popular, internationally as well as nationally. Various relics were gathered at the shrine, including supposed milk of the Virgin, fragments of the True Cross, and, above all, a wooden statue of the Madonna and Child, which became associated with miracle cures. The pilgrimage route passed through the small village of Houghton St Giles, about a mile south of Walsingham, where a chapel was erected as a wayside station. This became known as the Slipper Chapel (Plate 17), because it became the custom for pilgrims to leave their footwear there and proceed barefoot along the final 'holy mile'. Walsingham was brutally suppressed by Henry VIII in the sixteenth century, the statue burned, and the pilgrimage outlawed.

Revival of the pilgrimage place began in the nineteenth century, when Catholics reclaimed the Slipper Chapel, which was being used as a barn. In the 1920s, the vicar of Walsingham, Alfred Hope Patten, supervised the rebuilding of the shrine near the location of the original one; in the process, a Saxon well was discovered and Patten took this as a good omen. A garden was created next to the shrine, with the Stations of the Cross around it, and a statue of the Virgin was carved, copied from an ancient abbey seal held in the British Museum. The pilgrimage was revived, and today Walsingham has separate Catholic, Anglican, Methodist, and Greek and Russian Orthodox shrines, and considerable ecumenical and multi-faith cooperation is displayed. The main pilgrimage days are at the Annunciation (25 March), the Assumption (15 August), and Easter.

St Winefride's Well (Ffynnon Wenfrewi)

This well shrine in Holywell (Treffynnon), Clwyd, North Wales, draws on a twelfth-century legend woven around the seventh-century Celtic saint Winefride (Gwenfrewi), which states that when she fended off a rape attempt by Caradoc, a Welsh prince, her attacker became so infuriated that he cut off her head. Where it fell to the ground a spring of water bubbled into life, and where the blood spattered the moss turned red and produced a sweet odour of violets and incense. (It is interesting to note that the famed botanist Linnaeus listed a 'violet-smelling' moss exclusive to the area.) Hearing the commotion, Winefride's tutor, St Beuno, emerged onto the awful scene from a nearby chapel. He immediately cursed Caradoc, who dropped dead, then put Winefride's head carefully back in contact with her neck and shoulders. He prayed intensely until she became whole again and returned to life. Later, Winefride and Beuno blessed the well that had formed from the magical spring. Clearly, this legend contains allusions to the pagan Celtic myth of the living severed head. We can be sure that the well is a Christianised pagan site.

The well has been visited by pilgrims – including kings and other nobility – continuously since medieval times, the Reformation failing to interrupt the practice. One pilgrim route went from St David's in the south right across Wales to Holywell. Others came via Shrewsbury and Chester. Winefride's relics were kept in Shrewsbury but her shrine there was destroyed at the Reformation, and the saint's relics lost except for one finger, which was later divided between Shrewsbury and Holywell. The sacred, healing well is said to be the most complete medieval shrine in Britain, and consists of a large structure housing the spring, a chapel, and an ambulatory allowing pilgrims to circle the well before going to a bathing pool fed by the spring. The well continues to attract Catholic and Anglican pilgrims, as well as tourists, the curious, and those on personal pilgrimages. The site hosts several ecumenical pilgrimages, including one for the handicapped.

Mount Kailas

This 22,000 foot (6,700 metre) mountain is situated in the Himalayas in a remote part of south-western Tibet. Its pyramidical peak dominates the surrounding mountains, shining out like a beacon in the light of dawn. It is sacred for a fifth of the world's population: to Hindus it is the dwelling of the major god, Shiva, and his consort Parvati; Tibetan Buddhists know the mountain as Tise or Kang Rimpoche, Jewel of the Snows, home of the god Demchok and his female companion, Dorje Phagmo. The Jain sect of India call the peak Astapada, the mystical abode of one of their saints. Kailas is also sacred to the practitioners of Bon, Tibet's indigenous pre-Buddhist animist religion.

Hindu and Buddhist mythology cast Kailas as the earthly representation of the mythic Mount Meru or Sumeru, the World Mountain, the *axis mundi*. Mythically, a river flows from each of its four sides, defining the Four Directions, north, south, east and west, in accord with the geography of Paradise in many myths throughout the world. In actuality, four major, sacred rivers, the Indus, the Brahmaputra, the Sutlej, and the Karnali, have their sources around Kailas.

For thousands of years Mount Kailas has been the focal point of pilgrimage for untold numbers of people. Even to this day Tibetan pilgrims will circle the base of this exceedingly remote peak in devotional fashion using a most severe form of pilgrimage technique. From a standing position with hands held together in prayer, they kneel, bow down then lie on the ground, touching it with their forehead. They mark a spot with their nose, rise again and walk to that spot, then repeat the whole cycle. During the Cultural Revolution (1966–1976) of Mao Tse-tung, the monasteries around the foot of the mountain were destroyed, though some destroyed shrine sites on the pilgrimage route have been marked by rocks and boulders.

Relatively few Westerners have made the full Kailas pilgrimage. One who has is the American academic William Eddy. After much planning, he set off for the Himalayas, accompanied by his son and three other companions. With a Tibetan guide, they trekked for six days from Nepal to Kailas, gradually gaining in altitude from 9,000 to 15,000 feet (2,700 to 4,500 metres). They struggled along slippery paths, sometimes having to unload their pack animals in order to allow them to proceed. They passed through friendly villages, and crossed over the Nara La Pass, where they strung out some prayer flags. 'The physical and sensuous intensity of such an experience can only be shared with those who were part of it . . . In this sense the trip is an isolating experience that bonds you with the people who were there but separates you from those who were not,' says Eddy (personal communication), perfectly describing the sense of *communitas.* He found his first view of the white summit of Kailas across the blue-black waters of Lake Rakshas Tal to be 'magical'. It was June, considered to be one of the auspicious months for the Kailas pilgrimage, and Eddy and his companions found many hundreds of other pilgrims already engaged on their sacred journey round the mountain.

The circuit can be completed by the fit and zealous in one day, but those who use the prostration form of pilgrimage can take more than two weeks. These 'inch worms', as they are affectionately known, go with a friend who builds small bridges of stones when streams block the way so that the pilgrim need not interrupt the prostrations. Eddy made the important observation that this arduous form of pilgrimage was 'performed in joy, not as a form of martyrdom' (Plate 18). He and his companions started on the pilgrimage circuit, and camped after 10–12 miles (16–19 kilometres), at over 16,000 feet (4,800 metres). Next day they continued on, in a bitter wind, with Kailas 'like a living presence that loomed over our right shoulder'. As they continued, the path grew steeper and there was more snow underfoot. They passed a place called Tshiwa Tsel, where piles of rotting clothing were strewn around. It was here that every pilgrim made a small personal sacrifice – a piece of clothing, a lock of hair, a tooth, some blood, or whatever. At this place, the pilgrims tried to visualise their death. At the high pass of Drolma La, there is a huge rock painted with Buddhist and Hindu blessings and prayers, above which flutter strands of prayer flags – it is believed the winds blow the prayers to the corners of the Earth for the benefit of all living beings. For devotees, this place of barren desolation was a point of spiritual climax. 'For us,' recalls Eddy, 'it represented an achievement, of both mind and body, and to be amidst the honest and simple joy of the pilgrims was a privilege.'

PRINCIPLES AND PRACTICE

Principles

Pilgrimage viewed in a general context is a universal behavioural pattern that defies any attempt to impose some external rational logic in the form of a specific belief system. It is a meaningful, sacred activity *in its own right*. Gods, saints, religions, beliefs – they can come, go, or mutate, but the pilgrimage endures. Pilgrimage is not a function of religion; rather, religions (which are human constructs) make use of pilgrimage. So, as we have already indicated, we have to seek deeper levels of meaning, more fundamental principles, governing the pilgrimage impulse.

At one important level, the act of pilgrimage is metaphorical, a factor perhaps best used in Western literature by Bunyan in his *The Pilgrim's Progress.* The outer journey is the expression and stimulus for an inner pilgrimage. The goal of the pilgrimage is not, in the final analysis, a place, but the inner self of the pilgrim. As a Kashmiri woman mystic observed in the fourteenth century: 'I . . . went out far in search of Shiva . . . having wandered, I found him in my own body . . .' Similarly, Sufi mystics have invoked the idea of an inner Ka'ba, while Christian sages have argued that the true Jerusalem lies within. This may seem to indicate that physical pilgrimage is without value in any true spiritual sense, yet it is possible to dismiss the overt, literalist, and populist concept of pilgrimage and still see it as a practice, a yoga if you like, that can itself become a means of inducing an inner sacred journey. And this is the second deep principle underpinning pilgrimage. Pilgrimage, especially walking pilgrimage, can render the natural landscape meaningful in ways unfamiliar to modern people. Pilgrims journey outside their normal social structures and often in psychological and physiological states that can lay the groundwork for visionary insight. Perhaps we need to teach ourselves how to journey like this again, even if we strip away specific religious contexts and just preserve the spiritual and psychological core of the matter – physical process and liminality to encourage mental (and spiritual) changes, or at least alterations in perception.

Remember what the Koran urges: 'And proclaim unto mankind the Pilgrimage . . . That they witness things that are of benefit to them.'

Practice

To Be a Pilgrim

An obvious experiment to try is to take part in an established pilgrimage. It doesn't really matter whether or not you believe in the religious framework governing the pilgrimage you select or are able to gain access to – it is the spiritual development you are seeking, not a religion. And not necessarily even spirituality, if that word intimidates you, but psychological experience – changing your customary set and setting. It is from such changes that one gains fresh insights and perspectives, and new springs of creativity.

Plan out your pilgrimage expedition – perhaps as a vacation activity. You might have to travel some distance, even to a foreign country, and you have to find out the correct dates, who to contact (if you want to go on an organised pilgrimage), and so on. The information in the preceding pages of this part of the book will give you starting points, but you will need to turn the proposed pilgrimage into a carefully planned research project. If you have access to the World Wide Web, then that is a great help. If you do a search for, say, 'Pilgrimage' on a search engine or directory like AltaVista (http://www.altavista.com), you will get a list of literally thousands of Web and Internet sites containing personal accounts, photographs, information on pilgrimage routes and pilgrimage destinations both well known and utterly obscure in many countries and of many religions. There will also be contact information on many commercial operators who specialise in pilgrimage tours if you do not want to organise your own. As with all things on the Internet, you have to exercise caution and discernment – there is much rubbish, some dubious organisations, a lot of religions peddling their doctrines, as well as genuinely useful, inter-faith information. For a general directory I have found one on Google to be useful: http://www.google.com

You may want to access the Web for specific places, like Santiago de Compostela for example. In which case, put that in your search box (in inverted commas) – perhaps adding the word 'pilgrimage' after it. I found a couple of useful general Web sites related to Santiago:

www.humnet.ucla.edu/santiago/iagohome.html and http://webby.cc.denison.edu:90/modlangs/hnrs274/index.html.

If you have interest in British shrines, especially Marian ones, then the *Catholic Encyclopedia* has a good list (www.newadvent.org/cathen/13760a.html). The famous Marian shrine in Ireland is at Knock – see Plate 19.

A couple of hours of careful work on the Web, or in a library, or on the telephone, should get you started on the road towards your pilgrimage experience. I would recommend that for the purpose of this particular experiment you select an ancient and well-established pilgrimage destination, so you have the opportunity to experience places that have been drenched in devotion for centuries, and to observe how groups if not large numbers of pilgrims behave and respond. I would advise that you try to keep clear of being involved too intensely in the belief system governing the pilgrimage you embark on (remember that what really matters are the principles underlying all pilgrimages), while at the same time respecting the faith of other pilgrims who are devotees.

If you are unable or disinclined to actually participate in a pilgrimage, then you can at least try to visit a place that was an ancient pilgrimage centre, if only to absorb the qualities such sites usually possess – the sort of experience that the German composer Felix Mendelssohn had when he visited Iona in the 1820s. He was enchanted with the place, and wrote: 'When in some future time I shall sit in a madly crowded assembly . . . and the wish arises to retire into the loneliness, I shall think of Iona.'

This is, of course, one of the great reasons for visiting ancient pilgrimage places – their serenity, peace, and deep sanctity reinforced by countless pilgrims over the ages can live afterwards in the mind and heart, where they can be visited whenever the need arises in the turmoil of our lives. (The artistic fruits of Mendelssohn's Iona experience, incidentally, can be found in his *Hebrides Overture* (*Fingal's Cave*).)

Canterbury Trails

Another worthwhile exercise is to follow part of an ancient pilgrimage route even though not going on the pilgrimage as such. Such paths and tracks have taken on an aura of their own, and it is good to absorb this. The Camino to Santiago is a good example, and easy to find out about (see above), but let us here take the Pilgrims' Way to Canterbury.

There were several routes to Canterbury, with two main ones. Chaucer's motley group of fictional pilgrims in his *Canterbury Tales* took the route from London, starting out from Southwark, but the route that is now marked as the Pilgrims' Way on maps comes via Winchester in southern England. This is *The Old Road* that Hilaire Belloc famously and entertainingly explored around the turn of the twentieth century. From Winchester it runs in a direction slightly north of east through Alresford, Alton (along the main street here), Farnham, along the ridge known as the Hog's Back near Guildford, then onto the North Downs past Dorking and Boxhill, passing a little to the north of Reigate then on through Chevening, Otford, Wrotham, Trottiscliffe, Snodland, Burham, onwards to the north of Maidstone, through Detling, Thurnham, Boughton Aluph, in the porch of which church there was a pilgrims' resting place, Harbledown (probably Chaucer's 'Bobbe-up-and-doun'), where the Way runs through an Iron Age earthwork called Bigbury Hillfort, and so to Canterbury itself.

This route of roughly 100 miles (160 kilometres) makes a marvellous driving holiday, passing through or by so many ancient, charmingly picturesque and intriguing places as it does. (What are now ancient inns and chapels and the like naturally arose along the course of the Pilgrims' Way.) You can follow the general course of the route, occasionally stopping fairly close to the Way and walking sections of the path where it is well preserved or restored. The route as a whole in any case does not exist, but has been construed from surviving segments and documentary sources, and some sections are still speculative, or divert from the original course because of modern obstacles.

It *is* important to actually walk on the Old Road to some extent, though. Not only does it go through sections of countryside, some of which are still blissfully left alone by modern traffic, and provide some marvellous views, genuine old sections of it have a distinct 'atmosphere'. When Satish Kumar, editor of *Resurgence* magazine, travelled for a while on the Pilgrims' Way, he had a flash of what we might term transpersonal memory that made him feel he was 'in the company of those people who had preceded' him. This time-warping sense of companionship with people who used the same

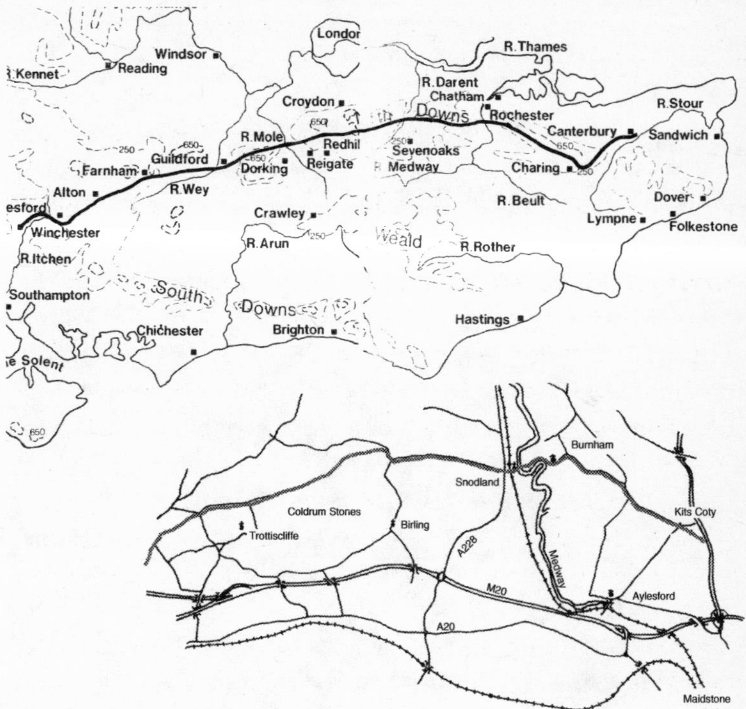

Figure 8: The general course of the Pilgrims' Way from Winchester to Canterbury, and details of the section from Trottiscliffe to Burham.

ribbon of space in the past can often occur when walking on old roads and tracks, and never more so than on ancient ways like this.

If you have only time for a brief visit to the Pilgrims' Way, then a particularly interesting section (though now unfortunately hedged about with modern road systems) is that which runs past Trottiscliffe, through Snodland to Burham. This section is immediately north of and parallel to the M20 motorway north-west of Maidstone. (Access north can be gained from Junction 3 of the motorway.) The reason this section is particularly to be recommended is that it drives home the fact that however old the medieval period might seem, parts of the Pilgrims' Way run on or close to the course of much older tracks. Indeed, it was Belloc's contention (with which most authorities now agree) that the Pilgrims' Way was in fact merely an updating – of its time – of a major east–west prehistoric ridgeway route through southern England, probably providing access to the great ceremonial centres of Salisbury Plain, where Stonehenge is located. The Old Road indeed. You can drive to the tiny village of Trottiscliffe, visit its ancient church which appears to have megaliths embedded in its Saxon foundations, and from there gain foot access to the Pilgrims' Way. This shortly passes Coldrum Long Barrow, a Neolithic chambered mound (Plate 20). Following the old course of the Way (ignoring the North Downs Way, which shares sections of the Pilgrims' Way) brings you to a paved length of the old pilgrim's route that leads hard by Snodland church, at an ancient crossing of the River Medway. (Roman remains were discovered near this area, including what appears to have been a Mithraic temple.) On the other side of the river the Way used to lead up past Burham church and a mile or so further on from there crossed what is now the A229, which occupies the course of a Roman road. The Way then passed onwards via Detling (fragments of it approaching Detling are marked on the Ordnance Survey Landranger map 178). There is now no way of crossing the river at Snodland, so the modern-day pilgrim has to cross either further north at Rochester where the M2 does so (this is not recommended), or go back south to the M26, travel east along it and take the A229 northwards at junction 6. About a mile along the A229 from the motorway is where the old Pilgrims' Way crosses; a few hundred yards from there is Little Kit's Coty House, also known as the Countless Stones. This is a collapsed Neolithic barrow, marked on Ordnance Survey maps at approximate grid reference 745603.

As you stand here, you will be acutely aware that you have followed a sacred trail that spans huge tracts of time, from the Stone Age through Roman, Saxon, and medieval periods. Sense the kinship of all the souls that have walked this way.

The Old Road is a line of information that transcends time but stays in place.

On Track

Quite apart from specific pilgrims' paths, *any* path that has some age to it can provide an experience of sacred journeying to anyone sufficiently attuned. In a literary study of paths, Kim Taplin suggests that 'because of their removedness from the human world and their closeness to nature, footpaths often induce that contemplative state which is the soil for visionary experience' (Taplin, 1979). This may well be why in the past certain pathways have themselves become shrines: the Samoyed in Arctic Russia had a sacred length of trackway in a wood that straddled a segment of their annual migratory route where they turned trees bordering the track into shrines; in France, a pathway known as Yries was still being venerated with offerings as late as the seventeenth century, and Anglo-Saxon chronicles record paths and tracks named after spirits in the English countryside. Any area of the Earth that was inhabited in the past will have such tracks.

As you walk an old track be alert to what the English poet Edmund Blunden called the 'sounds, scents and seeings' to be had on a country walk. Similarly, in the poem 'Small Paths', Bobi Jones points out that paths can 'teach the pupils of the eyes' about the wonder and detail of nature all around. And even if one follows the same path on more than one occasion, it is a different experience each time – 'It isn't the same shout you hear across the hedge / Calling the cattle; it isn't the same breeze . . . ' (Jones, 1987).

The use of a path to develop a sense of sacred journeying is basically the same as a yogi using a mandala for meditation: it is a physical tool to enhance your consciousness. It just requires a change from our utilitarian attitude towards paths and roads: they can be a means of getting from one place to another in the inner as well as the outer world.

Apart from traditional country paths in European landscapes, there are many other types that can fulfil the same purpose. In North America, for instance, the courses of some of the old Indian trails have been recorded. The famous case is Broadway: more than merely a road that runs through the theatre district of Manhattan, it stretches long distances north through upstate New York. But a visit to a reference library anywhere in the States is likely to elicit useful regional information on local Indian trails. (See also Part Three.) In Australia, some of the Aboriginal dream journey routes have been mapped, at least in part. Dig out the relevant information, gain any permissions that may be necessary, and walk in the ancient ways – even if for only a short distance. Wherever you live, you are likely to find an ancient track somewhere that has – or more likely, had – more than utilitarian purposes, if you are prepared to undertake the necessary research.

Slowing Down

In addition to deciding *where* to conduct your sacred journeying, there is also the matter of *how* you do it. The first thing that what we might call 'sacred walking' teaches us is to *slow down*.

We tend to forget that today we usually experience the landscape at speeds unknown to our ancestors. We flash through in motor vehicles and trains, or fly in aircraft through the skies, disconnected from the land altogether. We rush hither and thither – to and from work, going shopping, picking up the kids from school, and so forth. 'By increasing the speed at which we pass through the landscape,' warns geographer Jay Appleton, we '. . . may greatly alter the time-sequences which are an integral part of our perceptive experience of it' (Appleton, 1975). This is shown up more starkly with traditional peoples. For instance, Gary Snyder recalls that when he was being driven through the outback of Australia in a truck with a Pintupi elder, Jimmy Tjungurrayi, the Aborigine started telling him about Dreamtime stories concerning features in the landscape they were passing through. The old man was talking so rapidly that Snyder could not keep up with the narrative issuing from his lips. Snyder eventually realised that the stories were 'meant to be told while *walking*, and that I was experiencing a speeded-up version of what might be leisurely told over several days of foot travel' (Snyder, 1990). Similarly, Bruce Chatwin observed that an Aborigine known as Limpy who was travelling in a vehicle with him across bush country suddenly became animated and started babbling out of the window. It turned out that they had just crossed a point on a dream journey route or 'songline' known to him, and he was attempting to rush through the couplets associated with the place that he had learned at walking pace and was now trying to accommodate within the much shorter time frame afforded by the Land Cruiser as it rolled along (Chatwin, 1987).

Learning to Walk

Try to link the physical act of walking to mental exercise. You may have thought you learned to walk when you were a toddler, but don't kid yourself. It can be a deeper, subtler activity than simply putting one foot in front of the other. Pilgrimage was always about more than that. James Lovelock, the originator of the 'Gaia' theory, which posits that the entire Earth is one single integrated system like a living organism, has written: 'The simplest way to explore Gaia is on foot. How else can you so easily be part of her ambience? How else can you reach out to her with all your senses?' (Lovelock, 1993).

Walking is a healthy physical exercise, certainly, but here we are dealing with what Thoreau wrote of in his essay 'Walking', in 1862: '[T]he walking of which I speak has nothing in it akin to taking exercise, as it is called . . . ' Walking for its own sake, as a method of meditation, is considerably undervalued. Many people appreciate that it can help clear the mind and resolve problems, as indicated by the Latin phrase *solvitur ambulando* (loosely, 'you can solve it by walking'), but its mental effects can go deeper than this. The already cited wayfarer Philip O'Connor emphasised this in his account of tramping, remarking that the prolonged act of 'unproductive walking' (walking that is not directed at exercise or destinations) produces cyclical alternations of thought, emotion, and sensation that are somehow linked. The tramp, he explained, 'drifts sensuously in the rhythm of walking'. He even found that startling mind-change experiences could occur, so that 'mental fireworks will gloriously light the mind – but quickly the world will attach the inner light to outer phenomena . . . The speed of transit between inner state and outer appearance is a feature of tramping . . .' (O'Connor, 1963). In similar vein, the poet John Keats remarked on the sense of 'excited reverie' he experienced during country rambles.

When Thoreau wanted to go for one of his meditative walks, he would set off intuitively in a direction rather than plan a route out. He felt that there is a 'subtle magnetism' in nature that one can attune to at any given moment. You can do much the same for your first attempt at sacred walking. If you performed the practical experiment in Part One ('Round in Circles'), where you found out what direction felt 'good' to you, then that might be the one in which to set off. For this exercise, it doesn't so much matter where you walk, in town or country, but how you do it. A half-hour walk would do fine. Don't have any particular destination in mind – a circular route might be best. Walk alone and at an easy pace.

Use all your senses as you walk. If you are in familiar territory, make an effort to notice new things, details in the surroundings that you have missed previously, perhaps because you normally drive by, or your eyes are fixed and you are preoccupied when you normally walk this route. Seek out those missing features; glance to your side, look above the horizontal, and if you look downwards, ensure that you do so consciously, paying attention to every detail – though take care not to walk into something! Follow your nose, too, and take in the smell of foliage, the scent of flowers in the hedgerow or the park, the stench of uncollected garbage, or whatever the olfactory environment happens to be. You can also use the sense of touch while walking. In addition to trailing your hands along railings, leaves, or other objects you pass, try to feel the air moving over your face or exposed arms and legs. Be aware of the breeze or wind. And keep an ear cocked: be alert to the sounds around you – distant traffic, perhaps, or the cry of birds, a dog barking, insects buzzing, the rustle of leaves, the sound of your own breath, the noise your feet make on the ground. Monitor your senses like this constantly; take in as much multisensory information as you can.

Work this effort into your rhythm of walking. Feel that rhythm. If it is not comfortable and easy, smooth off its rough edges. Allow your breathing and movement to become as one. Become aware of how you are moving. What kind of contact are your feet having on the ground? Are you going up hill or down dale? Does the ground slope to your left or right – is it really horizontal? Notice forces of gravity on your body as you move, the subtle pull this way or that. Work it all into your gait and breathing pattern.

All these attempts to be aware can combine into a powerful way of quietening the usual chatter of your mind, which is the very aim of meditation. In this case, though, not only does your mind not have time to chatter in its incessant, abstract way, it is forced to attach itself to your body and your senses. This is important, for the mind loves to float off by itself – we have all had the experience of not being aware of what we are walking or even driving through because we are 'lost in thought'. This exercise is about *not* being lost, of not forgetting where we are. It is a powerful form of embodied meditation. Like all meditation, it can be difficult at first, but when you do manage to get all the factors hanging together, there will be a moment on your walk – if not the first attempt, then later ones – when your consciousness will light up. The more you do it, the more frequent and extended those moments will become. You don't have to travel to the Holy Land on a pilgrimage, you just have to realise that you are already walking through a holy land. You can walk to the inner Jerusalem just as readily as to an outer shrine.

Light and Dark

Try walking the same route – preferably in a rural area – in daylight and at night. Observe the different sensory impressions you receive. The dominance of the visual sense is reduced at night, so it is easier to use hearing and smell to greater effect, and in any case the scents of plants and flowers are stronger at night, and the environment is likely to be quieter and contain different, or transformed sounds. Country parson Francis Kilvert recorded stopping on one of his regular nightly walks to listen to 'the rustle and solemn night whisper of the wheat, so different to its voice by day'.

Walking on the Spot

When Pacific islanders are navigating in their remarkable way on the open ocean, one of the mental tools some of them employ is to visualise themselves as staying still, with the sea passing beneath their canoe, distant islands (real and mythic ones) floating by, and the sky rolling itself over them. It is the world that moves, while they stay at the still centre. It can be a fascinating experience to apply this principle to your walking. Try to imagine that you are not actually moving through space; instead, try to feel that you are 'walking on the spot'. Imagine the ground as a kind of giant roller turning beneath your feet, so that although you are moving your legs, placing one foot in front of the other all the time, you are not actually moving forwards through space. You are moving, but you are still.

It is of course difficult at first to counteract the overriding logical knowledge you possess that it is you who is moving. But ask yourself, is that really the case? Is it not a fact that you are always *here*, however far you walk, drive, fly? Try to tune in to this different kind of logic for a while; try to tune in to *here*. In a half-hour's walk, if you make a regular effort, you will slip in and out of this perception of walking on the spot numerous times. Persist, because when you make it happen for long enough it is a startling effect, I assure you. Suddenly, walking becomes effortless.

It is Zen in the art of walking.

Pilgrimage in Mind

Pilgrimage is as much a mental act as a physical one – it is particularly important to emphasise this for those who are unable for one reason or another to go on one, or even to undertake the physical walking-perception exercises suggested above. So much is this so, that Sophronius, Bishop of Jerusalem from 634 to 638, wrote poems (*Anacreontica*) about walking through the Holy City during a period of exile. It was an act of memory and imagination. The Jerusalem liturgy can be undertaken as a soul journey, in the mind.

Mental forms of pilgrimage can begin with a very simple visualisation exercise: recall the street where you live, or some other street or road very familiar to you. Imagine yourself walking down it – slowly. Stop occasionally here and there, look around, then continue. Do this exercise as often as you can. When you can hold the visualisation well, move on to conduct a mental pilgrimage to some special, physically real destination – one that you have visited in the past, so using memory, or one you have seen pictures of and read about, so using imagination. You might even use a map or atlas to help give structure to your pilgrimage. (Indeed, visualising yourself moving through a territory depicted on a map is in itself a valuable exercise.)

When you have become reasonably proficient at this kind of exercise (for quite a number of people, visualisation of this sustained kind can require some practice), move on to this next one, which is more powerful. It involves dream *incubation* – the deliberate 'programming' of dream material. As the last thing you do before closing your eyes to go to sleep, read the following visualisation slowly and carefully – perhaps two or three times. (You could even read it out and put it on an audio tape that can be played close to your bed, so you can listen to it with your eyes closed.) The visualisation is based on an actual Celtic holy well in Cornwall, England:

> You are walking down a straight path through a wood. You have been on a long pilgrimage, and you are tired. Nevertheless, your heart is full of joy and expectation, because you are near your journey's end. You continue on, walking down the long straight path. The foliage is thick around you, and the branches of the trees arch over your head, making the path seem like a long, straight green tunnel. You continue on along the path – walking, walking. The green gloom around you is

> both eerie and enticing, giving an aura of mystery. You can smell the earth beneath your feet and the foliage around you as you walk. As you progress along the living green tunnel through the heart of the woodland, you begin to notice trees on either side of the path festooned with strips of cloth – you know these are votive offerings, indicating that the holy place you are going to must be only a short distance up ahead. Indeed, you can see a patch of light ahead of you at the end of the straight, green tunnel of trees. You approach it, closer and closer. Suddenly you emerge from the tunnel and you are standing in a woodland clearing. In the middle of this is a small, ancient and ruined chapel. You hear the tinkling sound of running water. You walk round the old ruined chapel and find an entrance. You go inside. The chapel is roofless. In one corner there is a large stone basin into which is running a dribble of water. You walk over to the basin, and look into the gently shimmering clear pool of water it contains. It looks like dark crystal. This is the ancient, holy, and healing fount to which you have been making your long, long pilgrimage. Peer into the water – can you see your reflection in it? Slowly slip your hands palms uppermost into the living pool of water; feel the coolness of the sacred liquid. Bring out your hands and dab the moisture around your eyes and onto your lips. Go over to the middle of the chapel floor, which is covered in grass, lie down, and drift off to sleep feeling safe and content, knowing that you are at your journey's end.

After reading this a few times, close your eyes and go through the whole visualisation in your mind – repeatedly if necessary – as you fall asleep. The visualisation contains specific, key imagery and motifs that can stir the unconscious mind. Try this exercise at least once a week, and more frequently if possible. Your aim is for the visualisation to be harnessed by your dreaming mind, where the power of the unconscious can come strongly into play.

For many people, the visualisation will soon start to produce strong dreams, but if you find this is not happening for you, then there are specific measures you can take to help the process. One is to go to sleep after having a meal containing a good pinch of ground nutmeg – something like spinach pie, or even vanilla ice cream with the nutmeg sprinkled on it. Alternatively, you can fast all day then sprinkle essential oil (nutmeg or clary sage) on your pillow just before going to bed. If it turns out that you are simply too tired at night to go into sleep in the controlled manner required by the exercise, then try it as you take a daytime nap (morning naps are best for this).

Probably the most powerful technique to use is to set your alarm to wake you an hour or so before your normal time in the morning, go through the visualisation exercise, then let yourself fall back to sleep again. The reason for doing this is that the longest period of REM (rapid eye movement) sleep, denoting dreaming, occurs towards the end of the sleep cycle, and by interrupting it like this you can fall back straight away into that mental state. In this manner, not only will you almost certainly pick up the visualisation in the dream state, you might very well enter into a *lucid* dream state, in which you become conscious within the dream. When this happens, the dream scenery takes on a level of reality indistinguishable from waking reality, and far stronger than even the most vivid of normal dreams. You will actually feel the ground beneath your feet, you can touch the leaves and feel their waxy texture, and can even allow yourself to float gently along the path. The chapel will appear as real, three-dimensional architecture, and the water inside will feel truly wet. Of course, because the show is now being orchestrated by the vastly powerful unconscious mind, anything can happen, and you might find yourself being taken anywhere, and meeting all kinds of apparently real people and possibly other beings.

The real pilgrimage will have begun. Let your soul free.

3

SACRED GEOGRAPHY

How a culture maps its world says much about its way of thinking about its environment. In our brave new millennium we have our superb topographical maps, technical masterpieces; we have our satellites silently swooping through the heavens and peering down with electronic eyes; we have our hand-held, satellite-linked Global Positioning System computers, so even in the desert or jungle we can 'know where we are' to within a few strides. And yet, culturally speaking, we are in so many ways lost. We live uneasily with our planet, and we seem unable to stop ourselves damaging the habitat that sustains us. We all too frequently live and work in soulless, artificial environments, and our societies strain under internal pressures and frictions. There is clearly an important aspect of ancient wisdom that modern culture needs to reacquaint itself with – namely, that the mapping of the physical world needs to be integrated with a geography of the soul.

OVERVIEW

People who lived on Earth long before us, members of societies that in many cases lasted far longer than our modern culture, saw their world with their inner as well as outer eyes. The various types of mapping they produced we today lump together under the general label of 'sacred geography'. We generally consider such 'native' mapping as being inferior to our supposedly objective world-view, yet our modern maps contain various kinds of imaginary markings, such as grids of lines, demarcations of tropical zones and the equator, international date lines, various kinds of place symbols, a range of north poles, and scales. Lewis Carroll poked fun at this in *The Hunting of the Snark* with the Bellman's blank map of the ocean, a map the whole crew could understand because it was bereft of 'conventional signs', and in *Sylvie and Bruno Concluded* with a map with a scale of one mile to a mile 'which has never been spread out yet'.

In the following pages we consider some other geographies, other maps. There are many different ways to be in the world.

Mythic Mapping

Long ago, in many parts of the world, people saw their tribal myths, their spirits and gods, as embedded in the physical landscape around them. They had what the anthropologist Lucien Lévy-Bruhl called *participation mystique*, a local relationship with the land that surpassed mere utility and subsistence. 'The bond between a person and his (or her) country is not merely geographical or fortuitous, but living and spiritual and sacred. His country . . . is the symbol of, and gateway to, the great unseen world of heroes, ancestors, and life-giving powers which avail for man and nature' (A. P. Elkin, cited in Lévy-Bruhl, 1983). Lévy-Bruhl noted that to primary peoples 'Earth and sea are . . . as living books in which the myths are inscribed'. He quotes Paul Wirz's record of the places the natives of New Guinea associated with their mythic ancestors, the *Dema*:

> In most cases such spots have a striking outward appearance . . . some strange or unexpected aspect. In them occur unusual land formations, chasms, uplands. Swamps with sandbanks or gravel deposits . . . Curious noises may be heard in them . . . Occasionally people catch sight of strange apparitions, the *Dema* themselves, rising out of the earth, though mostly such visions are but fleeting and uncertain . . .

Lévy-Bruhl goes on to refer to another anthropologist, Bronislaw Malinowski, who found that virtually every 'conspicuous place' on Kiwai Island was considered to be the abode of a mythic presence of some kind. The landscape was filled with dramatic events, which gave it meaning. Lévy-Bruhl summed up such mythic mapping succinctly and memorably by saying that 'legend is captured in the very outlines of the landscape'.

Old place names can provide echoes of the mythic mapping of ancient landscapes. In Greenland, for example, Inuit (Eskimo) place names include Toornaarsutoq, 'The Place with Lots of Spirits', Angakkussarfik, 'The Place of the Initiation of the Shaman', and Tunisivik, 'An Offering Place'. Another Greenland place name, Iviangernat, meaning 'Twin Peaks Resembling a Woman's Breasts', highlights a form of mythic mapping common around the ancient world – the perception of likenesses or 'simulacra' of beings and figures in rock formations, hills, and mountains. In some cultures these were specifically associated with mythic themes. In Tibet, as just one example, the landscape is seen as containing spirits and deities, and this pre-Buddhist perception passed into later Buddhist sensibilities in the region. The holy area of La phyi in south-west Tibet is an important pilgrimage landscape made up of three mountains containing specific pilgrimage venues. The main sacred mountain at La phyi is thought of as the body of Vajravarahi, with a rock outcrop known as Ras chen seen as her head, the Seng khyams rock as her belly, and a rock in front of the bDud'dul cave as her knee. Samvara is another deity seen elsewhere at La phyi in the lie of the land. 'When asked to describe the mountain, local residents and pilgrims indicate rock outcrops which represent the deity's head and shoulders, while ridges on either are said to be his legs, the river that flows south from the place is said to be the stream of his urine, and so forth' (Huber, 1994). In the Indian frontier region of Himachal Pradesh, many significant features in the landscape are perceived as animal or human in form. A mountain and glacier facing Kardang Gonpa form a focus for meditating pilgrims and yogis: the mountain's double peaks are seen as the deity Khorlo Demchog yabyum, with the face, the eyes, and head of the elephant skin traditionally held by the deity clearly visible in the glacier. Double-peaked mountains were also seen as the breasts of the earth goddess by the ancient Greeks, and major sacred complexes such as the Acropolis in Athens, the Mystery temple of Eleusis, and Knossos and other palaces in Crete were built in sight

Figure 9: A depiction by Isle of Lewis artist Jill Smith of 'the Old Woman of the Moors', also known as the 'Sleeping Beauty', visible from Callanish. The moon is shown sequentially rising from the reclining figure, which is formed by the Pairc Hills.

of them and even oriented towards them. A similar landscape symbolism seems to have operated in Stone Age Europe as well – it has been noticed, for instance, that the skyline viewed from the Callanish stone circle complex on the Isle of Lewis, Scotland, is formed by a range of hills that give the appearance of a reclining woman referred to by local people today as 'the Old Woman of the Moors'. In Ireland, the rounded twin hills called the Paps (Breasts) of Anu, near Killarney, are still the focus of *Lughnasa* celebrations. In Egypt, fairly recent work by Egyptologist V. A. Donohue has startlingly revealed that rock faces and outcrops behind or in association with ancient temples along the Nile are in fact eroded natural features, sometimes slightly artificially enhanced, that were the simulacra of symbolic creatures and deities (Plate 21). These discoveries have blown away the false notion that the culture of ancient Egypt appeared 'suddenly' and 'inexplicably'. Indeed it did not; it literally grew out of the mythologised lands of the Nile.

In Australia, the Aboriginal perception of the topography as being formed by Dreamtime beings is now well known. A dome of rock with quartzite veins can be the head of one of these beings emerging from the ground; a gaping cave entrance can be the mouth of a grieving Dreamtime mother. Ancestral beings were transformed into place. 'They "sat down" and, however briefly they stayed, they became part of the place for ever . . . they *turned into* the place' (Morphy, 1995). A similar mythic sensibility existed in ancient America, too, and operated at varying scales. Take first, for example, a cavern in the Mayan and pre-Mayan Lol-Tun cave complex, in Mexico, where there are holes in the roof allowing dramatic beams of sunlight to enter. These punctuate a gloom in which can be seen weirdly shaped rocks and boulders, formed by the incessantly dripping water. Some of these look like human figures, and others like animals, including one massive boulder suggestive of a large catlike creature – perhaps a 'jaguar' or 'lion' (Plate 22). These formations have (undated) carvings of spirals and other geometric images on them, indicating an ancient response to the power of these suggestive forms.

The same way of looking could apply to something as large as a whole mountain or landscape. For instance, in Blackfoot Indian territory in Montana, virtually on the US–Canadian border, there is a distinctive peak called by the Indians, Ninaistakis, 'Chief Mountain'. On an associated ridge, smaller rock spires are known as Ninaki, 'Chief's Woman', and Ninaipoka, 'Chief's Child'. From certain angles, the mountain looks, variously, like a capped hat, a chief's topknot, or a traditional Blackfoot chieftain's headdress or bonnet. The Blackfeet consider it to be a place of great power, the home of Thunder-bird, or Thunder Chief, and, because a great vision was obtained on its summit by an ancestral elder, there are vision questing 'beds' in the form of rings of loose rocks, or slabs forming small platforms, on and around the mountain, at heights of up to 10,000 feet (3,050 metres). The name of the mountain is said to refer to a Blackfoot legend concerning a young chief who had to go into battle, reluctantly leaving his wife and baby. He was killed, and in desperate grief, the woman, carrying her baby, climbed the mountain peak and threw herself off. The configuration of one of the great rock faces forming the mountain's summit is such that the Blackfeet can see in it the form of the young wife with the baby in her arms. The myth is visible, wrought by nature in the mountain.

This ancient, mythologising way of perceiving or mapping the landscape has reappeared in a surprising form – that of modern advertising (see Plate 23)! But to traditional peoples it allowed their native territory to act as a *memory system*, encoding their tribal myths and legends, and bearing the imprint of their ancestors, thus reinforcing their cultural identity and sense of belonging. If such a landscape is destroyed or radically changed, or if a people are forcibly moved somewhere else, it occasions a kind of mythic amnesia that causes a society's cultural soul to die.

Symbolic Landscapes

Ancient Japanese sacred geography combined both mystical and political concepts. The role of sacred mountains, for instance, was related to sovereignty, because mountains identified as sacred provided a bird's-eye view of a territory to be conquered or protected. In turn, the ritual climbing of such mountains enhanced the legitimacy of a ruler over the territory he could view from its peak. Further, the holy mountains were the places where natural phenomena – stars, planets, Sun, Moon, water, fire – were observed, and these became symbolic of, and eventually appropriated by, the power of imperial rule.

Certain landscape configurations were sought in different places, and a kind of 'sacred template' of land formations evolved. Consequently, duplications of these basic place-formations became chosen as cult sites throughout Japan. An eighth-century example relates to a three-peaked mountain in the district of Kishima on the island of Kyushu. The peaks were associated with different deities, and every spring and autumn local people held hands and climbed the mountain in order to contemplate the landscape. There was dancing, drinking, and other festivities. This sacred geography was duplicated in Yamato in central Japan and in Kashima in the east of the country: the mountains were of similar appearance, the villages were oriented to them in a similar fashion, the same divine entities were worshipped, and similar rituals were conducted.

A third distinct nature-related belief that developed in Japan held that the landscape could 'speak'. This was based on the idea that the structures of the world and the human body were similar – that almost universal ancient fascination with the interactions between microcosm and macrocosm. It was felt that messages could be read in the marks and configurations to be found in nature – astrology and divination played a large part in this, and the art of landscape divination, feng shui, embodied some of this (see Part Four). 'The world was then conceived as a text to be decoded,' the scholar Allan Grapard remarks. 'What counted for people of the time was that there could not be a single natural phenomenon without its corresponding cultural "echo".' He goes on to observe: 'The rulers then came to be regarded as simple mediators of such transcendental powers, and sacred geography became a kind of political geography, since specific deities worshiped in shrines were considered to own and protect discrete geographical areas' (Grapard, 1994).

The basic idea of the land having the power of communication developed a more mystical dimension with Shingon Esoteric Buddhism in the Heian period (AD 794–1185). Its founder, Kukai, produced the first known Japanese account of the ascent of a mountain for spiritual purposes. He likened the natural landscape around Chuzenji Temple and lake to descriptions in the Buddhist scriptures of the Pure Lands, the habitation of the buddhas. This came to be taken to mean that a bodhisattva actually dwelled at the site. Kukai considered that the landscape not only symbolised but was of the same essence as the mind of the Buddha. Like the Buddha mind, the landscape spoke in a natural language, offering supernatural discourse. 'Thus, waves, pebbles, winds, and birds were the elementary and unconscious performers of the cosmic speech of buddhas and bodhisattvas; and mountains, springs, lakes, trees, flowers, stars, and vistas were morphological manifestations of the body of those divine entities that revealed to the trained eye the very essence which was thought to pervade the realm of natural forms,' explains Grapard.

Mountain mystics in the Kunisaki Peninsula, Kyushu, saw the landscape there as being the natural embodiment of the Lotus Sutra, a major Buddhist text. The peninsula's eight valleys were seen as landscape expressions of the eight scrolls of the scripture, twenty-eight temples were built to correspond to the twenty-eight chapters of the text, and it is said that as many statues were carved and erected as there are words in the Lotus Sutra. Walking in these mountains and listening to the natural sounds there came to take on the equivalence of reading the scripture.

India was envisioned as being the body of a goddess. This derived from a Hindu myth in which Sati, wife of Shiva, died of a broken heart as a result of being insulted by her father. Overcome by grief, Shiva scooped up Sati's body into his arms and commenced a crazed dance over the Earth. In an attempt to stem Shiva's agony, the other gods decided to gradually remove Sati's body from his arms, causing it to fall piece by piece to the ground. Where each piece fell became a holy place, and the focus for pilgrimage. Magical linkages between pilgrimage sites throughout India are also emphasised by other kinds of geographical mythic images. For example, one legend tells of a priest from Varanasi who cast his special cane into the well at Biraja, a pilgrimage site in Orissa. On returning to Varanasi, the priest found the cane floating in the Ganges.

Symbolic geography was also present in the Americas. A prime example has been well researched by the ethnographer-linguist Keith Basso (1987, 1996). He studied with the Western Apaches in the community of Cibecue, on the Fort Apache Indian Reservation, south-west of Flagstaff, Arizona. Basso discovered an unguessed power of place in the Apache territory: the names of places held great significance, and stories or legends attached to those places could even inform the social behaviour of the people. He found that for the Apache, the land 'stalked' the people, telling them tales to make them 'live right'. Place names were 'pictures' and stories related to them were 'arrows'. Everyone had learned the names of the places. 'White men need paper maps,' one Apache informant told Basso. 'We have maps in our mind.'

Basso, who recorded nearly 300 Apache places, noted Indians who would repeat the name of a place two or three times because 'those names are good to say', and he sometimes heard Apaches reciting long lists of place names quietly to themselves. Early on in his fieldwork, Basso, with tape-recorder and Apache guides, found he had trouble pronouncing a place name. But it doesn't matter, he said, as he had recorded one of the guides saying the name. 'It's matter,' the guide said quietly. The man went on to admonish the researcher. 'Our ancestors made this name. They made it just as it is. They made it for a reason.'

In his long and detailed fieldwork, Basso noticed that when his guides were showing and naming a place, they would mentally slip into the past and vividly reconstruct ancestral place-worlds in their speech. Basso found it to be almost like watching the events that took place at a location, or were supposed to have happened there. He also realised that the names and stories of some places demonstrated how the landscape had changed over the ages, including shifts in local climatic patterns.

The place names could be long, effectively forming sentences. Examples include: 'Green Rocks Side By Side Jut Down Into Water' (mossy boulders on a riverbank); 'Circular Clearing with Slender Cottonwood Trees' (a meadow); 'Whiteness Spreads Out Descending to Water' (a cliff by a spring); 'Line of Blue Below Rocks' (a mineral deposit). These were descriptive names, from which clan names eventually developed, but some place names marked locations where something instructive had happened. One such place was known as 'Shades of Shit', a tree-covered knoll generally avoided by the Indians. Brush-covered ramadas or shelters (the Shades) used to stand there long ago. They belonged to people who had farms below the knoll. They harvested much corn, but refused to share it with neighbours who had little. The neighbours became angry, and wouldn't allow the farmers to go anywhere, even to defecate, so they had to do it at home. Their shades filled with excrement, and they became ill, some of them almost dying. The neighbours pointed out that they had brought this sorry state of affairs on themselves by their selfishness, so the farmers finally agreed to share their corn. Basso could almost smell the stench on the breeze as his informants told the story with expressions of disgust on their faces. Basso was led to many other places with commemorative names, such as 'Two Old Women Are Buried' (a hill), 'She Carries Her Brother On Her Back' (a steep slope), 'Trail To Life Goes Up' (a butte), and 'She Became Old Sitting' (a cornfield).

The Western Apache have produced no historians that Anglo-American learning would recognise, yet those who know the place names and the stories are, of course, historians as far as the Apache are concerned, to whom place is more important than time – the reverse of modern cultural priorities. The land provided the framework for tribal memory and behaviour. If an Apache broke social rules, he or she was not openly rebuked. Instead, an elder would 'go hunting' for that person by drawing on the repertoire of topographical memory and start telling a story about a place. The story would be appropriate to the transgression committed by the tribal member, and contain an implied admonishment. The story or 'arrow' belonging to the place would 'shoot' the transgressor: the place would thereafter perform the role of a counselling elder to the person. Basso was told by informants who had left the territory for a time to seek work in big cities that out there in the modern world they began to forget the names and stories, and they forgot how to live right.

Marking the Spot

Research is increasingly suggesting that prehistoric rock art marks locations that had significance in ancient symbolic geographies. The Bushmen or San of southern Africa had a tradition of rain shamans, adepts capable of generating rain in arid areas by the use of magical ritual. Towards the end of the nineteenth century, a handful of ethnologists recorded snippets of information concerning legends and beliefs from the last of the now-extinct southern San who occupied areas of northern Cape Province, who had carved, pecked, and scratched imagery on rock outcrops at what appear to have been selected locations.

One informant told of his father, Xatin, who had been a rain shaman and who 'chipped' rock art, after the manner of untold generations. He did his rock engravings at a placed called !kann where animals came to drink before the arrival of the Whites. Other informants indicated that when the rain shamans wanted to make rain, they would 'go near the place at which there is water (a spring in a deep hole), for they know that the rain-bull is in that water' (Deacon, 1988). The 'rain-bull' was one of the images used by the San in their weather magic. This mythical creature was captured by the sorcerers and led around the country away from the waterhole in order to make rain. One of the informants made a pencil sketch of the rain-bull which looks remarkably similar to imagery engraved on dolerite boulders on the side of a low hill a short distance from a spring said to remain active even in times of severe drought. Also in the rock art are depictions of dancing men, two of them with animal heads.

Another rock art location also seems to associate with rain-making, though more obliquely. The Strandberg is a set of two large hills and one smaller one between the present-day towns of Vanwyksvlei and Kenhardt in South Africa. There is a concentration of rock engravings on the north side of the smaller hill. A San legend associates the Strandberg with the death of a mythical lizard who was broken to pieces as it tried to squeeze through the mountains. Its forepart became the western hill, its hindpart became the eastern hill, and its head became the low hill. Another San tradition claims that the lizard can affect the rain – 'it keeps its head towards the place where the north wind blows and bewitches the rain clouds'. Putting these fragments of traditional lore together, researcher Janette Deacon suggests that the concentration of rock engravings on the north side of the low hill, the lizard's head, relates to rain-making. These and other examples have caused her to come to the conclusion that San rock engravings associated with water-holes, north-facing slopes, and landmarks that have legendary connotations for rain mark the places where rain-making shamanic rituals took place.

In the mountains of northern Portugal, oral tradition still exists with regard to rock outcrops containing engravings and painted rock shelters. These natural locations are often given names, indicating their importance as landmarks for the existing peasant population in the region, and their role in defining villages' territories. Until recently, the peasants of the region would mark crosses and other symbols on boulders as territorial markers, a practice thought by them to have had its origin in the actions of their ancestors in immemorial times. Ancient rock art sites in the region are natural places – that is, unaltered features in the landscape. A recurrent folklore theme of the area identifies some of these places with legends concerning beautiful young Mooresses who are trapped in the rocks due to a magical spell. They are guardians of treasures, and only reveal themselves to humans on St John's Day (midsummer festival). Researcher Lara Bacelar Alves considers that these legends of 'Enchanted Moors' are a folk memory of local pagan deities and spirits associated with rock outcrops, mountaintops, springs, and rivers, and pre-Christian ritual activity (Alves, 1999).

Heaven on Earth

Much has been written about ancient astronomy, and there is no plan to repeat that here. It is more relevant in the context of this book to note that the observation of the skies by ancient peoples, and the orientation of their temples to Sun, Moon, or other astronomical bodies, was in the main not conducted for what we would recognise as scientific purposes, but rather for divinatory use (see Part Four), or religious and cosmological reasons. So the builders of Stonehenge were not erecting an observatory, they were keying their temple in to the great cycles of nature, making it a model of the universe and an expression of their cosmological beliefs. The temples, stone circles, and other sacred structures of antiquity were effectively stage sets incorporating astronomical phenomena for ceremonial and ritual activities.

This is well shown by the lunar-based organisation of the large Buddhist stupas in the Kathmandu Valley of Nepal. In a stunning research effort, Reinhard Herdick has found that with only one exception (Kirtipur, which is oriented towards a solar, solstitial point) the orientation and positioning of all the large stupas can be coordinated with certain key lunar rising points (Herdick, 1993). The Moon is associated with the Nepalese religious calendar and also with the cultivation of rice, and much ritual activity is governed by the Moon in one way or another. It seems that the whole system in the Kathmandu Valley was surveyed and organised from a small, flat-topped hillock with unobstructed views to the east that Herdick calls the 'measuring site', situated exactly midway between the two major stupas, Svayambhu and Kirtipur. Seven lines of stupa orientation intersect at this uninhabited hillock, which has a natural boulder oriented eastwards on it that was venerated by locals. Nearly all of the stupas are oriented to the Moon in two ways: by the angle of the stupa itself, and by means of alignments with other stupas, or between a stupa and the measuring site, leading to points of lunar significance on the horizon.

There are other, subtler factors, too. On top of each stupa dome is a boxlike superstructure (*harmika*), and this has the large eyes of the omnipresent Buddha painted on its sides (Plate 24). Herdick remarks that 'the intimation that the Buddha is looking towards a rising (or setting) heavenly body offers itself, as it is the *actual* direction of the gaze'. Incredibly, it also appears that the sizes of certain stupas varied in accord with the slight changes in the apparent width of the lunar disc at different points in its cycle.

The exact age of the lunar-based stupa geography in the Kathmandu Valley is not known, but lunar astronomy, calendars, and worship go back to at least Vedic times in India (first millennium BC). In accord with other researchers, Herdick concludes that it was the *sites* that had first significance, which was enhanced by the later erection of the stupas. He sees the first, oldest work at the measuring point as being the observation and systematisation of astronomical behaviour. The next step, over time, was to bring 'the heavenly phenomena into relation with the earthly environment'. Finally, there was the orientation of individual shrine structures.

Other examples of Old World astrogeography might include Mohenjo Daro, one of the two major cities of the Indus civilisation of the third and second millennia BC, situated in Sind in modern Pakistan. The axes of certain streets in this most ancient, ruined city were aligned to the positions that specific fixed stars occupied at the time.

In the Americas, the same urge to mirror heaven on Earth also existed. Again, this took many forms. The great, ancient city of Teotihuacán was laid out to strict astronomical criteria, as is described in more detail below. Similarly, the high Andean city of Tiahuanaco (c. 250 BC to c. AD 1000), situated close to Lake Titicaca in present-day Bolivia, linked topography to astronomical symbolism. Lake Titicaca was the mythological point of emergence for Andean peoples from the earliest times, and there are Tiahuanaco shrines on the islands of the Sun and Moon in the lake, and the ceremonial core of

Tiahuanaco was made into a symbolic island by means of a surrounding moat. The major ceremonial structures on this symbolic island are oriented to the four cardinal directions, with the east–west axis being particularly emphasised. The three sacred peaks of Mount Illimani were to the east, where the Sun rose. It set over Lake Titicaca. Doorways and staircases in the temples and sacred edifices relate to both directions, but favour the east. The most dominant monument in Tiahuanaco is the Akapana Temple, a terraced mound 56 feet (17 metres) high. Its summit (which was originally covered by a green gravel from mountains to the south) is the only place in Tiahuanaco from where Mount Illimani and Lake Titicaca are both visible. So what happens in the surrounding sacred landscape was repeated in miniature in the ceremonial core of the city.

Another way ancient Americans brought heaven down to Earth can be found on Mexico's Yucatán Peninsula, the heartland of the northern ancient Mayan empire. The Maya connected their ceremonial cities with straight ceremonial causeways that cut through the dense forest that covers the peninsula. There are many aspects to these remarkable features, but local archaeological investigator William Folan of Campeche University has collected data that indicate that certain of these ancient causeways aligned to the Sun, Venus and certain stars, such as Sirius (the brightest star in the heavens), Canopus, and the Pleiades or Seven Sisters constellation (Folan, 1991). Nor was it just alignments to heavenly bodies that figured in astrogeography. It could be more oblique than that. In northern California, for instance, the shadow of Simloki ('Soldier Mountain') was incorporated into the mythic world of the Ajumawi people. This prominent peak throws a shadow at solstitial and equinoctial sunsets that falls on certain sacred places in the valley to its east. The shadow was thought of as being an actual spirit, and there used to be a tradition in which braves would try to race it as it spread across the valley floor in order to gain supernatural power.

Sunwatching was another ancient American practice; this survived long enough in Pueblo Indian societies like that of the

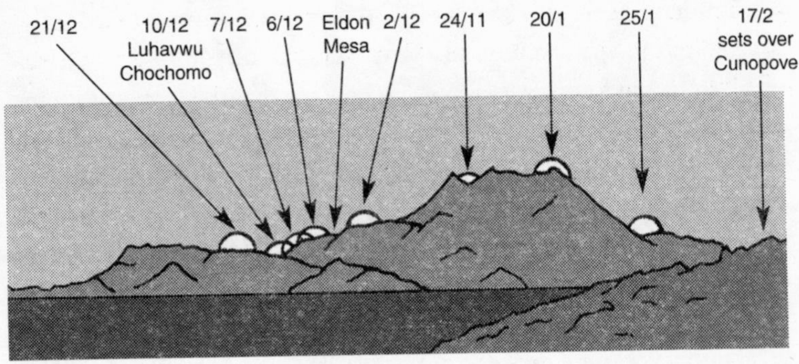

Figure 10: A Hopi solar horizon calendar as viewed from Walpi pueblo. (*After Alexander Stephen and Griffith Observatory.*)

Hopi to be studied by anthropologists. Sunwatching was conducted by special priests who made observations from specific locations and kept a tally of the Sun's rising points throughout the year. Sunrises on key times of the agricultural or ceremonial calendar were noted against distinctive skyline features such as mountain peaks, notches, rock outcrops, or even artificial markers. Sometimes, the key dates were further 'fixed' by allowing the sunbeams at those times to enter certain buildings and strike carefully positioned markers fitted to the interior walls.

Such horizon calendars were well known in the Old World too. European farmers made similar observations, in a more secular context, marking sunrise points at key agricultural times, or even using the Sun as a timepiece by noting its daily progress along a familiar skyline – *points du jour*. Medieval monks routinely used the position of the Sun and stars against skyline features, and the roofs of monastery buildings, to indicate times for prayers and observances. This practice seems to have existed from at least the fourth century in Europe, when it was used by John Cassian, who had acquired the method in the monasteries of lower Egypt. Medieval Christianity used astrogeography in a number of other ways, too.

Churches were supposedly oriented to sunrise on the festival days of the saints to whom they were dedicated. Although this does not seem to have been universally practised, and the procedure seems to have fallen out of use altogether at some undetermined date, a survey of 300 medieval churches did show that a significant number were accurately aligned to sunrise on their patron saint's day. It seems this practice could involve features in the landscape surrounding the church. So, for example, the very old St Piran's Church in Cornwall was oriented to a prehistoric earthwork over 2 miles (3.2 kilometres) distant. Examples in France included churches whose astronomical orientations pointed towards other churches in the vicinity.

The astronomical dimension of church siting could take even more dramatic turns. In the Alps, as an outstanding example, there is a fifteenth-century church at Elm, beneath the Tschingelhorner mountain in Switzerland. A natural rock tunnel 60 feet (18 metres) wide pierces the peak. Local legend tells that the feature was created when St Martin hurled his staff after a giant who had stolen some of his sheep. Around the equinoxes, the Sun shines through St Martin's Hole and falls on Elm church, illuminating its spire for about two minutes. The sunbeam stretching from mountain to

Figure 11: Elm Church and sunbeam, Switzerland.

church is 3 miles (4.8 kilometres) in length. This solar effect is also accompanied by a lunar one during the course of the 18.6-year lunar cycle (Bischof, 1990).

Although this phenomenon would have been occurring long before there was any church – any Christianity, in fact – it demonstrates that church builders did seek out astronomical symbolism. This is further endorsed in that there are, apparently, four more similar examples of this kind in the Swiss and Austrian Alps.

Faithscapes

As was indicated in Part Two, the journeying through the landscape could be as important a feature of traditional walking pilgrimage as arrival at the destination. Toni Huber has noted that the landscape associated with the Tibetan pilgrimage centre of La phyi referred to earlier is 'geography . . . written as theatre'. Her own diary of a journey to the region notes features such as a rock with a deep hole in it said to have been caused by the Buddhist saint Milarepa, when he drained a nearby lake (now a dried-up lake bed). A whole body of legends centred on these features was narrated by her guide.

> The natural topography over which the pilgrim must pass is reinterpreted and infused with a sacred significance through its association with the legendary scenarios of the past. This is indicative of the kind of presentation with which Tibetan pilgrims are equipped by guides as they approach holy places and travel pilgrimage routes. (Huber, 1994)

In addition to the mythologising of pilgrimage landscapes, the addition of artificial features, the careful placing of stations on the pilgrimage way, and the use of human art could enhance their meaning in terms of the pilgrimage involved. The Indian pilgrimage scholar Rana P. B. Singh has coined the term 'faithscapes' to describe such choreographed landscapes (Singh, 1991, 1995). They are strongly associated with pilgrimage centres in India, a prime case in point being Varanasi, which has fifty-six pilgrimage circuits, of which five are the most popular and trace a sacred design or cosmogram on the landscape, linking various shrines. There used to be fourteen Sun shrines (*adityas*) and research by Singh and John McKim Malville (1995) suggests that these formed alignments between them to sunrise positions on solar calendrical and Hindu symbolic days in the year. These seem to link with a whole symbolic journey, the plan of the sacred city, and, astrologically, to parts of the body. This seems to relate to a pre-Shiva period, and the Sun shrines and temples were razed in the twelfth century. The locations of the fourteen shrines remained in the communal memory, however, and today the positions are marked by small features such as Sun discs, lotus-form stones, or images of Surya (the Sun god). The linking pilgrimage route, though, has fallen into virtual disuse. With these findings in mind, it seems pilgrims trace out a cosmically significant pattern during their devotional visiting of the temples, and it is telling that the word for a cosmogram, *kashi*, was also the ancient name for the city territory of Varanasi.

The sacred Indian landscape is even more strongly choreographed at Braj, a cultural zone demarcated by language, customs, and topography. It is a mixed woodland and pasture area, and the sacred Yamuna River flows through it. The ancient city of Mathura, associated with Jainism, Buddhism, and Hinduism, is contained within the zone as are other sacred centres such as Brindavan, Gokul, and Govardhan, among others. In all there are some 4,000 shrines. Mathura is regarded as the place where Krishna was born to imprisoned parents. In the fields around Brindavan, Krishna grazed his cattle as a cowherd, and flirted with the milkmaids. He subdued demons in the forests, performed magical feats, and played tricks – called *lila*, or divine play. Indeed, within Braj every event in Krishna's life has been associated with a place – even specific fields are mentioned in the legendary texts concerning Krishna. Animistic elements of nature religion have also been absorbed into the Krishna tradition (so we have Krishna urging his contemporaries to worship a mountain rather than Indra, for example). Krishna, the Hindu god of love, could seduce the flora and fauna of the landscape as well as women with his flute playing. Krishna's favourite lover was Radha, who became his consort in legend, representing his Shakti or feminine principle. Certain places within the 'faithscape' are where Krishna and Radha held their trysts – there is even one temple that pilgrims are not allowed to visit after dark so as not to disturb Krishna and his consort in their lovemaking! The full pilgrimage starts and ends at Mathura, and involves a 185 mile (296 kilometre) circuit, passing through all the places in the faithscape where events in Krishna's life took place. (There are, of course, shorter pilgrimage routes as well.) During the monsoon period of July and August, pilgrims flock to Braj to witness *Ras Lila*, a form of dance-drama in which events in the life of Krishna are played out. They are spectacle and liturgy combined.

Various temples lay claim to specific parts of the Krishna mythos: the Kasava Deo Temple, for instance, is said to have the original stone on which the Lord Krishna was born 3,500 years ago. The 500-year-old Radha Raman Temple houses an image of fossilised stone, said to be inhabited by the god; he is awoken each day prior to sunrise by singing priests ringing bells, is bathed and dressed, and offered fruit, milk, and other foods. Then Krishna slips out of the effigy to roam free in the surrounding landscape.

The idea of the choreographed pilgrimage landscape holds true elsewhere. There are hints of it in Ireland on the old Brandon Mountain pilgrimage route on the Dingle Peninsula, mentioned in Part Two. The ancient Gallarus Oratory, a drystone construction shaped like the upturned hull of a boat, is set a short distance off the Saint's Road at the precise point where the summit of Brandon Mountain is visible rising over an intervening ridge. The geography surrounding the pilgrim seems to have been carefully planned to give meaning.

So too at Mount Sinai, Egypt, the Horeb of biblical record where Moses saw the burning bush and received the tablets of the Law. This was the focus of pilgrimage from at least the fourth century, reaching a climax in the sixth century, when the entire topography of the area was marked with sacred or significant spots where the pilgrim might pause to pray. This pilgrimage destination, with the monastery of St Catherine at its centre, became a form of 'theology fixed in space' (Coleman and Elsner, 1994). Pilgrims moved from one sacred site to another, 'tracing a biblical narrative through the landscape'. They visited mythologised places such as the rock where Moses struck water, the site of the burning bush, the spring where Moses watered sheep, the cave where Elijah fled from King Ahab, and the peak of Mount Sinai itself, where a small church marked the spot on which Moses received the tablets of the Law. A series of prayer niches was built along the pilgrimage route up the mountain where the path joined another path, or at places where pilgrims might glimpse a view of the distant peak, their goal.

The Geography of Death

There are a variety of funerary landscapes around the world. In Britain, for instance, there are about a hundred known earthen monuments called 'cursuses' (Latin for racecourse). They have become so eroded that most are visible only as crop markings in aerial photographs. They are large monuments, usually of a regular form, often straight, and always linear, and can stretch up to 2 miles (3.2 kilometres) in length. Their function is unknown, and they present a genuine archaeological mystery.

What may be of significance is that they represent a Stone Age example of a funerary geographical motif that involves ground markings or structures displaying direct linearity associated with burial sites that can be fragmentarily traced in western Europe right through to the medieval period.

In the Bronze Age, there were stone rows on places like Dartmoor, Devon, that linked burial sites, or, at least, passed through them. Sometimes the rows were single, sometimes double, and, occasionally, multiple in parallel. As with the cursuses, their purpose is simply unknown, but some association with death seems to be clearly indicated. A telling feature is that many of the rows have larger stones standing at their ends, and these have been termed 'blocking stones' because that is what they look as if they are doing. But blocking what? The answer might be that the rows depict spirit paths or enclosures of some sort. Perhaps it was thought that the spirits of the special dead who were interred at the sites linked by the rows could move along or within the stone rows, but their return to the land of the living was prevented by the blocking stones. We cannot know for sure, because these monuments are prehistoric – before documentation. All we can do is try to interpret them, but this idea of blocking spirit movement is found in the original forms of feng shui (see Part Four), the ancient Chinese system of landscape divination, where straight landscape lines of any kind were thought to facilitate the movement of spirits, specifically troublesome ones, and houses and tombs had to be protected or shielded from such 'arrows' in the land. The same idea is also implied in old Ireland in that if one built carelessly, a house could block a fairy path. It could also be that the cursuses were similarly spirit ways or precincts associated with the spirits of the dead buried in the associated long barrows.

In the historical era in Europe, the Vikings built straight ritual paths to wheel dead chieftains along to their burial places, and throughout medieval Europe there was a great tradition of funerary paths. The *dodenwegen* ('death roads') or *spokenwegen* ('ghost roads') of Holland were dead-straight paths that led to cemeteries, and in eastern Germany and Poland there was a folk belief in spirit paths or *Geisterwege*. These were invisible paths linking actual cemeteries along which the ghosts of the dead were thought to drift. These supposed ghost paths led in dead-straight lines across country. In the Harz Mountains of Germany there is a curious medieval stone path (*Steinweg*) that leads in a straight line to Iron Age burial sites (*Ringwalls*). Why these older sites should have been linked by a medieval feature is another mystery, but it might be of significance that the Harz were associated with witchcraft in the popular imagination.

In Britain, funerary routes were called, variously, lyke or corpse ways, coffin lines (in Cornwall), and church paths, among other appellations. They were designed for walking funerals (or funeral processions using a horse) leading from outlying farms and homesteads to the main parish church cemetery. To conservative historians, these corpse ways were simply pragmatic ways the rural poor took their dead to burial during the medieval period, but the existence of specified spirit roads and ghost ways in Europe – some of them not even physical realities – that similarly led to cemeteries gives the lie to such an exoteric and over-simplistic interpretation. Many corpse ways may indeed have been simply the means to take someone to burial, but some at least, and the idea itself, were associated with all kinds of beliefs and practices aimed at ensuring the ghost of the dead person did not haunt the corpse way, or try to make it a two-way road by wandering back home along it from the cemetery. Corpse ways emerged from a matrix of ideas that was deeply impregnated with ancient spirit lore. (For further information and deeper discussion on all these features and more, see Devereux, 2001.)

SITE EXAMPLES

Teotihuacán

This ruined ceremonial city is situated in the Valley of Mexico 25 miles (40 kilometres) north-east of present-day Mexico City. The foundation of Teotihuacán dates back to at least the first century AD, and its builders are unknown to us. The much later Aztecs considered it their spiritual home, and it was they who named it Teotihuacán, 'Birthplace of the Gods'. The city was one of the greatest in the world when it flowered between the fourth and seventh centuries AD, and its temples, shrines, plazas, dwellings, and workshops covered some 10 square miles (26 square kilometres).

Its main north–south axis is marked by a great road now referred to as the Street of the Dead, which leads to the impressive Pyramid of the Moon at its northern end. This pyramid is slightly smaller than the 200 foot (61 metre) tall Pyramid of the Sun, which stands on the eastern side of the Street of the Dead (Plate 25). However, the axis is not a true north–south one, for it is skewed 15.5° east of north. This was a great puzzle for archaeologists for many years, especially as it became apparent that the whole layout of the city had been made to slavishly adhere to it – even the river was canalised to make it run according to the axial plan of the city (Plate 26). The answer came in the 1970s, when a cave was discovered by chance beneath the Pyramid of the Sun. Its lava tube passage led into a four-lobed cave. There was clear evidence that both passage and the natural chambers had been modified for ritual purposes from before the city was built. The really interesting finding, though, was that the cave's entrance passage happens to align to the setting point of the Pleiades, a key constellation in the religious skylore of most ancient Mesoamerican cultures. The people who occupied the area that was to become Teotihuacán had obviously placed great importance on the natural orientation of the cave, so it became a ritual place and, later, they built the Pyramid of the Sun over it, set to the same orientation.

It was this astronomically significant line that had set the groundplan of the whole city, not the Street of the Dead, which had simply been set at right-angles to the Pleiades line. Surveyors' 'bench marks' were found pecked on rocks and the floors of buildings marking the crucial alignment (Plate 27).

The urban geography of Teotihuacán is a classic case of heaven being imaged on the earth.

Borobudur

This great Buddhist temple, dating to c. AD 800, is a marker in multiple sacred geographies. First, its site, formerly a Hindu holy place and probably an indigenous sacred spot before that, is located in the geographical centre of the island of Java, clearly identifying it as an omphalos, a sacred centre (see Part One). Second, looking south from the top of the vast terraced structure of Borobudur, the steep Menoreh mountain range forms a skyline ridge reminiscent in shape of a man lying on his back, his chin, lips, and nose clearly delineated. Local lore says that this is the figure of Gunadharma, the supposed architect of the temple. There is no historical evidence to support the existence of a man with this name, which has survived only through local oral tradition. The landscape has been mythologised, just as in many other ancient places around the world.

The third form of sacred geography is the alignment that Borobudur plays a part in with two other temples some distance to the east – the temples or *candi* of Pawon and Mendut. '[A] straight line can be drawn from Candi Borobudur through Candi Pawon to Candi Mendut,' the Indonesian architect Soekmono observes. 'Moreover these three monuments are the only Buddhistic temples within a five kilometre [3 mile] radius from Borobudur' (Soekmono, 1990). It is not, therefore, a chance alignment. It is a fact further emphasised in local legend, which states that the three temples were connected by a covered passage for religious processions. A procession is still performed, with the participants starting out from the Mendut end of the line. A pathway links Mendut to Pawon on the alignment, and an approach avenue to Borobudur has been constructed on the course of the line. There is also the site of a no longer extant fourth temple that fell on the alignment.

Rame Head

The tiny fourteenth-century chapel of St Michael perches atop a remarkably conical hill (Plate 28) on this headland on the south coast of England. Records show that the chapel had the St Michael dedication from its foundation. It provides an excellent example of astronomically inspired medieval Christian sacred geography, for it orients to a conical rock outcrop called the Mewstones rising out of the sea about 5 miles (8 kilometres) away. These rocks marked sunrise from the position of the chapel on St Michael's Day (29 September) in the fourteenth century.

PRINCIPLES AND PRACTICE

Principles

Our modern maps are imaginary props that support our view of our world. They use symbolism that describes physical terrain, but they miss out much else that we actually *experience* in being in the environment – they do not record the interactions between place and memory, myth, and imagination. We never really experience the world around us in the neutral manner our objective mapping insists upon.

We don't have to dispense with our maps – indeed, we shouldn't – but we can perhaps learn to appreciate other ways in which people have seen their surroundings. We can enrich our present world-view and perhaps usefully modify it with the additional dimensions provided by how the ancient mind mapped its world, investing the topography with dreams and myths. As a culture, we moderns no longer exteriorise our inner lives in the natural world; we no longer see the world in soulful ways. That leaves the environment exposed, naked, and vulnerable to our actions. The antidote is to try to ensoul our world-view. To put that another way, to experience at least briefly geographies other than the one laid down for us by our present culture. This would hold out the possibility for new and perhaps more wholesome world-views to develop in the future, for without the opportunity to experience alternatives, such developments are less likely to occur. It may be true that we can only do this now at an individual level, but individuals make up societies, and societies create cultures.

Practice

Sacred Sights

Arguably the first and most important practical experiment you should attempt is to acquaint yourself with archaic geographies. To see as if with the eyes of the ancients.

This necessitates a visit to an ancient, preferably prehistoric, monument. The procedure is basically to keep both inner and outer perception 'in sync', and being prepared to see an extra dimension to the physical geography. 'To see and move around the monuments invokes a brief encounter with a totally different culture which inevitably generates both intrigue and wonder' (Richards, 1993).

Initially, you might want to consider how you approach an ancient sacred site. Christopher Tilley, one of the leading lights in the new 'cognitive' school of archaeology, has commented that all too often we locate a monument or a site on a map, drive there, and after perhaps being hours on the road, park as near as we can to the place.

> In the case of all but a few well-preserved chambered monuments the result is inevitably disappointing: a few overgrown stones or a low mound covered with rank vegetation in summer is hardly inspiring. You acquire little sense of the feel and character of the land. A monument or place encountered in the course of a walk between places is an altogether different matter. Approaching it slowly, from different directions . . . it is possible to observe in a much more subtle manner the way in which it is related to its physical surroundings, the lie of the land. (Tilley, 1994)

Choosing the ancient site for your experiment is another important matter. It ideally needs to be in a natural setting, and one that has been changed as little as possible from when the monument was constructed. 'A megalith in an urban environment does not work, it has no aura,' Tilley opines. He goes on to describe his feelings when visiting certain monuments in southern Sweden that are in modern, built-up environments: 'It is as if the modern buildings surrounding the tombs detract from them as signifiers of the past, deconsecrate their space' (Tilley, 1993).

When you are at your selected monument, what will you be looking for? Let us follow Tilley again for a few moments as he looks at a range of Stone Age monuments in the area around the Preseli Hills in the extreme south-west of Wales. These are the hills from where the bluestones of Stonehenge purportedly came. Tilley discovered that the monuments needed to be approached from certain angles for their landscape relationships to become apparent. At Morfa Bychan, a group of four burial chambers, it was a natural rock outcrop that was prominent and to which the monuments related. The chambers were invisible at a distance, but the natural place was visible from far away. In short, the sacred places of the ancestors were placed alongside landmarks. In exploring the area, Tilley worked out that there had been a path of movement along the Welsh coast from landmark to landmark.

So it is that such subtle relationships between monuments and their natural surroundings can yield glimpses into forgotten geographies. One truly can partially re-experience the ancient mental world-view. Tilley has written on his investigations at other Welsh monuments. By studying a range of prehistoric long mounds in the Black Mountains of eastern Wales, for instance, he was able to find patterns in their orientations – they were either in parallel to the courses of rivers, or pointed to prominent spurs on mountain ridges. And there have been ample other observations at British prehistoric sites. Archaeologist Frances Peters found that solitary standing stones – monoliths or menhirs – scattered across the landscape of West Penwith, the tip of the Cornish peninsula, were in most cases precisely intervisible, sometimes over considerable distances. She concluded that the stones had been purposely positioned along contours, perhaps marking out prehistoric boundaries. 'None of this would exclude a ritual function,' she points out. 'The positioning of the menhir might be part of the ceremonial associated with it' (Peters, 1990).

Figure 12: One of several 'coincidences' between the shapes of stones and skyline noted by John Glover at the Castlerigg stone circle, Cumbria.

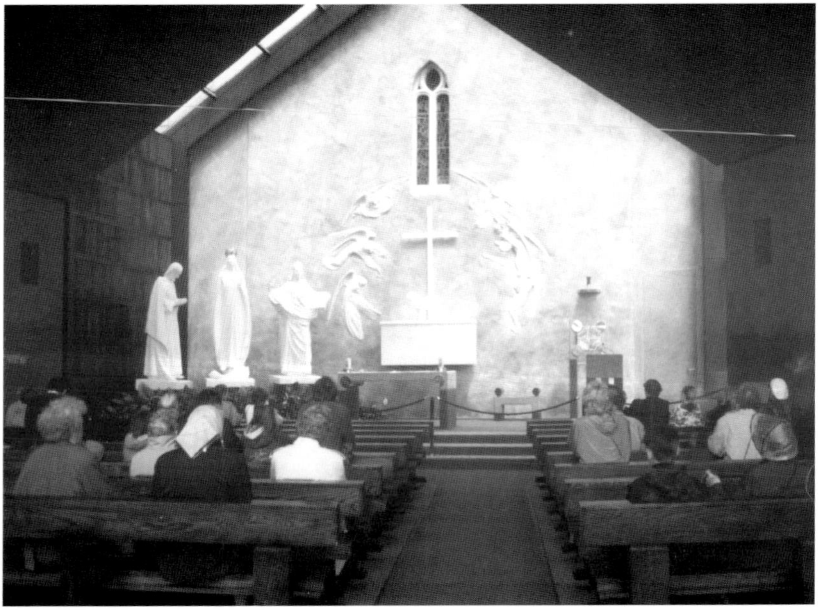

19: A vision in stone – Knock is a major Marian shrine in Ireland. A vision of the Virgin along with other figures and an altar with a lamb and cross on it was witnessed in 1897 at the gable end of the church. Here we see pilgrims in the modern chapel built onto the end of the older church looking at a reproduction of the vision constructed against the wall of the church.

20: The Neolithic Coldrum Long Barrow, adjacent to the pilgrims' 'Old Road' to Canterbury, showing that the route was used in Stone Age times, long before Christianity. See Part Two.

21: Rocky crag forming the simulacrum of a human profile at the pre-dynastic rock-hewn Temple of Min, Egypt. Min became the Roman Pan. (*Anthony Donohue*)

22: The so-called 'Lion Rock' in the Mayan ritual cave of Lol-Tun, Yucatán, Mexico. This vaguely zoomorphic rock was venerated in ancient times, judging by Mayan markings made on it. See Part Three. (*Sol Devereux*)

23: This advertisement for cafédirect, the people who sell coffee directly on behalf of the growers, shows the mountain peaks behind the Inca temple-citadel of Machu Picchu from an unfamiliar angle, revealing the simulacrum of a human profile. Although this image has been slightly enhanced by digital means, it merely underlines the fact that a profile looking skywards is, indeed, truly visible in the crags overlooking this mysterious Peruvian site. An interesting case of modern technology underscoring the ancient mythic vision of Native American peoples. (*Courtesy of cafédirect*)

24: The all-seeing Buddha eyes on a stupa in the Kathmandu Valley, Nepal. They play a part in the remarkable lunar-based sacred geography in the region – see Part Three. (*Chris Ashton*)

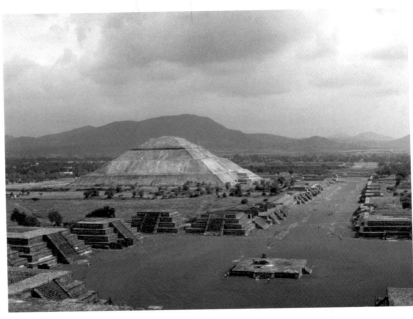

25: Looking south down the Street of the Dead towards the great Pyramid of the Sun, Teotihuacán, Mexico, from the top of the Pyramid of the Moon. A ceremonial city laid out to an axial sacred geographical scheme oriented on the Pleiades constellation – see Part Three.

26: A river runs through it . . . Even this was canalised so as to make its course conform to Teotihuacán's axial grid, based on the Pleiades. See Part Three. (*Sol Devereux*)

27: Looking down at one of the remnants of a surveying mark in Teotihuacán marking the 'Pleiades Line'. See Part Three.

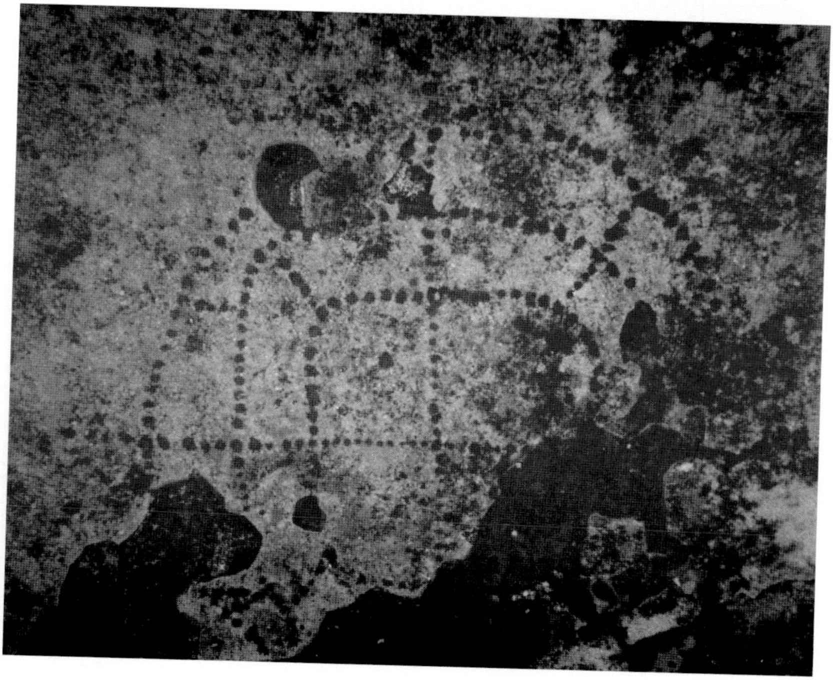

28: The tiny medieval St Michael's Chapel atop its conical hill by the sea at Rame Head, Cornwall. The chapel is oriented on a specific sunrise position – see Part Three.

29: The outline of a bird-shaped effigy mound marked out in the snow at Effigy Mounds National Monument in north-eastern Iowa. See Part Three. (*U.S. National Park Service*)

30: The labyrinth-engraved slate known as the Troy Stone as displayed in the Witchcraft Museum, Boscastle, Cornwall. See Part Three. (*Jeff Saward/Caerdroia*)

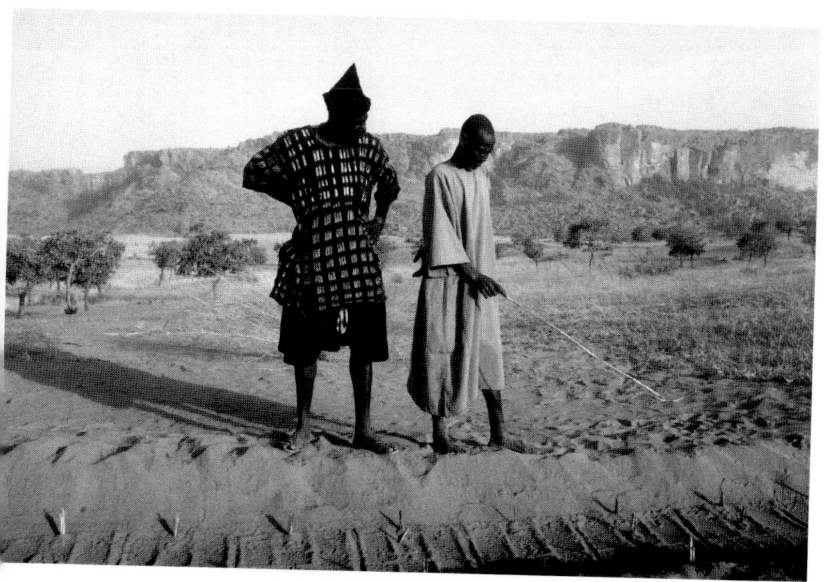

31: A Dogon diviner interprets animal tracks on his geomantic grid for a client. See Part Four. (*Edward Parker/Hutchison Library*)

32: A British feng shui expert, Derek Walters, uses a *luopan* (specialised compass) in the area around Stonehenge to see if the famous monument exhibits any feng shui aspects. See Part Four.

33: The Stone of Fal (Lia Fail), the royal divinatory stone on the hill of Tara, Ireland. See Part Four.

34: Head in the clouds . . . See the exercise on cloud divination, 'Cloud Nine', in Part Four.

What might you expect to discover by looking at or from an ancient monument? Well, photographer John Glover noticed that the shapes and relationships of a number of the stones in the Cumbrian stone circle of Castlerigg precisely echoed the contours of the skyline beyond them, as if they were megalithic signposts, directing the eye to particular places in the surrounding mountainous landscape. He also discovered that a 2 mile (3.2 kilometre) 'shadow path' was cast by the tallest stone at the circle at the summer solstice sunset; this shadow also pointed out distant natural features and sacred places. Again, archaeologists studying a standing stone by Loch Finlaggan on the Isle of Isla off the west coast of Scotland found by geophysical survey that a stone row had aligned to the menhir, creating a line of sight that led to a notch on the skyline that exactly framed the breast-like peaks of the Paps of Jura on a neighbouring island. And, as third example, simply by looking I found that the profile of the giant prehistoric mound of Silbury Hill in the Avebury complex in Wiltshire related in a specific way to the skyline when viewed from associated prehistoric sites. This led to the discovery of a remarkable natural optical phenomenon at Silbury at sunrise at certain periods of the pre-Christian agricultural calendar. I have written extensively about this elsewhere (Devereux, 1992a; 2000), so I will not do so again here: the simple point I wish to make is that it is possible to see things at or from ancient monuments that no one else has noticed for thousands of years.

The above examples all relate to ancient British sacred sites, but the same principles naturally prevail at others elsewhere. We have already briefly mentioned the association between ancient Greek temples and split-peak, breastlike mountains, thought to have been seen as symbolising the Mother Goddess (Scully, 1979). So go to Eleusis (associated with the split-peaked Mount Kerata), or the Acropolis in Athens (from where the saddle-peaked Mount Hymettos is viewable) on the Greek mainland, or to Knossos (Mount Juktas), Phaistos (Mount Psiloritis), and Gournia (local breast-shaped hills) in Crete and see for yourself. Experience a mountain as a goddess. Or, again, visit the Valley of the Kings in Egypt and stand before the Temple of Hatshepsut, and try to discern the gigantic images of a pharaoh and a cobra in the craggy rock face rising behind it. Or visit monuments like the *Steinkisten* in northern Hesse, west of

Kassel in Germany: these take the form of long stone chests, comprised of upright slabs set in the ground. There is usually a 'soul hole' cut through an end slab. At Züschen, the axis of the *Steinkisten* and its soul hole align exactly to the Wartberg a few miles distant, its peak jutting prominently above the horizon.

The potential of ancient sights at ancient sites is enormous. In every country that has them, use the old places like magnifying glasses through which you can pore over the maps of the ancient soul.

Dream a Little Dream

Whether or not you are successful in noticing any secret sights at the monuments you visit, be sure to bring the great, dark lens of your subconscious mind into play. I have elsewhere likened prehistoric monuments to fragments of dreams we can only half remember. It is useful to treat them in that fashion, and it makes the idea of using dream consciousness more relevant. The dreaming mind can notice things overlooked by waking consciousness; it has different priorities. It also is a form of mythic consciousness, and so can put you closer to the type of cognition used by the ancients. It is quite feasible that the site you visit and your subconscious mind can engage in a dialogue that the waking you is totally unaware of.

So how do you make use of the subconscious mind? The simplest way is to take a nap while you are visiting a sacred place, if circumstances allow you to do so. I have on several occasions found a ten-minute nap to provide information about a place I would not otherwise have been aware of. A more organised and structured way of using the dreaming mind is to take a lot of photographs on print film at the site – from all angles, details and general views, looking into and out of the monument, and a panorama of the surroundings. Collect any other memorabilia of the place as well – such things as an essential oil that reminds you of any characteristic scents associated with the place (the aroma of cypress, wild flowers, damp earth); take a leaf from a weed growing at or near the site, or a small pebble or pinch of sand or soil, if that can be done without damaging the site or its environment (and *never* take any archaeological material). Then, on one or two set nights for several weeks after your site visit, before settling to sleep, take out these memorabilia and immerse yourself in them. Go over your memories of the place. In this way, you might be able to incubate a dream about the monument. Keep a notepad handy by the bed, and immediately on awakening jot anything down that you can remember you have dreamed about the place.

Continue this for several weeks to see if you can compose a dream account of your visit to complement your waking recollections. They may turn out to be two very different yet complementary narratives.

Walking Sacred Geographies

There are sites that allow you to directly experience still-extant sacred geographies. Take the holy isle of Iona off Scotland's western coast, for instance. It is a most spiritually evocative place, and has been the destination for pilgrims for many centuries, and is still. (The Iona Community informs of events on www.iona.org.uk or you can write to The Iona Community, The Abbey, Isle of Iona, Argyll, PA76 6SN, UK. Include a stamped, self-addressed envelope if from Britain, or an international postal reply coupon available at post offices if from elsewhere.) On Iona, the life and actions of Columba and his monks created a sacred geography on the island, and scholars have tentatively mapped this out (Yeoman, 1999). There was the circular banked ditch or *vallum*, still visible today, that encircled the original monastic community, there is Cnoc an t-Sithean, the hill where Columba prayed and was seen to discourse with the flitting white forms of angels, there is the Bay of Coracles where Columba first landed, and near which is the Cairn-of-the-Back-to-Ireland, the monument to the saint's exile from Ireland. There is little doubt that Columba's huts would have been seen as shrines, and there were many crosses erected around the island. Though most of these were destroyed at the Reformation, the remarkable ninth-century St Martin's cross survives intact, with a few other restored ones. From the harbour on Iona a road called Sraid nam Marbh ('the Street of the Dead') runs to the Reilig Odhrain burial ground, and on to the monastery and Columba's shrine. 'This cobbled road was the grand processional route used by funerals and pilgrims, marked by a trail of ornamental crosses, chapels and burial grounds, with side-paths leading off directing pilgrims towards some of the satellite sites,' Scottish archaeologist Peter Yeoman explains.

A much older example of walkable sacred, funerary geography can be found close to Stonehenge. After visiting the monument itself, find the track marked as a by-way running along outside the western boundary of the car park. After a few hundred paces along it you will encounter a National Trust noticeboard marking the course of the Stonehenge Cursus, and giving a 'bird's eye' view of the great earthen linear monument from that position. If you look to your left (westwards) you will just be able to make out the now faint signs of the outer banks of the feature. You can actually stroll down the cursus – I advise you do so from the western end in the Fargo tree plantation where there is a curious false long barrow (Neolithic earthen burial mound). At the other end of the cursus nearly 2 miles (3.2 kilometres) away there are the remains of an actual long barrow. If the line or axis of the cursus is extended beyond that eastern terminus, it passes through a standing stone known as the Cuckoo Stone, and the site of a former timber henge monument called Woodhenge.

Walking east, feel the mystery of this monument, which was old before the great stones of Stonehenge (visible to your right) were erected. What was it all about? Did ancient priests conduct processions along this obviously special, sacred route, or was it designed to contain the ancestral spirits? Are you treading a spirit path? Trust your intuition.

And keep your eyes open – look ahead to the distant eastern horizon as you walk. There is a range of hills on the skyline, and the cursus aligns directly towards them. One of them is now known as Beacon Hill. Beacon hills were selected in Elizabethan times because they were particularly intervisible locations – key sighting points. Did the cursus builders 5,000 years ago use this Beacon Hill simply as a sighting point, or were they acknowledging it as a sacred peak? Again, listen to what your intuition whispers to you.

There are walkable ancient sacred geographies still surviving in many other places around the world, too. In the Americas, for example, there are ritual landscapes containing highly mysterious giant effigy mounds left by unknown Indians about 1,000 years ago (Plate 29). The outlines of these fairly low, earthen mounds form the shapes of bears, birds, wolves, panthers, and human–animal hybrid figures, as well as a variety of abstract, geometric shapes. Not all were for burial. Although many have been destroyed, some still survive – especially in Iowa and Wisconsin, but also in various other parts of the United States and Canada. In some cases

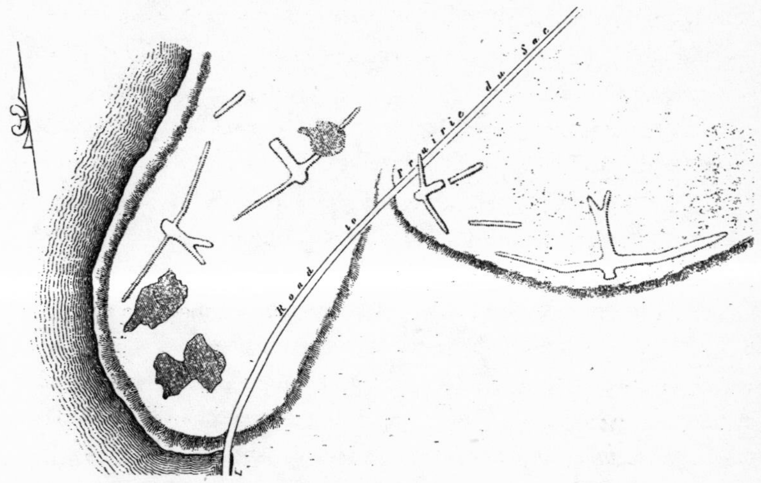

Figure 13: A few of the many Wisconsin effigy mounds surveyed in the nineteenth century by I. A. Lapham. (Detail.)

boulder outlines were used rather than shaped earthen mounds. A particularly atmospheric effigy-mound site to visit is the somewhat isolated and lonely Lizard Mound County Park just north of West Bend, Wisconsin (phone 414–335 4445). Many mounds in the shape of birds and animals are scattered amongst woodland here, and it is an eerie experience to walk among them – a bizarre sacred landscape indeed. A larger though more structured effigy mound park is to be found on the banks of the Mississippi at the Effigy Mounds National Monument just north of Marquette in Iowa. Here, you can walk for miles among giant terrestrial effigies of bears, birds, and geometric shapes.

Whether in the Old World or the New World, get out and about and explore the spiritual geography of long-lost cultures – of other, older worlds. Experience using another kind of map.

Cosmic Connection

You don't necessarily have to venture out to remote sacred sites in order to experience a touch of sacred geography. Bring it into your own home. Start by making a note of when and where the Sun shines into your habitat, be it house, apartment, cottage, mobile home, or bedsit. The bigger the place, the more windows or skylights it has, then, obviously, the more instances you will have to check. Take particular note where sunlight strikes on key times of the ancient solar calendar – sunrise, sunset, or noon at the solstices (21 June and December), and the equinoxes (21 March and September). Likewise for the cross-quarter days marked in the 'Celtic' calendar as *Imbolc* (1 February), *Beltane* (1 May), *Lughnasa* (1 August), and *Samhain* (1 November). These are only approximate dates, but they will suffice. Note where the sunlight falls at such times, or nearest to those times that your windows afford, and place a marker of some sort there. It could be a golden image of some kind, perhaps one you create for yourself from art materials, a piece of stained glass or plastic for translucent colour, or a glittering object like a crystal, or whatever you can manage – even a bowl or glass container of water. Or you could place a shadow-throwing object at a suitable location in your home – even a sundial for those moments in time. Use your inventiveness.

As time rolls by, and you become immersed in your daily routine and concerns, a glint of sunlight in some corner of your dwelling, a glow from a wall, or a meaningful shadow created by one of your solar-significant artefacts will suddenly remind you of the larger cycles of time that frame all our lives. Your now astronomically activated domestic sacred geography can pull you up short, putting things in perspective. It is what the builders of the ancient temples did. Over and above the rounds of our lives, we belong to something bigger. Remember and celebrate that fact.

Bringing Sacred Geography Within

All sacred geography is an externalisation of inner states and ideas; a projection of the mind onto the land forming mindscapes. You can reverse the process in a number of ways. A key one is by using the unconscious mind through dreaming techniques already described. Another, to be described here, is to take a specific piece of sacred geographical design, the labyrinth, and use it as a meditational tool. This is an old and tried method, as we shall see.

The labyrinth is one of the smallest examples of sacred geography, but it has been used in many contexts. The origins of large-scale labyrinths laid out in boulders, or smaller versions carved on rocks, are in the mists of time. Prehistoric rock-carved labyrinths are to be found on rock faces in Val Camonica, Italy, and at Pontevedra, Spain, and labyrinths created from rocks laid out on the ground occur in Iceland and the Baltic region, including Russia. Some of these are probably prehistoric: a group in the Solovecke Archipelago is thought to date to 4000 BC, and meander patterns – from which the labyrinth configuration can be developed – have been found on carved mammoth ivory figurines from Siberia dating back c. 20,000 years.

One recorded use for the stone labyrinth in Baltic areas was as a spirit trap. The Saami of Lapland would walk round labyrinths in order to ensnare evil spirits that might be following them. The spirits would be unable to escape from the labyrinth when the person stepped out of it.

The best-known example of the feature type is doubtless the Cretan Labyrinth, the lair of the mythic Minotaur, a fearsome half-man, half-bull creature. This was at Knossos, one of a number of Minoan palace-temples on Bronze Age Crete, and centre of a bull cult. Although the original form of the Cretan Labyrinth is not now known, late prehistoric Cretan coins show a classic labyrinth design. This design became popular with the Romans, who employed it for mosaic floor patterns.

There was a labyrinth revival in medieval Europe, primarily in the forms of open-air turf labyrinths and as tiled designs on the nave pavements of Gothic cathedrals such as Chartres.

The turf sites are formed by grassed earthen ridges creating a gully between them that serves as the path. They measured up to 60 feet (18 metres) across and were usually circular, though square and other rectilinear shapes also existed. Several hundred such sites have been documented, but only about a dozen still survive, in England and Germany. Folklore also indicates that turf labyrinths (often, if incorrectly, referred to as 'turf mazes') were typically incorporated into spring fairs. They were situated on village greens, near churches, and sometimes at remote sites such as hilltops, perhaps suggesting pagan origins. One documented account describes a game in which young men would race one another through a labyrinth to be first to reach a girl standing in the centre. Another records a festival at a huge former labyrinth site in Poland in which a man would hop around the labyrinthine path while trying to drink a glass of beer!

The centres of turf labyrinths were typically occupied by a mound or a tree. The tree seems to be an expression of the World Tree – one of the many images of the Word Navel. But there were exceptions – for instance, available documentation indicates that a now destroyed labyrinth in Shrewsbury had an archaic drawing of a face in its centre.

The cathedral labyrinths were used as penance paths, and the name sometimes given to them was 'the road to Jerusalem'. At least some of the turf mazes shared this function, and there is evidence that monks did penance on their knees in the great Saffron Walden turf labyrinth in Essex, England.

The labyrinth design also makes its appearance in the Americas. Labyrinthine spirals and meanders appear in Anasazi and Hopi rock art in the American south-west, and are etched into the desert surface at Nazca in Peru. Meanders also appear in pre-Columbian decorative art.

The reason why the labyrinth pattern has appeared in various parts of the world in different eras is because it seems to relate to a deep, archetypal pattern in the unconscious mind, and so is universal to humanity. Psychologists have reported on the spontaneous production of the labyrinth pattern in the dreams of patients, and one writer, Geoffrey Russell, has described an experience in 1944 when he was transported into a mystical, visionary state while listening to music in which he saw a glowing mental image. Not knowing about the labyrinth pattern at the time, he described his vision as looking like 'a pair of kidneys stuck together'. He was later able to identify this as the classic labyrinth pattern.

It is because it is a powerful and deep-rooted mental construct that the labyrinth design can be used as a means of entering light trance states, as in meditation. A portable divining tool used by Celtic wise-women, for instance, was a labyrinth design carved on a piece of slate or stone. The woman would trace her finger around the sinuous line into the centre of the labyrinth and out again repeatedly while humming a tune, until she entered a trancelike state for the purposes of divination. These labyrinth stones – or 'Troy stones' – would be handed down from mother to daughter, or transferred woman to woman, through the generations. An example is to be seen in the Witchcraft Museum in Boscastle, Cornwall (Plate 30). It was given to the museum's former owner (the late Cecil Williamson) by a woman from a

Figure 14: Plan of the former turf maze or 'Shepherd's Race' at Boughton Green, Northamptonshire. It was 37 feet (11.3 metres) across.

nearby farm, who had no longer any personal use for it. She was the daughter of a wise-woman known as Kate 'the Gull' Turner, who had inherited the stone from a 'sea witch' in the Isle of Man, who in turn had received it from another known wise-woman.

It is this meditational aspect of the labyrinth we will make use of here. At the top of this page is a traditional labyrinth pattern. (If you find it too small to use here, you can always enlarge it by photocopying it.) Unlike the maze, there is only one path to follow in a labyrinth – you cannot get lost, even though the route is circuitous. So start your finger at the bottom of the design where the path (the white line) opens at the edge. While intoning a humming sound – perhaps an extended 'omm' – let your fingertip slowly trace the path round and back, round and back, until it reaches the centre. Then, still humming, trace the path out again. Keep repeating this activity while having as your mental orientation that you are travelling a sacred geography as in a pilgrimage into the deep, silent recesses of your spiritual being. With some dedicated effort, practice and persistence, your unconscious mind will recognise the timeless pattern and allow you to use it as royal road into its secrets. In other words, you will enter a light trance state. Use it wisely.

4

DIVINATION

The word 'divination' derives from a Latin term meaning 'god-inspired'. Although usually equated with telling the future, divination has also had many other applications, such as seeking cures to illness, gaining knowledge and personal insight, obtaining answers to specific questions, selecting kings and priests, and even directing the placing and founding of buildings. Although it is nowadays generally treated as a fun thing, like newspaper horoscopes one does not have to take too seriously, in the past divination was a mainstay of human cognition. It was the way things were done. We will see that divination can still be a useful psychological tool if handled in an appropriate manner, and can offer extended ways of knowing.

OVERVIEW

Humanity has found many ways to conduct divination, fortune-telling, prophecy, seership, or whatever other term one wishes to use. In his *Mysmantia* of 1652, John Gaule listed some fifty-three different categories of divination, and that was far from being exhaustive. We may be fairly familiar with the reading of tea-leaves or coffee grounds, crystal-gazing, and palmistry, but as odd as these may seem to be, they pale in comparison to other methods that have been employed, such as bubble-watching, sneezing, and thumb-sucking, and monitoring the coagulation of cheese (tyromancy), the creaking of doors, or even tummy rumbles (gastromancy). Despite its multifarious manifestations, though, there are basically only two types of divination, one that involves the interpretation of chance elements in relation to objects, creatures, conditions, or events, and another in which the diviner enters a trance state and receives the divinatory information from within – this is more accurately called prophecy or oracular utterance. Cicero, a Latin philosopher of the first century BC, called the first kind of divination *entechnos*, that which can be taught, while the latter was *atechnos* or *adidactos*, a natural gift rather than a learned one. Quite often, though, both types can run together, with the trained diviner or seer being also a natural prophet, with great intuitive abilities. As J. R. Porter has suggested with regard to Hebrew prophecy, 'the one, the prophet, replaced the other, the seer', both possessing 'distinct, though no doubt overlapping , features' (Porter, 1989).

The techniques of divination themselves can be simple and homely, or highly structured and sophisticated systems. Both kinds have intermingled through the ages.

Trance Divination

A variety of methods based on hypnotic gazing at lustrous surfaces were used by diviners to access the prophetic trance. The use of crystals (scrying), mirrors (cathoptromancy), and bowls or dark pools of water (hydromancy) was common in many ancient cultures. It is recorded that in Hungary, seers would use a fingernail smeared with poppyseed oil or even spittle to provide a reflective gazing surface, in order to find lost animals and objects or buried treasure, or to divine for money. Mirror divination was practised by Thessalaian seers, who would hold up a glass to the Moon before using it for divining. The remnants of copper, bronze, and sheet-metal mirrors, or the lead surrounds of glass mirrors, have been found at various ancient Greek and Roman sanctuaries, bearing inscriptions or reliefs relating to a variety of goddesses. These seem to have been either votive offerings or divinatory artefacts. The chief emblem of the Mayan god Tezcatlipoca ('Smoking Mirror') was obsidian, the black volcanic glass used for divination by ancient Mayan priests and seers. Obsidian mirrors dating back to c. 6000 BC have also been uncovered in the much different context of the Çatal Hüyük archaeological site in Turkey. Shiny, dark surfaces similar to obsidian were obtained by seers in some cultures by moistening the surface of a piece of slate. Non-reflective 'mirrors' like this have been found in a variety of archaeological contexts around the world and are sometimes referred to as 'shamans' mirrors'.

In Tibet, there is a method known as *dkyil-'khor*, which consists of constructing a mandalic form with rice on a round metallic surface then wiping the surface clean. (A mandala is a meditational design basically consisting of a circle – usually quartered – with a centre.) A special bowl used for this procedure is called a *sa-gzhi* in Tibetan, and is made of silver or copper with symbolic engraving and often with a gold inlay around the rim. It is used upside down, and its base consists of a flat, matte-finished surface upon which the rice mandala is constructed. Over three months at a Tibetan retreat, ethnopsychologist Charles Laughlin achieved the method's initiatory requirements of producing 100,000 rice mandalas. He used a shaving mirror fixed to the base of a saucer, and created his circular designs using yellow long-grained rice. The process required concentrated, rapid activity. Laughlin found that when this demanding process had got under way he would have powerful lucid dreams almost every night. (Lucid dreams are those in which one becomes fully conscious inside a dream while remaining physiologically asleep.) The dreams were all mandalic in some way, having circular peripheries and dynamic centres through which Laughlin could oftentimes glimpse scenes (Laughlin et al., 1992).

There are many other types of trance divination, especially as conducted by the oracles and sibyls of antiquity, but these we shall consider separately later on.

The Body Divine

Diviners through the ages appropriated anything that could facilitate their practices, and the human body itself was not exempt. In China, for example, there was – still is – divination by bodily sensations. A shiver, a burning ear, or a flushed cheek can all be decoded to yield information as to one's fortune. A tic in the eye has different meanings depending on when it occurs. So at 8 a.m., for instance, the hour of *Ch'en*, a tic in the left eye means a close friend will visit from a distance. If the tic is in the right eye, though, it foretells of a minor injury. The *T'ung Shu*, the Chinese almanac, has charts for all times of the day. Likewise, a ringing in the ears has different meanings depending on the time it occurs, and whether the left or right ear is affected. In post-Renaissance Europe, reading the moles on a person's face was considered a form of divination – moleosophy. This was also practised in China. There was also metoposcopy, divination of a person's character and destiny by making a correspondence between the lines on his or her forehead with planetary symbols.

The body part best known for its divinatory potential is the hand. There is a very ancient north European tradition, based on a Scandinavian legend which may itself be alluding to earlier beliefs, that by placing a thumb in the mouth a person is enabled to discover 'that which he did not know' (Davidson, 1989). It seems that throughout northern Europe the thumb was thought to be sensitive to supernatural influences, and it is noteworthy that one of the witches in Shakespeare's *Macbeth* refers to 'the pricking of my thumbs'.

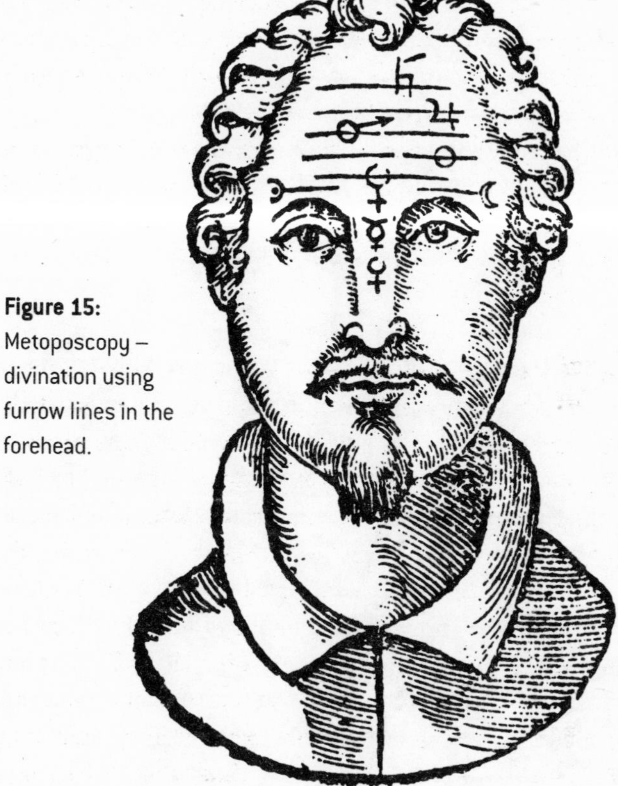

Figure 15: Metoposcopy – divination using furrow lines in the forehead.

The study of fingernails, or onychomancy, is another form of divination, but it is the hand itself that has become most associated with divination because of the continued popular practice of palmistry, or chiromancy. In this method, the various lines running across the palm of the hand, the forms of specific parts of the palm, and the shape of the fingers and hand as a whole are thought to be freighted with meaning concerning a person's mental state, character, past experience, and future prospects. Chiromancy has obscure origins, but it is mentioned in Indian Vedic texts of c. 3000 BC, and it was known to ancient China, Tibet, Persia, and Greece. It is said that Aristotle discovered a text on palmistry while studying in Egypt.

Animal Magic

Mantic practitioners through the ages have often turned to the non-human world of living creatures to seek means of divination. Birds were particularly popular, often being seen as 'messengers of the gods' due to their ability to flit and fly through the vault of heaven. The classic example of divination by studying the behaviour of birds was Etruscan and Roman augury, and we will shortly explore that further. The Chinese also had augurs, as did the ancient Maya – the Yucatec Mayan term *mut* relates to both bird and augury, and the Dresden Codex, one of the ancient Mayan bark-paper books, shows a goddess with the muan owl (screech owl), the quetzal, and other birds, referring to good or bad auguries. Bird divination was conducted in the Celtic world as well, and the Iron Age priesthood we call the Druids is believed to have practised augury, telling the future from the flight or songs of birds. Some memory of this seems to have survived in folklore in the Celtic lands. The wren, for instance, was known as *drui-en*, 'Druid bird' (Spence, 1945), and in Welsh it is called *dryw*. Ravens and doves likewise were associated with divination – perhaps because of the distinctive voice-like sounds they make. Celtic folklore has it that if a raven or crow cries above a bedroom in a house a distinguished guest will visit; if it calls from the north-east end of the dwelling, the place will be burgled, and if at the door, strangers or soldiers will come. Some Celtic folk would defer a journey if they happened to look out of a window and see a single crow. A 1697 account by J. Toland describes a then current Irish belief that if one should encounter a raven with white feathers in its plumage, and it should fly off to the right while croaking, it was a sign of extreme good fortune, and any enterprise could be undertaken with confidence (Spence, 1945). But as we shall note later on, birds were often associated with death omens.

The mole has long been associated with divination in numerous cultures, often in connection with death. In many districts of the British Isles, the sudden, unexpected appearance of a molehill in the garden was taken as an omen of a death in the family. If a mole burrowed under an outhouse, then that meant the death of the mistress of the house within a year. Pliny noted in the first century AD that the mole, 'permanently blind, sunk in other darkness also, and resembling the dead', was considered to be an extremely important divinatory animal in Persia, Greece, and Rome. While it was particularly credited with the power to predict death in some cultures, the mole had a contradictory body of healing lore attached to it as well. So strong was this, in fact, that throughout Europe there was a tradition of throttling moles in order to gain their healing virtue. Sometimes, the creature's paw was bitten off while it was alive so that it could be used as a talisman. Some healers would stick a finger into a dead mole's body throughout the night in order to acquire healing power.

Quite lowly creatures also figured in divination. In Scotland, divination by worms used to be practised. At a healing holy well at Ardnacloich, for example, the sick person 'if he bee to dye, shall find a dead worm therein, or a quick one if health be to follow' (Spence, 1945). In Africa, the Azende of the Congo region consulted termites. Two leafy branches would be stuck into a termite mound while a question was addressed to it. The branches were left in place overnight. The 'yes' or 'no' answer to the question would be revealed the next day depending on whether or not the leaves on the branches had been eaten by the termites.

A pagan Celtic tradition required the seer to wrap himself in an animal skin when lying down to sleep in a special spot in order to seek a prophetic dream. In Norway, the seer would go to a lonely forest, lay a freshly flayed ox-hide on the ground, and draw nine squares around it while reciting various spells. He would then sit on it and await the appearance of spirits who would tell him the future.

Then there was haruspicy, studying the entrails of a sacrificed animal, a speciality of both the Etruscans and the Druids, and hepatoscopy, 'reading' the liver of an animal. We know this latter method goes back at least 4,000 years to Babylonian times because archaeologists have found clay models of animal livers divided into sections and marked with cuneiform writing for the purposes of divination. An Etruscan bronze model of a liver was found at Piacenza, dating to c. 100 BC. It was divided into forty areas, each given an association with one of the elements or a god – these included Tin, Tul, Selva, and Cul, the Etruscan deities of the cardinal directions. The shape, condition, and colouring of the liver would be taken into account when the diviner inspected it, along with the characteristics of vein markings and any other distinguishing features.

To the Bone

Bones and shells have been used in a variety of ways in a number of cultures. In Africa, bone divination is widespread and cuts across tribal and cultural boundaries. Two basic types are practised. One involves a set of four bones, often cut from the hooves of oxen or cattle, but also fashioned from horn, ivory – and even wood. Each of these has a decorated 'positive' side, and an undecorated 'negative' one. They are further differentiated into other oppositions, such as senior and junior male, and senior and junior female. The diviner throws the bones like dice in response to a

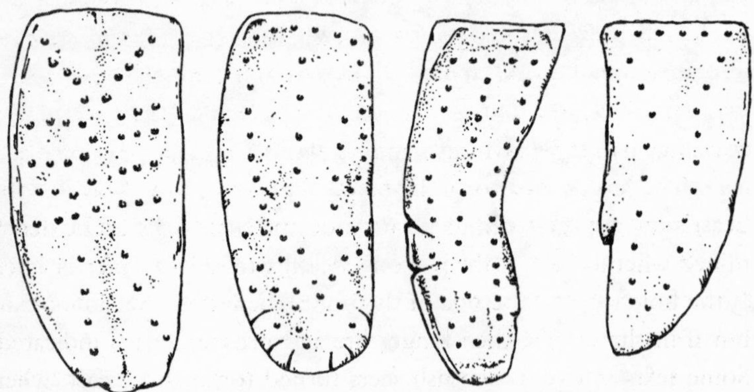

Figure 16: Divination tablets, *tlhabana*, as used by the Tswapong of southern Africa. The markings are burnt into the tablets. In this set, left to right, the tablets represent senior male, junior male, senior female, and junior female respectively. (*Courtesy of Richard P. Werbner; Werbner, 1989*)

client's query and interprets the mix of oppositions. Each combination or 'fall' has a name or 'praise', and the specified praise-poem is recited when the fall has been identified. The other method uses up to sixty astragali – the knucklebones of various animals, such as hyena, antbear, antelope, lion, baboon, sheep and goat. Each has its meaning. Sometimes seashells, tortoiseshell fragments, and selected stones are mixed in with the set. In the main, there is a bone from the male and female of the species involved, but this duality is avoided in particular cases, such as there being only one bone from the antbear, as this creature is associated with the ancestors. When the pieces are cast, the diviner has to interpret the outcome from the way the various pieces relate to one another in the fall.

In the course of his training, the apprentice bone diviner is required to obtain his own set of bones, cut from the raw flesh of the animals involved, and these are then subjected to various treatments, such as placing under a white ash in moonlight, in order to strengthen their divinatory properties.

Scapulomancy – the use of the shoulder blades of animals as divinatory tools – was practised by several cultures. In the Highlands of Scotland it was known as *slinneineachd*, and the right blade-bone of a black pig or sheep was considered the most suitable. It was thoroughly boiled so that all the flesh was removed, and then it was carefully inspected for its special markings. Various types of markings had their own meanings, such as a sale, a fight, or whatever. The largest hole or indentation represented the grave of the beast's owner, and from its position on the bone it could be determined whether or not the person's death would be sooner or later. If the hole lay near the side of the bone, then death was imminent, but if in the centre, then longer life and prosperity was indicated. Some texts state that Scottish seers turned towards the east 'when divining futurity from the lines, shades, or transparence' disclosed by a shoulder blade.

In early China, the cracks appearing in a fragment of heated tortoise-shell would be interpreted and the resulting divination scratched onto the shell – over 100,000 pieces of such incised shell and bone dating back to the second millennium BC have been uncovered.

Simple Twists of Fate

Most forms of divination invoke chance, but some methods use the random element in more naked ways than others. Cledonomancy, the use of chance remarks or happenings, is a case in point. In Roman times, one form of this involved going to the temple and making offerings before the statue of Hermes. The enquirer whispered a question in the effigy's right ear, then, blocking his or her own ears, left the temple and made for the street or market place. The first words that were heard on unblocking the ears had to be interpreted as in some way providing a response to the question. Another method was empyromancy or capnomancy, the study of smoke, especially that rising from incense. One could even select the lavatory as the place to divine one's fate – scatoscopy involved the inspection of excrement, while uromancy required dabbling in the meaning of urine.

A more wholesome divinatory method that relies strongly on randomness is tasseomancy, or tea-leaf reading. Tea bags are no use for this method, of course – the beverage has to be brewed from loose leaves. When the cup is drained, the pattern of clusters made by the dark, soggy dregs can be interpreted. This is accomplished by simple visual cues leading to various associations. So for example, a wiggle of dregs might suggest a snake, which in turn could indicate that one is in danger of being duped in business or other circumstance that might be relevant at the time. A crosslike shape warns of an enemy, a shape like a cat might indicate good luck. Sometimes, the dregs form patterns that can be read as initials – these suggest particular people, of course, and the meaning can be interpreted by studying accompanying configurations of dregs.

Water was often used as a convenient medium for divination. In Europe, divinatory readings were made by studying the shapes created when oil or molten wax or lead was poured into water. Coins, pins, or pebbles cast into water were also popular divinatory methods, particularly with regard to any bubbles that arose or sounds made.

Many love divinations rely on randomness – which is, perhaps, not entirely reassuring. In Northumberland, a girl wishing to know whom she would marry would seek a leaf from an ash tree that had an equal number of divisions on each side. If she found such a rare leaf, she would recite: 'Even, even, ash / I pluck thee off the tree / The first young man I do meet / My lover he shall be.' Another method was for a man or woman to spin a knife with a white haft on a table. If it stopped with the blade pointing towards the diviner, the future mate would be dark-haired, if the white handle, then he or she would be fair-haired.

Figure 17: Diviner and oracle blocks from the pages of the *T'ung Shu*, the Chinese almanac.

One of the most pervasive categories of divination was, and remains, sortilege – the casting or drawing of lots. It is also one of the oldest – it is mentioned in Homer's *Iliad*, and probably reaches back to dawn of human society. The old Hebrew term *qasam* refers to divination, and is equivalent to the Arabic *istiqsam*, meaning divination by lot. We have already noted the throwing of oracle bones, but many other objects were used around the world in various systems. In China, a variety of lot-based systems have developed from antiquity. One system makes use of two kidney-shaped wooden oracular blocks or cups called *chiao* which each have a flat (Yin) and a concave (Yang) side. Before a session the blocks are waved through incense smoke. After a question has been silently put to the deity, the blocks are thrown forwards and upwards to land on an altar. If they land with one having its flat side and the other its hollow side up, it is a positive sign, *Sheng*. Two flat sides down is negative, *Kai*. Two hollow sides down is a qualified 'no', generally indicating a poorly couched question.

Accessing the venerable I Ching (The Book of Changes) requires the casting of yarrow stalks or coins in order to obtain negative–positive, Yin–Yang, combinations that identify a pair of trigrams out of the eight on offer which between them provide sixty-four hexagrams identifying a broad range of conditions. This highly sophisticated system allows for subtle modifications.

The casting of beans and seeds was used widely around the world for divination.

Reading patterns in scattered beans was prevalent, for example, in Transylvania (Pocs, 1999). The Maya, too, used beans and seeds. The Codex Borbonicus shows priests as diviners, *chilanes*, casting maize seed on a mat. To this day the highland Maya still cast red beans, *mech*: an odd count indicates a positive answer, an even count a negative answer. One Mayan scholar, the late Linda Schele, described her own with a Mayan diviner in Chichicastenango, Guatemala (Freidel et al. consultation, 1993). After Schele had posed her question, the old man asked her to speak her name out

The Eight Trigrams of the I Ching

In combination as upper or lower parts of a hexagram, these give rise to 64 hexagrams (8 x 8).

Chien (The Creative: strength, heaven, father, south)

—

—

—

Chen (The Arousing: movement, thunder, first son, north-east)

– –

– –

—

K'an (The Abysmal: danger, water, second son, west)

– –

—

– –

Ken (Keeping Still: rest, mountain, third son, north-west)

—

– –

– –

K'un (The Receptive: yielding, earth, mother, north)

– –

– –

– –

Sun (The Gentle: penetrating, wind/wood, first daughter, south-west)

—

—

– –

Li (The Clinging: light-giving, fire, second daughter, east)

—

– –

—

Tui (The Joyous: joyful, lake, third daughter, south-east)

– –

—

—

loud, then gathered his bright red beans into a pile, and swiftly, with deft turns of his wrist, divided it into smaller piles. He then arranged the piles into groups of four forming two rows lined up on the small table in front of him. All the time he chanted prayers, pausing occasionally as he listened to the 'lightning in his blood'. He gathered the beans together and laid them out three more times in quick succession, asking Schele's name each time. The man finally gave Schele his divined response to her question, an answer that she found to be 'utterly unexpected'.

One of the classic forms of sortilege is geomancy, the casting of handfuls of soil. It is a method of great antiquity, at least as old as ancient Greece, and is still practised in many parts of the world. In the simplest and most direct form of geomancy, the diviner marks a circle, square, or grid with his finger on the ground where the particles of soil are to be thrown. Muttering appropriate incantations, the geomancer shakes a clutch of soil in his left hand then casts it down and studies the patterns of particles that have been produced. Interpretations accord to learned formulas. Sometimes the diviner will mark the divining area with lines or sigils to aid his analysis of the patterns. After the divination has been given, the seer clears the ground. Geomancy has taken varying forms at different times and places. Sometimes pebbles, twigs, seeds, beans, or other small objects are used. Even animal tracks: the Dogon of Mali, West Africa, leave a grid drawn on soft, sandy ground overnight, and in the morning inspect it for animal tracks (Plate 31). The type of animal that made the marks, and their positions on the grid are together taken into account.

Arabs use sand, as might be expected, and it was probably the spread of Islam that helped carry the art of geomancy we know most about today around Africa and ultimately to India and Europe. Among the first European texts on geomancy were *Ars Geomantiae* and *Geomantia Nova* written in the twelfth century by Hugh of Santalla, in Aragon, Spain, a region that had been conquered by the Moors in the eighth century. Geomancy became a popular form of divination in medieval Europe, and as *Goral Ha-hol* (the lot by sand) or *Hokmah Ha-nekuddot* (the science of points) was also incorporated into the Jewish tradition of the period. Around the turn of the sixteenth century, the astrologer and occultist Heinrich Cornelius Agrippa connected geomancy with astrology. Western geomancy developed into a system in which random points marked on paper are converted into a combination of figures (see 'Principles and Practice' below).

Aeromancy is the interpretation of atmospheric phenomena, of portents. The Chinese were great portent watchers. Comets, meteors, and eclipses were all grist to the Chinese diviner's mill, as were fireballs, lightning, ball lightning, and what we today would call UFOs, or, at least, unexplained aerial phenomena. When stars and stones fell from heaven over Shaanxi province in AD 164, Xiang Kai warned the Emperor that he needed to mend his ways. His Highness was not too pleased with this advice, and promptly jailed the seer. The Japanese, too, took aerial events as omens. In 1606, fireballs were repeatedly seen over Kyoto, and one that looked reminiscent of a wheel hovering near the Nijo Castle was widely interpreted as a portent. The Aztecs were rattled by signs and wonders in the heavens in the decade before the Spanish arrived in 1519. Among the portents was an unexplained brilliant light that stayed in the sky for months, and a thunderbolt which supposedly caused a fire in the Temple of Huitzilopochtli in Tenochtitlán. The Europeans likewise saw unusual heavenly phenomena as signs from God foretelling great events – usually, disasters. As in China, fireballs, meteors, and other luminous phenomena were thought to be fiery flying dragons. The *Anglo-Saxon Chronicle* entry for AD 793, for example, tells of 'terrible portents' that appeared in Northumbria. There were 'exceptional flashes of lightning, and fiery dragons were seen flying in the air'.

Weather lore is a survival of aeromancy. In Wales, for instance, thunder in February predicts a marvel during the summer, while changes in the appearance of the Sun, such as refractive effects, warn of disaster. There was also a more interactive divination tradition in France and central Europe in the form of wind magicians or 'cloud leaders' who could supposedly control meteorological phenomena such as hail. They also held shamanistic wars or 'night battles' with sorcerers in other areas who were trying to steal rain. The spirits of these weather magicians – known in some parts as *tempestarii* or *tempestatum ductores* – were believed to fly up to the clouds when they were in trance.

Divination and Death

In Europe there is a large repository of lore related to death omens, and birds figured prominently in this. Salisbury Cathedral, as an example, was reputed to attract mysterious 'White Birds'. These albatross-like avians were said to appear whenever a Bishop of Salisbury was about to die. There were reports of them in 1911, accurately foretelling the death of the then bishop. A similar event happened at Dornoch, Scotland, in 1816. A large cormorant was seen to settle on the steeple of the parish church, and this was viewed by locals as warning of the minister's death, which duly occurred a few days later. A white bird was said to appear before the death of a member of the Oxenham family of South Zeal, Devon, and family deaths in 1743 and 1873 were supposedly presaged by this omen. In north-east Scotland, a crow alighting on the roof of a house was deemed to presage an impending death there. In Tibet, likewise, ravens were seen as harbingers of death if they made a nest in a person's house.

There is a great range of other kinds of death omens in folklore and tradition. A curious one related to the wedding veil. Even as late as 1939 in Nottingham, it used to be the 'done thing' for wedding-dress makers to work a long strand of fair hair through the veil they were embroidering. If it went right through without breaking, a long and happy marriage was indicated, but if it broke at the beginning, the bride would die early, and if it broke at the end, it would be the husband who would die. Another extraordinary example of death divination was a way of foretelling the fate of a sick person in Scotland. Two holes were dug in the ground, one representing the 'living grave', the other the 'dead grave'. The poor invalid was placed between the two without being told which was which. If the person turned to the living grave he or she would survive, but if to the other, death was certain to be the outcome.

Among many other bizarre traditions, the belief that the appearance of strange lights was a harbinger of death is noteworthy. Classic in this regard is the Welsh tradition of the corpse light or candle. At the turn of the twentieth century, an old Welshwoman who spoke no English told the great American folklorist W. Y. Evens-Wentz about such lights seen in and around Nevern, in south-west Wales, the region where the bluestones of Stonehenge are thought to have originated. She claimed that corpse candles appeared like 'a patch of light', usually about 'as big as a pot', and were not a flame 'but a luminous mass'. A pale green one was seen in Nevern just before the death of the local doctor. (There might be something over and above mere superstition involved here, as in the 1990s residents of the hamlet of Nevern reported being pestered by a light the size of a basketball.) Traditionally, the corpse light would appear outside the house of the soon-to-be-deceased, then wend its way to the nearby graveyard. Sometimes, however, the light might intercept the unfortunate person in the street. The rule seemed to be that if a strange ball of light was encountered, one should stand stock still or look preoccupied in the hope that the light would pass by.

As might be expected, November Eve – Hallowe'en, the pagan Celtic *Samhain* – was identified as a time suitable for divination, for it was traditionally when the barriers between the worlds of the living and the dead could be temporarily breached. Prehistoric burial mounds were considered to open and their inhabitants free to walk abroad at that time, and in Wales it was said that a spectre sat on every stile.

Naturally, the eerie evening was ideal for divining who would die in the forthcoming year (for *Samhain* was the pagan Celtic New Year). There was a distinct form of divination in Britain known as the 'Church Porch Watch' or 'Churchyard Watching'. As well as on

Hallowe'en, it could be conducted the next day, All Saints' Day, or New Year's Eve, Midsummer Eve, or Christmas Eve. The preferred time, though, was St Mark's Eve, 24 April. The seer, alone or accompanied by inquisitive village folk, would stand in the churchyard between 11 p.m. and 1 a.m., in sight of the church porch or door, and during the night a spectral procession of those local people who were going to die in the forthcoming year would be expected to appear, passing through the entrance of the church. An ear would also be kept open for prophetic murmurings from within the dark and empty church. It was recorded in 1673 that during one Church Porch Watch in a Yorkshire village, two seers observed as many as 140 souls drift into the church. Later that year, the plague broke out in the village. Although anyone could try their hand at the Church Porch Watch, there were seers who specialised in it. One such was Margaret Dove, known as 'Old Peg Doo', who 'used to watch on St Mark's Eve, in the north porch of the Priory Church, Bridlington'. Other famed churchyard diviners included 'Milkey Lawrence' of Flamborough, and Ben Barr of Northamptonshire.

In the Netherlands there was a related tradition, involving a specialist group of diviners known as 'Precursors', who were said to be able to see future funeral processions moving along that country's special corpse ways known as 'death roads' (*dodenwegen*) or 'spook roads' (*spokenwegen*).

Death-related divination in one form or another has been practised by virtually all ancient and traditional cultures. Take the Kwaio of the Solomon Islands in the Pacific, for example. They see illness and other misfortunes as often being due to displeased ancestors. Their diviners, therefore, have to contact the ancestors when attempting to help an ill person or someone in trouble seeking their advice. They use a method called *arina*, which involves collecting green cordyline leaves and drying them over a fire. The leaves are then stripped from the midrib into half-widths, knotted, then 'magicked'. After discussion with his client, the diviner then starts asking the ancestors, the *adalo*, a series of questions to find out the cause of their displeasure and the remedy. As he does so, the diviner wraps each leaf round the index finger of his left hand and pulls it with the other till it breaks. Where the knot comes relative to the break point determines whether the ancestor has replied to each question in the affirmative or kept silent.

Death by sacrifice, whether of humans or animals, was often used for divination. The pagan Celtic Druids killed their sacrificial victims by stabbing, impaling, shooting with arrows, burning, or drowning. They then either divined from the entrails of the victim, or practised hieromancy – studying the person's death throes, the angle the eyes took at death, or the patterns created by blood issuing from the body. The Aztecs incorporated similar forms of divination in their sacrificial religion.

Divination by means of communication with the spirits of the dead is called necromancy. The classic example of this black art that is often quoted is the Bible story about the 'witch of Endor' who raised the soul of the dead Samuel to seek knowledge of the future from it on behalf of Saul. This indicates the antiquity of the practice, as does the description of a necromantic ritual by the Roman dramatist Seneca, telling of a burnt offering and a blood-covered altar. In his *Pharsalia*, written in the time of Nero, Lucan describes how the witch Erichtho prepared for a necromantic operation by squatting in tombs and surrounding herself with gobbets of flesh and other body fragments from children's funeral pyres. She sought a fresh corpse because it would have its lungs in workable shape, as old corpses 'only squeak incoherently'.

Various forms of necromancy developed in Renaissance and post-Renaissance Europe. Bodies or body parts would be appropriated and magic sigils marked on them as parts of rituals aimed at conjuring departed souls. According to some forms of necromancy, the operation could take place at locations such as isolated crossroads, ruins, lonely forests, or windswept moorland, as well as churchyards. Churchyard necromancers would prepare themselves for several days before opening a grave: they might dress in musty grave clothes, eat dog's flesh and black bread baked without salt, and drink unfermented grape juice.

The Church was very hostile to necromancy, equating it with raising the Devil, and it is only in relatively recent times that the idea of ghosts has been conceptually separated from that of demons.

Modern spiritualism is the more benign ghost of necromancy. The modern medium uses trance in order to contact the spirits of the dead on behalf of living relatives, to seek reassurance for them and any information the dead soul may wish to pass on. Other, non-trance methods of spirit divination also exist within spiritualism, such as the ouija board or the practice of planchette (see below).

Place and Divination

The founding of cities and buildings, especially temples, was usually accompanied by divination in former times, and certain types of location and directions had divinatory associations.

Etruscan diviners (haruspices) possessed a doctrine of orientation. This is also evidenced in their augury and skylore which we will touch on shortly, and in their role in the founding of Etruscan and Roman towns, which was described in Part One. The street layout from a centre was due to surveying, but the founding of that centre point, the ***mundus*** or navel point, resulted from an act of divination.

In the world of the ancient Maya, the diviners used a variety of divining stones, the clear crystalline ones among them being referred to as 'stones of light' which are still used today by the highland Maya to ascertain the true location of the four corner points in an area, especially when that area has to be cleansed ready for ceremonial activity. We need have no doubts that this recalls the practice of the diviners who first laid out the holy, ceremonial cities of the ancient Maya, and we have already noted (Part One) that these had subtle centre points or 'navels'.

Animal behaviour was used by diviners in many ancient cultures in order to determine the appropriate location for a building or town. The legend concerning the founding of the Aztec capital, Tenochtitlán, is replete with such references. The Aztecs were wandering, seeking their ancestral homeland. A priest had a vision

Figure 18: Zeus Ammon.

in which he saw that the sacred spot was marked by a large nopal cactus on which an eagle perched. As they combed part of the Valley of Mexico the next day, they saw an eagle sitting on a cactus and this was recognised as the sought-for sign. At the spot they erected a simple platform with a reed temple as a shrine to their deity. This spot later evolved into the great pyramidical temple, the Templo Mayor, of Tenochtitlán. The ancient Greeks, too, had myths about animals leading humans to the place where a city was to be built – a white sow figured in some legends. The oracle temples at Dodona and Thebes were said to have been built on locations flown to by doves that uttered in human voices. Another legend tells of a ram leading an army to a spring in the Libyan desert and then promptly disappearing. The spot became the Oracle of Zeus Ammon.

A faint echo of probably pagan divination by animals is also preserved in certain folktales concerning the founding of Christian churches, such as in the Sussex village of Alfriston. The church there stands on an ancient Saxon mound on the Tye, the village green. Legend tells that the building's foundations had originally been started at another location nearby, but each night the stones laid that day were mysteriously thrown through the air to land on the mound on the green. Concerned at this supernatural occurrence, the villagers were at a loss as to how to proceed. Eventually a village elder noticed four oxen sitting on the Tye with their rumps touching, thus creating a cross shape. The folk of Alfriston took this as a sign, and built their church at that spot with no further trouble.

Divination also played a part in the founding of humble dwellings. In Ireland it used to be the custom even up to the nineteenth century for a new spade to be stuck in the ground at the selected spot before building began. If it had not been removed overnight by the fairies, then it was safe to begin construction. Another Irish foundation divination involved the throwing of a hat into the air when a strong wind was blowing, and building wherever the hat happened to fall. There was a measure of wisdom to this, in that the spot so indicated was probably one that was sheltered from the winds, and so suitable for habitation.

The founding of buildings carried a great deal of symbolism over and above mere structural considerations in former times, and was seen as a powerful, even magical act in many parts of the world. When a traditional dwelling is planned in India, for instance, an astrologer selects the point directly above the head of the mythic snake that supports the world – perhaps an echo of the serpents that entwined some of the Greek *omphaloi* (Part One). A peg is fashioned from the wood of the khadira tree and driven into the ground at the designated spot by means of a coconut in order to pin down the chthonic serpent. A foundation stone is then placed over this position, and this is understood as being the centre of the world. This idea is basically inherent in cornerstones and foundation stones of buildings everywhere, even if this is now largely forgotten in the modern world.

Certain kinds of places were specifically associated with divination. Norse seers would seek out prehistoric burial mounds. They would sit on the mounds, and enter a trance state in order to communicate with the spirits there. The practice was called *utiseta*, 'sitting out'. This was also conducted at the meeting and parting of ways, for throughout old Europe, crossroads – particularly ancient and isolated ones – were seen as places of divination. One divination tradition held that if a person went to a crossroads at Hallowe'en, New Year's Eve, Christmas Eve, or some other similarly auspicious 'betwixt and between' time, and rested his chin in a forked stick, spirits of the dead would become visible drifting by.

Certain prehistoric standing stones, especially holed stones, had divinatory lore attached to them, as did holy wells and springs – the origin of the latter-day idea of the 'wishing well'. Springs and waterfalls were among the favoured places selected by Celtic seers to go in order to have prophetic dreams, as they were considered to be entrances to the otherworld, and they were similarly so regarded by other peoples around the world.

Feng Shui

Perhaps the form of ancient place divination whose name is best known today is feng shui, as in the latter years of the twentieth century it became popular in the West as an adjunct to interior design. Its ancient nature is, however, more complex than that. The term itself means 'wind-water', and was highly regarded in ancient China as a system of landscape divination. Today, popular feng shui as practised in Singapore, Taiwan, Hong Kong, and the West tends to have a rather simplistic and superstitious nature, relating to the traditional subject in much the same way that a newspaper horoscope relates to the venerable ancient art of astrology. Its roots reach back three millennia or so to animistic Taoist (Daoist) influences which in turn derived from shamanism. The precursor versions were essentially forms of ancestor worship and spirit lore. It was believed that keeping the spirits of the ancestors happy was a way of ensuring their helpful influence on the living, so the siting of tombs became an important consideration. A practice began to develop that became increasingly intricate and formalised, and which eventually spread to the siting of houses and major buildings as well.

The basis of feng shui as such began to emerge around the third century BC, and had assumed its most complete form by the tenth century AD – though it continued to evolve in subsequent centuries. Underlying the system, like ancient Chinese philosophy in general, is the concept of yin and yang, the feminine (negative) and masculine (positive) principles of the universe whose interactions make all creation. The function of feng shui is to control or influence the flow of chi for the betterment of the living and the dead. Chi (*ki* in Japan) is a complex concept for the Westernised mind to handle, and it is usually reduced to some unspecific notion of 'energy'. While this is a workable interpretation, it is probably better to think of chi as a generic concept covering the signs of an invisible force of animation as expressed in phenomena and ideas like breath, motion, spirit, life force, and so on, the negative of these being stagnant, bad or *sha chi*. In short, the same sort of characteristics that can be exhibited by wind and water. That chi also had its roots in ancient spirit lore is revealed by such feng shui features as images of fearsome demons and mythical creatures placed as protective devices either side of doorways.

Feng shui has two basic traditions woven through it, the 'Form' and 'Compass' schools. The Form School is the oldest, and deals directly with the topography. The feng shui diviner (*hsien-sheng* or *kan-yu jia*) brought in to find the most propitious site for a tomb or dwelling would look for a spot where a harmonious confluence of chi forces already existed or could be engineered. The yin element in the landscape was symbolised by the tiger, the yang element by the dragon. The forms of the land could be interpreted by the diviner as to which augured well or those that were potentially harmful. Rocky hills and mountainous places, and valleys, canyons, or rivers with convoluted courses, are yang places where chi rushes like a tumbling mountain stream. Flat or swampy country has excessive yin, possessing sluggish or stagnant chi. Direct, linear features such as roads, ditches, dykes, ridges, rows or avenues of trees, fencing, or lines of telegraph poles, are 'secret arrows' along which chi tends to be conducted. Such a direct line oriented on a dwelling is likely to bring strife and bad luck to the household, and even supernatural disturbances such as poltergeists. A balance of yin and yang is required. The ideal location for tomb or dwelling is in gently rolling countryside (the 'true dragon'), with no harsh, straight elements, the building angled to the wind, sun and hillsides in an manner approved by the canons of feng shui, and the same with any bodies of water. If the ideal spot could not be found, the feng shui diviner would attempt to create a better balance of factors by physical manipulation such as altering the slope of a hill, planting trees, or modifying the courses of rivers or streams. If the landscape was extremely flat, a depression could be made in the ground to collect chi, or fountains or ponds created, as water can attract and conduct chi. Sharp, tinkling sounds are yang, so wind chimes can be put up, or babbling little waterfalls engineered. If a straight feature pointing towards the entrance of the building cannot be altered, then it can perhaps be screened by trees or a low wall. Failing that, special mirrors can be placed on the door or gates, or fearsome 'doorway gods' images or effigies used.

The Compass School puts a more formalised veneer on basic feng shui, and brings in factors such as planetary aspects, the traditional five Chinese elements (wood, fire, water, earth, metal), the time of year, star patterns, compass directions, and astrological symbolism. This is incorporated in the reading of the landscape and makes for a complex divinatory system. Among other instruments, this school makes use of a special compass, as the name implies, the *luopan* (*lo'pan*) (Plate 32). This usually consists of a square tablet of wood, often lacquered, set into the centre of which is a magnetic compass. This is surrounded by concentric circuits, from five to thirty-eight of them depending on the complexity of the instrument. Each of these provides specific information on the stars, elements, and so forth that have to be brought into correspondence.

The Victorian Europeans who came into contact with feng shui on their visits to China introduced it to the attention of their home audiences in various books and papers. They often referred to feng shui as being a system of geomancy, which led to the earth mysteries enthusiasts of the next century adopting that term to mean sacred geography rather then the actual meaning described earlier. Feng shui continues to be practised in parts of south-east Asia, though it is officially discouraged in China. As we have noted, it has also achieved fashionable status in the West, but it is not completely portable, despite claims to the contrary, as many tenets of feng shui relate specifically to former Chinese conditions. So, for instance, a house with a narrow frontage is said to have good feng shui, but this was because taxes were assessed on the width of a house's frontage in China.

Formalised Divination

Feng shui can be seen as a formalised system of divination that was virtually a cultural institution. Among examples of institutionalised divination elsewhere was the Aztec system of *tonalpohualli*, 'counting the days', involving a 260-day cycle. This repeating round of days created a sacred almanac that is thought could have originated as far back as the Olmec in the first millennium BC, or even earlier. Long before the Aztecs, the Maya similarly used the calendar as a formalised cultural tool for divination. They employed a 'great cycle' system, referred to today as the Long Count, which started on the curiously early date of 3114 BC. Two calendars were used within this great cycle: the sacred round of 260 days (*tzolkin*), and a solar calendar (*haab*) of 360 days plus five more of bad omen. These calendars were 'meshed' together, taking fifty-two years for the same combination of days to repeat, a process today's scholars refer to as the Calendar Round. (The Aztec term for this period was *xiuhmolpilli*, meaning 'year bundle'.) The Maya had divinatory systems relating to both the 260-day cycle and the solar calendar.

In long-ago northern Italy there was the great system of Etruscan augury, which was part of what the Romans called the *disciplina Etrusca*, the 'Etruscan Discipline'. This included the study of entrails and the practice of sacred surveying, as already noted. Public divination involved the observation and interpretation of atmospheric and astronomical phenomena, and the flight and calls of selected birds in certain sections of the sky, as well as the behaviour of sacred chickens kept in the temple, to help govern the running of affairs of state (it was important to know whether the gods approved of certain actions). Etruscan diviners were highly regarded by the Romans, and they were allowed full rights in Rome, where the augur wore a mantle with a purple border, and his 'staff of office' was a rod, called a *lituus*, which had a curved top slightly reminiscent of a shepherd's crook. It is from Roman accounts that we know of the practice of Etruscan augury. In this, the diviner faced south, from a high point, a sanctuary, or a tent that limited the view of the sky. (The actual point used for observation was itself part of the Etruscan doctrine of orientation or surveying.) He would hold his *lituus* at arm's length to visually mark off a segment of sky, the *templum*, in which the movement of birds was considered significant. The diviner would then observe any omens that presented themselves. The flight of such birds as the eagle, buzzard, and vulture was particularly noted, as were the calls of crows and owls, among other birds.

The tarot is another highly formalised type of divination, and takes the form of a symbolic system of cartomancy – divination by cards. Its origins are not certain, having been documented only since late medieval times in Europe, and is popularly associated with gypsy travellers and fortune-telling. It is in fact a complex and sophisticated system of archetypal, symbolic imagery that is, therefore, in a sense, timeless. Tradition has it that the method developed in Babylonia, and that after the destruction of Alexandria in Egypt as a centre of esoteric scholarship it was used as a means of universal communication between adepts coming from different traditions and linguistic backgrounds. The system is based on elements in the cabbala, specifically correspondences between the letters of the Hebrew alphabet and the paths of the Tree of Life.

The tarot pack consists of four suits, Wands, Cups, Swords, and Pentacles, each containing fourteen cards, plus twenty-two trumps called the Major Arcana, containing images given titles such as The Magician, The Hermit, The Hanged Man, The Tower, The Devil, Strength, and Temperance. Each trump card is assigned a number between one and twenty-one, and there is zero – The Fool. Each card contains a complex image or symbol that has acquired a dynamic set of meanings allowing flexibility in interpretation.

The term 'tarot' derives from *Tara-Rota*, the Wheel of the Law, and in an individual reading the system basically comments on a person's progress through life, which involves a maze of complementary and opposing forces and influences. In a deeper and larger sense, it charts the dynamics of the cosmos, both inner and outer. When used in fortune-telling, the sitter selects seven cards from a cut and shuffled tarot pack and these are laid out by the tarot reader. Interpretation relates to meanings attached to the images on the selected cards, which way round the cards are placed, and their relationship one to another. It is a system that relies on skilled intuition on the part of the tarot reader at least as much as on rote meanings assigned to specific cards.

Astrology

The best-known type of formalised divination today is undoubtedly astrology. The term covers a range of more or less similar divination systems designed to plot the influence of heavenly bodies on Earthly events, and on the fate of human beings. More flippantly, astrology could be described as astronomy with esoteric meaning: its practice requires objective astronomical knowledge combined with an established canon of interpretative information. Its origins must reach back to the time when human beings first gazed at the night sky. There can be little doubt that the astronomical orientations of the great prehistoric megalithic monuments like Stonehenge were part of an astrological science now lost to us.

Forms of astrology appeared early in Indian and Babylonian records – the *Vedas* and cuneiform tablets respectively. When Alexander the Great conquered Babylon in 331 BC, he found that there were astronomical records there dating back to 2230 BC. From about the fifth century BC, the Babylonians had produced horoscopes – charts of the heavens for an exact time and place on Earth. Indian astrology used the fixed stars as its basis rather than the planets. By c. 400 BC, the Indians had formalised a lunar zodiac of twenty-seven equal 'mansions' – a system notionally based on the constellations through which the Moon appeared to move each month. The role of the Indian astrologer combined astronomy, mathematics, astrology, and meteorology. However, it was the Greeks, interacting with both India and Mesopotamia, who developed Vedic star-lore into a fully astrological system. The Arabs derived much of their astrology from Babylonian sources, and it was primarily through the Arab world that Europe acquired the astrological knowledge that has developed through the medieval and Renaissance periods into the Western tradition recognised today.

Modern Western astrology is essentially based on the ecliptic – the apparent path the Sun, Moon, and planets take through the sky. The Sun needs its full solar year to traverse it, but the Moon rushes along it every month. This celestial path can be visualised as a band cutting across the sky at an angle of around 23.5° to the plane of the Earth's equator, which means that it shifts its position through the year, seemingly rocking up and down, so that in the northern hemisphere it reaches its highest point in the southern sky in midsummer, and its lowest point in midwinter – the two solstices. For astrological purposes, the ecliptic is divided into twelve sections spanning thirty degrees each. These relate to the set of constellations through which the ecliptic travels, giving us the 'signs' of the zodiac: Aries, Taurus, Gemini, Cancer, Leo, Virgo, Libra, Scorpio, Sagittarius, Capricorn, Aquarius, Pisces. Each of these has its own 'meaning' in astrological terms, representing certain properties and characteristics. The annual cycle of the zodiac in astrological terms begins at 0°Aries, the 'spring point', meaning the vernal or spring equinox (21 March). In other words, the first 30° division to follow the point on the ecliptic where the spring equinox occurs is the constellation Aries, the Ram. At least,

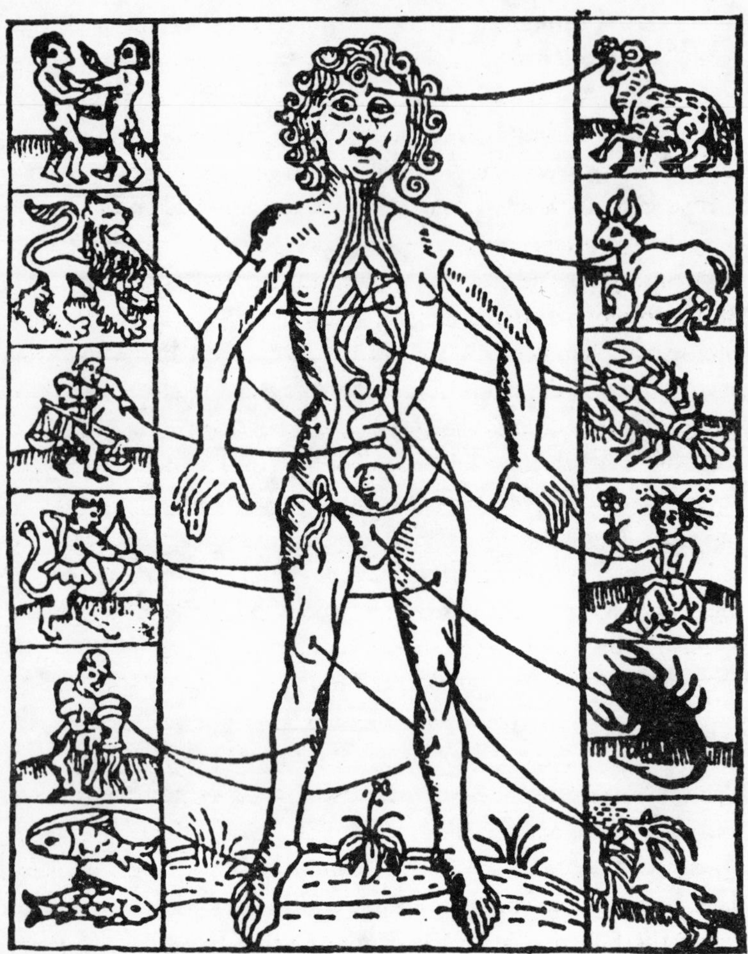

Figure 19: One aspect of astrology tries to associate parts of the body with zodiacal signs, as indicated here in this fifteenth-century diagram.

this was true at the time the zodiac was established, but because the Earth wobbles slowly on its axis, like a spinning top that is slowing down, a phenomenon called the 'precession of the equinoxes' takes place which causes the rising and setting points of stars to shift over the ages. In practical terms, this means the zodiac is gradually moving backwards through the constellations, so that today '0° Aries' is actually in Pisces. The signs of the zodiac are, therefore, somewhat notional nowadays. This is obviously of no use in objective modern astronomy, but the signs of the zodiac are still of great importance in astrological – divinatory – terms.

The zodiac, then, is the framework for astrological divination, but when a specific horoscope is being cast, other, dynamic factors come into play. The most important of these are the driving forces of a horoscope – the planets. These used to comprise the Sun, Moon, Mercury, Venus, Mars, Jupiter, and Saturn, the known planets of the ancient world, but modern astrologers have added Uranus, Neptune, and Pluto. As with the signs, a set of meanings and qualities is attributed to each planet.

Then there are the twelve 'houses'. These are divisions or arcs of the full round of the sky, the celestial sphere (which can be visualised as like two cosmic planetarium domes stuck together and enclosing the globe of the Earth). Various methods exist of dividing up the celestial sphere as locally observed, and a knowledge of spherical geometry is required, but in actuality most astrologers simply consult a Table of Houses in regard to the latitude and longitude coordinates involved.

Each house has a cusp or boundary, and the cusps of the first, fourth, seventh, and tenth houses are identical with what are sometimes called the 'four angles'. These are, respectively: (i) the ascendant, representing where the ecliptic cuts the horizon in the east, or where the Sun rises at dawn; (ii) the mid-heaven or zenith point (known in astrology as the *Medium Coeli* or MC), where the Sun reaches its highest point – 'Sun at noon'; (iii) the descendant, the setting point in the west; and finally (iv) the nadir (*Immum Coeli* or IC), the opposing point to the zenith – 'Sun at midnight'. As with the zodiacal signs and the planets, each house has a set of given meanings, which in turn modify the separate meanings of the signs and planets coinciding with them.

Finally, there are the 'aspects', which are the angles of separation between the planets on the great circuit of the ecliptic, as viewed

Planetary Attributes and Correspondences
(Some of these differ a little between astrologers)

Sun: Nobility, authenticity, glory. Ruling authority. Gold/orange/yellow. Heart; thymus.
Moon: Instincts, intuition, psyche, changeability, feelings. The public. Silver/white/grey. Stomach, chest, womb; lymphatic system.

The 'Ancient' Planets
Mercury: Intelligence, communication, reason, observation. Journalists, communicators. Yellow-brown/blue-grey/violet. Tongue, bowels; thyroid and pulmonary system.
Venus: Beauty, physical attraction, sentiment, love, sex, attainment. Artists, performers, young women. Blue/indigo/green. Nose, liver; arterial system.
Mars: Energy, courage, initiative, aggression, competitiveness. Military personnel, surgeons, engineers. Red/scarlet/carmine/magenta. Kidneys, genitals; cerebro-spinal system.
Jupiter: Development, success, humour, generosity, expansion. Teachers, legal workers, merchants, travellers. Purple/violet/indigo/cobalt. Thighs, hips, pituitary; involuntary muscular system.
Saturn: Limitations, contraction, severity, separation/death, inflexibility, inhibition, concentration. Black/grey/sage green/dark brown. Governmental or institutional systems, hermits, old men, labourers, beggars. Spleen, bones, lower legs and ankles; cerebral cortex and skeletal system.

The 'Modern' Planets
Uranus: Inventiveness, creativity, transmutation, revolution, violence. Electric, fluorescent, or bright colours. Aerospace and electronic technicians, inventors, political revolutionaries. Reproductive system.

Neptune: Romanticism, idealism, deception and self-deception, compassion, dissolution or melding. Lavender/mauve. The socially vulnerable, musicians, visionaries, mystics. Pineal gland.

Pluto: Transformation, contained or hidden power, destructive force. Blood red/black. Miners, psychiatrists, criminals, dictators, corporate business. (But is Pluto a planet or an errant moon of Neptune? This astronomical uncertainty mirrors the lack of clarity by astrologers.)

from the Earth. In any given horoscope, the angular relationships known as 'conjunction' (the approximate same location in the sky) and 'trine' (120° apart) are seen as good, positive aspects, while planets 'square' to one another (90° degrees apart) or in 'opposition' (180°) tend to have bad, negative, or difficult aspects.

The complex interactions of all these factors – the planets, signs, houses, angles, and aspects – have to be considered when the astrologer is reading a horoscope. It is an intricate divinatory ecology.

Astrology has a number of divinatory applications. The one most people are familiar with is the natal chart, the horoscope for the moment of birth. How the various astrological factors are arranged at a person's birth is believed to give the basic 'blueprint' of the personality, characteristics, positive and negative attributes, potentials and restrictions, and strengths and weaknesses. By calculating the movement of the planets as they leave the natal position, the skilled astrologer can develop further insights about how that life is likely to unfold. For a natal chart to be really accurate, though, as astrologers point out, the exact time and place of a person's birth needs to be known. Consequently, the generalised 'Sun sign' horoscopes published in newspapers can never give more than a diffuse indication, at best.

Other forms of astrology include 'horary astrology', designed to answer specific questions put by a person. In this, a chart is made for the moment the question is asked. Then there is 'mundane astrology', the purpose of which is to examine trends affecting nations, organisations, groups, political parties, and so forth. A chart can also be created for a place – if one wants to know how a particular building will fare, for instance. 'Electional astrology' is a way of casting and interpreting charts in order to divine the best times for commencing a specific activity, such as starting a business, setting out on a journey, getting married, engaging in a legal matter, and so on. Similarly, charts can be arrived at for given events, such as a natural disaster, the onset of an illness, an accident, or a period of economic depression.

Oracles

The term 'oracle' derives from a Latin verb meaning 'to speak'. As a noun it is variously applied to persons, animals, objects, or places.

People referred to as oracles are usually those given a specific social status and who utter in trance states. Such individuals served at oracle sites, as we will discuss below, but sometimes they were viewed as oracles simply in their person. As one of many such examples around the world, we might cite the female oracle or ***dianyal*** in the Hindu Kush (a western extension of the Himalaya). She would inhale the smoke from burning cedar prior to uttering her prophetic statements. Sometimes, specific persons were identified as being able to incarnate the voice of the gods. In Hawaii, for instance, it was formerly the tradition that the king would utter oracular pronouncements from within a wicker structure. Again, when an epidemic struck a region in Cambodia, it used to be the case that villagers would band together to search for a man who they considered had temporarily become the channel for the deity, in order to find out how to combat the illness.

Occasionally, specific animals were resorted to as oracles. Classic in this regard was the living bull-god oracle of Apis at Memphis in ancient Egypt. The sacred bull was identified by special markings. When one died the animal was embalmed, and the priests of the temple would travel the land seeking a calf with the requisite markings to replace it. The way the oracle worked was that the outcome to a question or petition was indicated by whether the creature accepted or refused the food that was offered to it, or which of two stalls it would go into after the food had been offered. Pliny records that early in the first century AD Germanicus Caesar, a Roman general and nephew of the Emperor Tiberius, received a negative response when he consulted the sacred bull. The Roman duly suffered an untimely death near Antioch, Turkey.

Certain objects could be perceived as being oracular agents in their own right. The post-Conquest Maya of Quintana Roo, as an example, had a wooden image known as the 'Talking Cross', which formed a focal point for them in their resistance of the Spanish encroachment. On rare occasions, the object could 'talk' on its own, but more often it had a human interpreter. The phenomenon of Talking Crosses emerged several times after the Conquest, nagging the Indians to throw off the foreign yoke. It was a development of a pre-Columbian tradition of talking statues, like the oracle of Ix Chel on the island of Cozumel, off the Yucatán coast. This took the form of a life-sized clay statue of a woman, and was reputed to be able to speak. The Spaniards who saw it claimed that it had a hidden door behind so that a Mayan priest could furtively enter the effigy and pretend to speak as the voice of the goddess in answer to questions and pleas put to the idol. An account from the second century AD similarly tells of statues in Canaan (ancient Syria and Palestine) that moved in order to indicate 'yes' or 'no' answers to questions.

The primary sense of 'oracle' is a *place* where prophecy took place. Such locations typically were reputed to have vapours or waters, or issued sounds in one way or another. They also tended to have brooding, elemental 'atmospheres', conducive to altering the mood and inducing awe in those who visited them – the late Julian Jaynes, the Princeton psychologist, dubbed them 'hallucinogenic places'. Most had resident priests or priestesses who conducted the oracular interpretation, but some oracle sites also 'spoke' directly to the enquirer, as we shall see.

Just when specific places became identified as having oracular characteristics is unknown, but we can probably trace the tradition in Europe back to the Stone Age. Near the group of Neolithic chambered cairns (stone mounds) on the Loughcrew Hills in Westmeath, Ireland, for example, are a couple of rocks referred to locally as 'the Speaking Stones' and 'the Whisperers', which could suggest that a faint folk memory of some oracular function remains attached to the monuments. This is echoed in the suggestion of Welsh archaeologist Frances Lynch that the passages of prehistoric chambered mounds were used for communication rather than simply for access. This has been supported by acoustic tests made at such sites, showing that their chambers resonate at around 110 hertz (cycles per second), which is comfortably within the male vocal range (Devereux and Jahn, 1996; Devereux 2001). Similarly, it has been noted that a room in the Hypogeum, a remarkable subterranean Neolithic temple-tomb hewn out of solid rock in Malta, gives particularly resonant echoes, causing speculation that it may have been used for oracular purposes. But the golden 'age of oracles' belongs to ancient Greece and the Mediterranean region in general, from the latter half of the first millennium BC until the first few centuries AD.

There were many important oracle temples throughout the Greek mainland, and foremost among these were Delphi (see below), and Dodona, dedicated to Zeus. The ruins of Dodona stand near the foot of Mount Tomaros. It was claimed that Zeus spoke through a sacred and 'voiceful' oak tree. It seems it was the rustling sound made by wind blowing through the tree's foliage that was the god's 'voice'. Although this was the primary oracular form, other methods were introduced to respond to queries visitors wrote down on strips of lead. (There were so many such petitions that the temple priests and priestesses selected them by lot.) Among these other forms was a 'sounding brass', a cauldron or basin that was made to reverberate and the ensuing sound interpreted. One description of how this was done says that a statue was placed over or near the sounding brass, and when the wind disturbed special chains attached to it, they struck the brass vessel causing it to vibrate. A third form of divination was by the interpretation of the murmurings of a spring or fountain at the site. Another 'direct' oracle was that of Trophonius, on the side of a mountain at Lebedeia, not far from Delphi, where there are soaring precipices and rocky ravines. Before descending to the oracle itself, the supplicant prepared by spending a number of days in a special building near the oracle, eating a certain diet, bathing only in cold water, and making sacrifices to Trophonius. The attendant priest would divine the entrails of the sacrificed animals to let the supplicant know the most propitious time for him to visit the oracle. He was then led down at night to a river, where he bathed and was anointed with oil; then he was taken to two fountains, called Forgetfulness and Memory, and given draughts prepared from them (these may have contained psychoactive herbs). The visitor would then pray and make offerings before a secret statue of Trophonius, and finally he would proceed to an enclosure which contained an artificially constructed 'chasm in the earth', as the second-century Greek writer Pausanias described it. Entering this, the enquirer went down a ladder and was confronted by a fairly small hole, which he had to struggle into feet first. He then slipped rapidly down to a cavern and shrine. The supplicant learned of the future 'sometimes by sight and at other times by hearing', Pausanias states, somewhat enigmatically. It has been suggested that the cavern was seething with snakes, and that priests whispered prophetic messages to the frightened, confused, and possibly drugged enquirer. It has also been suggested, though, that the voice of Trophonius was a roaring underground stream or flume. Suppliants were said to return 'paralysed with terror' or semi-conscious. The priests would then help the enquirer to a special seat near the shrine, where they helped him interpret his experience.

Apart from the other famous sites on the Greek mainland and islands, such as the oracle of Apollo and Artemis on Delos, there were important oracles in neighbouring lands as well. On the west coast of Italy, near present-day Naples, was a pre-Roman oracle of the dead (*nekyimanteion* in Greek) close to Baiae. This was rediscovered as recently as the 1960s. It is an underground complex carved by human hand out of the solid rock, and is now referred to by scholars as the Great Antrum. It seems that those consulting the oracle were ferried across an artificial underground river, enacting the supposed crossing of the mythic River Styx by the dead on their entry to the underworld. Seances were held in an inner chamber beyond. Turkey had a number of important oracle sites, among them the oracles of Didyma and Claros. At the Oracle of Apollo at Claros, the enquirer was taken at night down a passage leading from the temple to a subterranean complex. The narrow passage twisted and turned like a maze. When the enquirer reached a hall, he would sit there while the priestess went on to drink from a fountain or spring that was said to impart prophetic inspiration.

Sibyls

The term 'sibyl' is a composite Greek noun deriving from the words for 'god' and 'advice' or 'message', and is applied to the women who belonged to a tradition involving often itinerant prophetesses in classical antiquity. They appear in ancient Asia Minor, Egypt, and parts of Europe, especially Greece. The origins of the tradition are unknown; it may have started in Mesopotamia, but the earliest historical evidence indicates the existence of sibyl-like prophetesses in Syria c. 700 BC.

Sibyls claimed to be the mouthpieces of the gods, and some of them even boasted that they were related to certain gods. It was rumoured that they could attain extraordinary longevity. A sibyl was not possessed like a medium, but was more like a clairvoyant. They were, therefore, distinct from the priestess, the Pythia, of the Apollo temples like Delphi, who went into ecstatic trance – though there seems to have been some mixing and matching of the written prophecies of both traditions. Sibyls uttered their rather ambiguous prophecies in verse, and tended to concentrate on the fate of nations and cities, and major events like the outcome of wars or impending natural disasters such as earthquakes and plagues, rather than dealing with specific questions about their fates from individual, ordinary people.

Sibylline utterances were written down and circulated among the general population by the *chresmologoi*, the 'tellers of oracles', who quite probably massaged some of them. For centuries, the Roman state possessed books of prophecies in Greek verse now known as the Sibylline Books (*Libri Sibyllini*), and whenever there were disasters or disturbing portents, they were consulted – even at relatively late dates, such as when Rome was threatened by the Gauls and Hannibal. It may have been Etruscan influence that persuaded the usually hard-headed Romans to resort to these prophetic texts. The developed form of Sibylline prophecy, containing earlier material, was collected together in the sixth century AD in the form of the *Oracular Sibyllina*, but it is unlikely that pagan scholars would have been familiar with the prophecies in this form.

Despite the tradition that sibyls were wanderers, particular places were often associated with specific ones (though it seems that these were usually composite identities comprising the utterances of different prophetesses). An example of this is a remarkable hewn-out grotto with extraordinary carved features in Campania, Italy. Thought to be the oracular shrine of the Sibyl of Cumae (Demophile), it consists of an artificial passageway reaching 150 yards (137 metres) into (and roughly parallel with) the cliff-face, the 'Euobean Rock'. This *dromos* is 8 feet (2.45 metres) wide and 16 feet (4.90 metres) high, and has a trapezoidal section narrowing towards the roof. The passage leads through an arched entry into a high-ceilinged room lit by an aperture on one side, and on the other an opening leading into a further chamber where it is thought the sibyl uttered her prophecies. On each side of the entrance lobby to this chamber are benches carved out of the rock walls. There is some evidence that doors were once fitted between the various chambers and passages.

Discovered in 1932, the grotto corresponds to descriptions given in Virgil's *Aeneid* (first century BC), if some poetic licence is allowed, and in other classical literature. Virgil wrote of the sibyl's voice issuing from a 'hundred mouths', and this may have been an allusion to apertures running down one side of the *dromos*, together with the window niche in the main chamber. A legend also claims that the sibyl wrote verses in response to questions on leaves laid out in order on the floor of her cave, but when the enquirer entered, the breeze blew the leaves into fluttering confusion.

Dreams and 'Temple Sleep'

Deliberately encouraging dreams for divinatory purposes is called 'incubation' (from the Latin *incubare*, 'to lie down upon'). When practised in specific religious and cult contexts, it is also sometimes called 'temple sleep'. There is some evidence that dream incubation may have been conducted by both Mesopotamian and ancient Jewish seers. The Babylonians considered the Jews as potent dream interpreters, and this is indicated by the biblical story of Daniel, who was called on to interpret the dreams of King Nebuchadnezzar. The Talmud, the collection of rabbinical literature dating to the fifth century BC but including earlier material, contains over 200 references to dreams.

The ancient Egyptians certainly practised incubation: a person seeking a dream would go to a special temple, fast, offer special prayers, and conduct rituals so as to encourage a divinatory dream. It was common for dream candidates to invoke the help of appropriate gods shortly before going to sleep by writing their names on a piece of clean linen, then burning it. Ancient China, likewise, had incubation temples, and these were active up to the sixteenth century. They were often used to assist political and governmental processes, and state officials would spend a night at such a temple prior to important meetings or negotiations. In Japan, too, the emperor would formerly have had a dream hall in his palace, where he would sleep on a polished stone bed called a *kamudoko* whenever he needed help in resolving some state matter.

The ancient Greeks called dream incubation *psychomanteia*. Dream interpretation, called *oneiromanteia* (oneiromancy) by the

Greeks (*oneiros* being the Greek word for dream), came to be considered an art of civilisation. In the fifth century BC, Hippocrates, the father of medicine, wrote an essay called 'On Dreams', in which he commented on the astrological, psychological, and physiological aspects of prophetic dreams. Greek temple sleep was aimed mainly at finding cures for illness, and accompanied the rise in popularity of the healing god, Aesculapius, son of Apollo. Over 300 temples were dedicated to him throughout Greece, the first one in Athens, and the most important one at Epidaurus. The Romans generally adopted Greek oracular practices, and temple sleep was no exception, so it is not surprising that 'dreaming' temples have been found scattered through the Roman Empire.

The Islamic world was familiar with dream divination, because the Prophet Muhammad had used dreams for religious and military purposes, and the Koran states that the study of dreams is 'the prime science since the beginning of the world'. Although Muslims did not practise Greek-style incubation, special dreams were sought by reciting special prayers during the day, a procedure known as *istikhara*.

Dream divination has had a bumpy ride in the Christian world. It fared well initially, but gradually came to be frowned upon. The fourth-century saint Jerome considered the practice to be pagan, and equated it with witchcraft. In the thirteenth century, St Thomas Aquinas warned against dream divination, considering it to suffer from demonic influence. The Protestants also officially decried dream divination – Martin Luther felt that sin and Satan were the 'fathers of filthy dreams'. In the 1500s, the Calvinist Gaspar Peucer provided a little more balance, in that while he felt dream divination was dangerous for the common folk, divine dreams could be received by holy patriarchs and prophets.

The use of dreams for divination continues as strongly as ever in some countries, such as India. This is exemplified at the Shiva shrine of Tarakeswar, an hour's train ride north of Calcutta. It attracts 1,000 pilgrims daily. The goal of the pilgrimage is the shrine of Taraknatha (the local name of Shiva). Some of those with chronic or incurable diseases undertake dream incubation at the site, a procedure known as *dharna* in Bengali. This ritual is conducted under the guidance of an officiating priest of the temple. The sick person enters a fast and lays down in a specified location to sleep and perchance to dream of Taraknatha explaining how the illness can be cured.

SITE EXAMPLES

Delphi (2)

We visited this remarkable Greek temple in Part One, where we considered it as an exemplar of the sacred centre, with its omphalos stones and founding legends. It also provides the classic example of a Greek oracle site. Its fame spread throughout the ancient world, and people seeking divinatory guidance came from far and wide to consult the Pythia, the prophesying priestess of Apollo. Visitors included mighty kings and generals and representatives of city states, as well as common folk, and so the oracular pronouncements issuing from Delphi dealt with a wide range of matters, from affairs of state, wars and political intrigue, to everyday personal problems. The oracular or mantic sessions took place in the adytum or inner sanctum of the Temple of Apollo, which received waters from the Kassotis spring.

Scholars are not completely clear as to what the mantic procedure was exactly, but as best as it can be reconstructed it seems the first stage was to sacrifice an animal and check its entrails to see if the omens for a consultation were favourable. (It is claimed by some, though, that instead of actual sacrifice, cold water was thrown on a living creature and interpretation was made of its shivering.) If the signs were favourable, the enquirer was taken into a room adjoining the adytum. This may have been the oracle chamber, but this is not certain. No women were admitted apart from the priestess herself. Questions were submitted written on

Figure 20: A Delphi Pythia or priestess divining the answer to a question put to her by a client. (*Image from the Vulci Cup, fourth century* AD.)

lead strips. The priestess prepared for a mantic session by bathing in the Castalian spring at the foot of the mountain and then burned laurel leaves, barley, and myrrh on an altar before entering the oracle chamber or *manteion*. It is also probable that she chewed a laurel leaf. Attended by the *hosioi*, 'holy men', she seated herself on a special three-legged stool or tripod with a bowl-like seat. Traditionally it was said that this device was to span the fissure that Koretas had originally discovered, allowing the fumes issuing from it to rise up to the priestess causing her to fall into prophetic trance.

The problem of the trance-inducing fumes, the *pneuma enthusiastikon*, has long exercised scholars. Some have argued that the idea of vapours issuing from the ground was simply a legend, and that in reality drugs were used. First suspect was, naturally, laurel. But Albert Hofmann, the man who synthesised LSD, has examined the plant and found no evidence of chemically active principles that could induce trance. Various other psychoactive plants have been suggested, but the most likely candidate is henbane: the Greeks consecrated the herb to Apollo, and it was used as a trance-inducing herb from Sumerian times up to the medieval period in Europe. C. Scott Littleton, an American professor of anthropology, has studied a stone slab in the Delphi temple complex that has three rectangular depressions indicating that was where the metal tripod was situated, and a hole going through its middle. He has found the interior surface of the hole to be partially charred, indicating that *some* sort of smoke had passed through it. He suggests that psychoactive herbs were burned in a basement beneath the oracle chamber, and their smoke vented up through the holed slab over which the priestess was seated.

Until recently the standard view of scholars was that there had never been fumes coming out of the ground, but the situation has recently changed. Due to road works in the vicinity of the temple, Professor Jelle Zeilinga De Boer, an earth scientist from Weslyan University, Connecticut, was able to discover active geological faulting around, and seemingly passing beneath, the Temple of Apollo. The rock on which the temple complex stands is limestone rich in hydrocarbons. This discovery opens up the real possibility that during seismic tremors, cracks in the rock could open up releasing toxic fumes of ethylene, methane, and hydrogen sulphide.

Perhaps the balanced view on all this is to consider that during the long life of the Delphic oracle, the functionaries there employed a number of mechanisms to keep the show on the road. There was certainly hype surrounding Delphi, and phoney prophecies were produced, but there may also have been authentic oracular sessions in which a fume-induced trance did take place. When conditions were suitable, that is, when there were seismic tremors (a common occurrence at Delphi), these fumes may well have been from the ground. When they were not available, however, they may have been substituted by smoke from burning psychoactive plants.

Epidaurus

This was the main sanctuary of Aesculapius in ancient Greece. It was partly a religious retreat and partly what we would today call a health spa, and like the hundreds of other Aesculapia in Greece, temple sleep or *psychomanteia* was one of its prime therapies. When patients resorted to the temple they had to undergo a period of purification, which involved copious washing at the springs that were a feature of all the sanctuaries of Aesculapius, then under guidance they would take herbal preparations and go to sleep in a special cell known as an *abaton*, hopefully to dream of the god Aesculapius. The temple environment was liberally filled with statues and carved reliefs showing Aesculapius and his daughters, and it is thought that in some cases harmless snakes slid freely across the temple floors, recalling the fact that a snake entwined around a staff was the god's emblem – the caduceus. By the time patients came to take their healing sleep, therefore, the set and setting of the temple would have created a powerful psychological state of expectation in them. In the dream, it was hoped that the means of a cure would be shown. The temple helpers were known as *therapeutes*, and may have conducted operations as well as help interpret dreams for the patients, for there is evidence that the floors of abatons were at times covered in blood. The therapeutes also sometimes applied poultices and ointments to the afflicted parts, and in cases of ear and eye complaints, a temple snake would be used to lick the eyelids or ears.

That cures were sometimes actually effected is indicated by the many votive models of limbs, heads, genitalia, and other body parts made from terracotta left with testimonial plaques by visitors who felt they had been cured. There are also forty-four contemporary records (or adverts) concerning specific healings, written on stelae recovered from the site. One Heraieus of Mytilene was embarrassed because he was bald, having 'not a hair on his head, but a great deal on his chin'. He slept in the shrine and 'the god, anointing his head with a drug, made him grow hair'. Another inscription tells that a man blind in one eye had its vision restored as a result of a dream visitation from Aesculapius. 'The god seemed to boil some medicine and, drawing apart the lids, to pour it in. When day came, he went out seeing with both eyes.'

Epidaurus is nowadays a grand and picturesque ruined complex. It is overlooked by a mountain that in myth was where Aesculapius was brought up and learned his healing arts. Worship of Aesculapius commenced at the site in the fifth or even sixth century BC, and it was an established complex by the fourth century BC. This included a temple, hotel, stadium, amphitheatre, a curious circular building called the Tholos, which may have housed the god's healing snakes, as well as the Enkoimeterion where the cells for the healing sleep were located. This was situated alongside a well so ancient it predated the temple itself. The sanctuary was ransacked in 86 BC. Eventually, the site was Christianised with a large basilican church.

As a footnote, it is worth recalling that the mole was widely associated with divination in old Europe. It is interesting that the Greek version of the name Aesculapius is derived from the ancient Greek word for the rodent mole, and it is even more intriguing that the Tholos had the interior layout of a molehill.

Men-an-Tol

Holed standing stones anywhere in the British Isles were typically resorted to by people in order to obtain omens before going on a journey, or in matters of life and death. Men-an-Tol in the Land's End district of Cornwall was one such that was consulted. The folk belief attached to the stone says it can be used as an oracle or for healing. If the latter, the sick person, usually a child, has to crawl or be passed through the stone's large hole, and then dragged three times round the stone. When used for divination, it was said that two

Figure 21: Men-an-Tol holed stone and outliers. These stones are now known to have been part of a stone circle. (*J. T. Blight*)

brass pins placed one over the other on top of the stone will acquire a peculiar motion when questions are addressed to it. These movements are then interpreted in order to arrive at a response. The tradition does not state it, but it must be assumed there were local 'wise people' who would have been proficient at such interpretations.

Recent discoveries about the stone have been made by archaeologists, showing that it was part of a stone circle. In 1999, it was subject to an attack by vandals using napalm. The stone itself would have to be consulted to find out what possible rhyme or reason there could be in such an action.

The Hill of Tara

This was the seat of the High Kings of Ireland in pagan Celtic times. It is situated in County Meath, and was the meeting place of five great roads from the Provinces of Ireland. It was a mesomphalos, a sacred centre. It is a multi-period site, and had its origins in pre-Celtic times – the Bronze Age certainly, and very probably the Stone Age, too, being a complex of earthworks and mounds on a hilltop. The ancient literature that refers to Tara's role in the determination of sovereignty, though, ultimately derives from the pagan

Celtic, Iron Age era. According to these sources, it was at this place that the initiatory rites for sacral kingship were held. Two elements of these are related to divination. One was the *Tarbhfhess*, or 'bull-sleep'. This was a Celtic version of temple sleep, used to divine who was the correct man to be the next king: a bull was killed and the appointed seer ate its flesh and drank a broth made from it. He then went to sleep while being chanted over by four Druids, and was expected to see the rightful king in a prophetic dream. It was said the seer would be slain if he made a mistake. The second part of the divination came when the prospective king had to touch the Lia Fail, the Stone of Fal (Plate 33). If he was the correct choice, the stone was said to produce a sound – a cry, or even a piercing shriek. A stone stands in the earthworks of Tara to this day, and most authorities think it is probably the original Stone of Fal, though it may have been moved from its original position on the hilltop. The magical monolith stands 5–6 feet (1.52–1.83 metres) tall, and is phallic in form – probably another allusion to kingship.

PRINCIPLES AND PRACTICE

Principles

In seeking the ruling principles involved in divination, it is important to filter out those aspects of the practice that down the ages have amounted to no more than deceptive procedures, manipulative or political utterances, deliberate obfuscation, and rank superstition: a real, underlying principle can only exist where a genuine process is taking place. Where this is the case, it can be seen that what is involved in divination is a structured procedure for reaching the unconscious mind. Divination allows the collection of information without involving the interfering intellect, yet nevertheless allowing it to translate the unconscious information through the symbolism, terminology, and methodology of whatever divinatory system is being used.

As we have seen, there are some divination methods that are simple and basic, while others are elaborate and complex. The only distinction between these levels is that the complex systems possess more intricate and sophisticated mechanisms for decoding the divinatory information; they provide a better scaffold for the intuition to scramble over, using layers of processing, archetypal images, and so forth. When trance divination is involved, the accessing of the unconscious mind is of course direct, but the multitude of non-trance methods allow a structured access without recourse to trance.

The type of language often associated with divination enhances this interaction with the unconscious mind. The verses of the sibyls and the Pythia, or the 'praises' of the African bone diviners, all allow a flux of ambiguous and paradoxical imagery with 'hanging meanings' to facilitate the essentially unconscious processing that divination invokes. Anthropologist Richard Webner calls this 'the poetics of divination'.

We have seen that oracle sites often use natural roaring sounds such as rushing water, wind in foliage, or reverberating echoes to provide an acoustic matrix within which a person can 'hear' divinatory information. Many of us have had experiences when in listening to a high wind or a roaring waterfall we have fancied we could hear voices calling. It is only a small step from that to a more organised and enriched form of 'communication' with the beyond, or whatever we choose to call non-mundane sources of information.

But what is the nature of the information supplied by the unconscious mind? It need not necessarily be paranormal – many matters a person seeks help with in divination really boil down to a need to observe, calmly and dispassionately, events, circumstances, and life trends in order to be able to make a fairly accurate assessment of what the outcome of a particular situation is likely to be. Divination can offer that kind of vantage point. Often the information we might be seeking is actually held in our unconscious mind – diagnosis of a health condition, for example, and what the body needs for it to be remedied.

There is, nevertheless, at least anecdotal evidence that genuine foreknowledge or precognition can also occasionally be accessed by the unconscious mind. A good example of dream precognition is the famous case involving Abraham Lincoln, the American president, who dreamt of his own assassination. A few days before John Wilkes Booth shot him, Lincoln dreamt that he was walking around the White House and encountered a grieving group of people around a body that had its face covered. He was told that it was the President, who had been killed by an assassin. Again, the famous writer Mark Twain (Samuel Clemens) dreamt of seeing the corpse of his brother Henry laid out in a metal coffin. On its chest, the body had a bouquet of flowers. Shortly afterwards, a Mississippi river boat exploded and Henry was among those killed. When Mark Twain went to see the body, it was laid out in a metal coffin in a temporary morgue. While Twain was there, a hospital worker came in and placed a bunch of flowers on Henry's body that was identical to the one Twain had seen in his dream. Another famous author, Charles Dickens, claimed to have had a dream in which he saw a woman in a red shawl who said, 'I am Miss Napier.' Dickens thought it had been a 'preposterous' dream as he had never heard of a Miss Napier. Yet that very evening, after he had given a reading, the woman he had seen in his dream appeared and introduced herself – as Miss Napier.

Yet another well-known writer was involved in an example of how the unconscious mind can supply information by inexplicable means. In

March 1970, a parapsychologist, Alan Vaughan, watched the author Kurt Vonnegut on TV. A couple of nights later, Vaughan had a dream about Vonnegut in which he saw the writer in a house full of children, and planning to leave on a trip to an island called Jerome. Vaughan sent a letter to Vonnegut in which he described the dream. Vonnegut replied, saying that on the night of the dream he had had dinner with Jerome B., the author of children's books, at which they had discussed Vonnegut's forthcoming trip to the British Isles. This case demonstrates particularly well how information from subconscious sources can often be associative in nature, and while being somewhat 'scrambled' still retain references to actual events.

Practice

Divination is traditionally bound up with firm beliefs that supernatural powers 'speak' through whatever form of divination is being employed. Even if we can no longer readily subscribe to that kind of belief, it can nevertheless greatly assist the effectiveness of divination if we at least adopt an ambivalent posture between traditional and modern terminology and concepts *while the process is actually taking place*. It helps the psychological set and setting, allowing more to be gleaned from the exercise.

One way of exploring practical divination is to experiment with a well-established method. Choose one that is accessible. You might decide, for instance, to explore palmistry, a method that is literally 'to hand'. There is no need for this book to go into this method, as it has many teachers, and there are numerous books on the topic. Another recommended divination system is the I Ching. In this, as we have noted, one casts yarrow stalks or coins in order to obtain combinations of the eight basic trigrams. Again, there are any number of versions of the I Ching, some of them lightweight and humorous, others more sober. My personal recommendation is the Bollingen version translated by Richard Wilhelm, with an introduction by Carl Jung. I have used the I Ching for thirty years, but only sparingly, at key points in my life when I truly need guidance. I've found that it always gives sensible advice, and is sometimes astoundingly prophetic – even when I have not wanted to hear the answer. I advise that you never use the I Ching in a flippant manner. This is illustrated by a true incident: a psychologist friend of mine many years ago was shocked that I actually consulted the I Ching. I argued that it could give helpful information, and challenged him to use it. He resisted at first, then did consult the oracle, asking if it was authentic. He obtained a response that said, in part, 'Do not mock the Sage'.

Indeed, any divinatory method should be approach seriously. A jokey approach tends to result in valueless responses. There can be a measure of fun involved, but not disrespect.

If you want to get down to divination straight away, a set of methods is presented below. The methods range from those that are fairly quick and easy to try out, to those that require a measure of sustained application and effort. Some are based on traditional techniques while others are highly innovative, but all of them will allow you to test the basic principles of divination and to develop your intuitive abilities. If you want an answer to a specific question, make sure you take time to phrase it clearly and well – careless questions lead to confusing responses, whatever the method of divination. And be aware that some forms of divination can be approached in a more general way, with an openness or 'reaching out' for precognitive insight or 'otherworld' guidance. Sometimes you don't know what it is you need to know!

One final comment before we consider the exercises: divination is a non-rational process, and it should never be relied on to the exclusion of rational, responsible thinking. It is best to use it as a supplementary information source.

Turning Over New Leaves

One of the simplest techniques of divination is bibliomancy – flicking randomly to a passage in a book while reciting a particular question or holding it firmly in your mind. It is best if you use some thick, dense tome, and one that you are totally unfamiliar with – perhaps something you pick up at a car boot sale or a secondhand bookstore. And make sure it is a book you have never read. When you have randomly selected the page, scan it to see if it contains subject matter, or a word, phrase, sentence, or passage that you can associate with the question in hand. Then allow your intuition to dwell on what you find in order to see if you can recognise a meaningful message that relates to whatever your query has been about.

Instead of flicking the pages of the book manually, you could write numbers equivalent to the number of pages in the book on slips of paper, place them in a container, then draw one out after you have posed your question.

Cloud Nine

Another simple – and enjoyable – form of divination is cloud reading, what the pagan Celts called *neladoracht*. You need to select your time and place for doing this. First, choose a day when the sky is scattered with interestingly shaped clouds – such as after a storm, or on one of those bright spring days that has fluffy white clouds scudding across the azure heavens. Find an open space where you have a wide view of the sky. Lie on your back and look up at the heavens. Have the question you are concerned about clearly in your mind, as you watch the clouds softly float past, watching them slowly change their outlines as they move. As children, we all saw castles in the clouds. Remember? Now that you are older, you will observe that clouds behave very much like thoughts, arising, moving, shifting their forms, passing by or dissolving away. Think of the sky beyond the clouds as the perfect enlightened state of mind, and the clouds as the scudding associations we all make in our thinking and which constantly cloud the essence of our nature. Let the clouds and your thought processes merge. Pick up on any shapes that lead to further associations, and let those in turn lead you to a better understanding of the problem or issue you are grappling with.

To accustom yourself to this technique, take a look at the photograph we supply you with (Plate 34). What different things do the shapes of these storm clouds suggest to you? Treat this as an exercise to develop your intuitive skills, rather than directly as a divination. Save that for the real thing, when the sky will be your limit.

Firing the Imagination

A form of divination very similar to cloud reading is the study of flames and embers – pyromancy. As well as the flickering, glowing, and shifting forms one can see in a fire, there are the additional factors of soporific warmth and the flicker of flames. The warmth encourages a dreamy state of mind which can be a helpful mental condition for divination, and the flicker effect can generate certain brain rhythm frequencies that also aid divination.

High and Low Spirits

Planchette is probably the simplest form of supposed necromancy, or spirit communication. Cut up paper into squares measuring roughly 1–2 inches (2–5 centimetres) across. With a felt-tip pen write a different letter of the alphabet onto each square. Arrange this alphabet around the edges of a tabletop, allowing as much of a gap as possible between each letter. You can also insert a slip of paper that says 'yes' and another that says 'no' and place these opposite each other in the circle of letters. Place a tumbler or sturdy wine glass upside down in the middle of the table. With a group of friends (a total of four or five people is optimum) sit around the table, each person resting a finger on the upturned glass. Start to collectively move the glass, so it slides smoothly around inside the ring of letters. One of you then voices a question. It could be as corny as 'Is anyone there?' What typically happens is that you initially feel yourself consciously moving the glass along with your colleagues, but at a certain point the glass seems to take on a life of its own. It will probably start moving faster and faster and more erratically, until it shoots off and hits one of the squares of paper, probably the one that says 'yes' if you have asked the leading question suggested above. Keep the glass on the move. Next you can ask: 'What is your name?' The glass will pick up speed again and start hitting various letters. This could spell out a name, but it is more likely to be gibberish at first, or even swear words and insults. It is almost like trying to tune in to a radio station more clearly, with the 'static' being nonsensical or foul words. For whatever reason, this unpleasant stage seems to nearly always occur. But if the group persists, and its intentions are serious, then this problematic stage is usually transcended and a point reached where the movement of the glass stabilises and coherent responses are made to specific questions with increased regularity.

'Hard' information can be obtained by this method, and it is a good idea to have at least one or two questions prepared that allow any answers produced to be quickly checked. When I was at college, a good many years ago, a group of us set up a formal enquiry into paranormal claims. I recall that on one occasion we conducted a planchette session in a small library in the college that none of us had visited before. When the session settled down and we began to get a more measured response from our tumbler, I asked, 'What is the third book from the left on the top shelf of the left-hand bookcase behind me?' The bookshelves were in a recess and the books on the shelf in question were not directly visible to any of us. The glass swirled around the tabletop, knocking various letters to spell out R-O-D-E-N-T. This didn't sound like a book title, and might even have been an insult, so when I went to check the designated book, I wasn't expecting too much. In fact, the title turned out to be *Of Mice and Men*. We were all duly impressed. This case also points up the fact that in planchette, as in other forms of divination, answers are by no means always direct, but can, as in this instance, use allusion or association. Dreams, likewise, tend to produce information of this type.

Some people do not like to use the planchette. Perhaps because of the foul language that so often occurs, there is a belief that the method tends to attract low-order spirits. Another school of thought considers that there are no spirits involved at all, but rather that it is the subconscious minds of the sitters that are engaged by the method – or even a group mind temporarily and unconsciously created by the sitters. Whatever the truth may be, it is probably sensible to hold a planchette session in a neutral place, rather than in a person's home.

Making Your Mark

A traditional system of divination that can be performed quite readily is the pen-and-paper version of geomancy. Start off by concentrating on the question you want answers to or at least guidance on. Speak it aloud or write it down. Then take a pen or pencil and very swiftly make sixteen horizontal rows of a random number of dots each. When you have done this, count up the dots in each row and write down the number in each case. The sixteen numbers you end up with will provide four geomantic figures (4 x 4) in this fashion: take the first four rows and for any even number draw two dots, and for any odd number, draw just one. So if the dots in the first four rows you made added up to, say, 7, 9, 4, 8, respectively, they would produce a geomantic figure like this:

*

*

* *

* *

In the Latinised lexicon of geomancy, this figure is known as *Fortuna Major*, a good sign as can be seen from the sixteen basic geomantic signs or figures and their meanings set out below.

Geomantic Figures and Their Meanings

*	* *	* *	*
*	* *	*	*
* *	*	*	*
* *	*	*	* *
Fortuna Major	Fortuna Minor	Caput Draconis	Cauda Draconis

*	* *	* *	*
* *	* *	*	* *
* *	* *	* *	*
* *	*	*	* *
Laetitia	Tristitia	Aquisitio	Amissio

*	*	*	* *
* *	*	*	* *
*	* *	*	* *
*	*	*	* *
Puella	Puer	Via	Populus

* *	* *	* *	*
* *	*	*	* *
*	* *	*	* *
* *	* *	* *	*
Albus	Rubeus	Conjunctio	Carcer

Fortuna Major (The Greater Fortune): Victory, good luck, overcoming odds, safety, security. Obviously, a very good figure indeed.

Fortuna Minor (The Lesser Fortune): Success, support, protection. A good figure.

Caput Draconis (Head of the Dragon): Inner happiness, access to esoteric knowledge.

Cauda Draconis (Tail of the Dragon): External happiness, progress in the world, a way out of a situation. This is not necessarily an entirely positive figure.

Laetitia (Gladness): Wisdom, joy, beauty, good health, equanimity. A very good figure.

Tristitia (Unhappiness): Misfortune, sadness, despondency, reduced circumstances.

Acquisitio (Gain): Profitable transactions, a positive outcome concerning a court case, an investigation, or other ongoing process, beneficial circumstances and influences in general.

Amissio (Loss): Depletion of resources, including health and property, money problems, theft, misappropriation.

Puella (Girl): A young woman, daughter, purity, softness, cleanliness. Can also indicate deceptive appearances, depending on context.

Puer (Boy): A young man, son, solidity, carelessness, argumentation. Quite a good figure if a combative situation is involved, but a somewhat negative one in many other circumstances.

Via (The Way): The way forward, way of life, way of the world, roads and paths, journey. A good sign in contexts involving travel, but otherwise should be seen as diminishing the positive potential of good figures obtained in the divination as a whole.

Populus (The People): Humanity, nations, society, crowds/mobs, audiences, congregations, organisations, groups, assemblies, reunions, mass opinions/movements. The positive or negative aspects of this figure depend on context.

Albus (White): Spirituality, high knowledge, insight, intellectual achievement, beauty, clarity, success in business or other endeavours.

Rubeus (Red): Earthiness, materiality, passion, temper, destructive behaviour, a warning.

Conjunctio (Union): Meeting, mutuality, connection, agreement, fellowship, integration, amalgamation, mergers, reunion, clarity of communication, receipt (of money, goods, news, tip-offs, etc.), making deals, getting a bargain. While generally a good figure, context is, as ever, of key importance.

Carcer (Prison): Confinement, isolation, being trapped, enslaved, forced to acquiesce, beset by difficulties, meeting resistance, limited or no options, restricted movement, no leeway, bound by the small print or other legalities, delays.

Proceed through all sixteen numbers deriving from your rows of random dots, so you end up with four geomantic signs. Then consult the panel of meanings shown here in order to interpret them, and try to apply those meanings to the question you asked in order to arrive at a general sense, a gestalt, as to the outcome of the problem you require help with.

As with all divinatory responses, geomantic meanings provide hooks to stimulate your own intuition and perception to come to bear on a question or problem with greater focus and intensity, and perhaps from unexpected angles. But if after much application you simply cannot make any kind of relevant sense of the meanings of the four geomantic figures you have cast, the system allows for a finer breakdown of interpretation. For this, you have to derive further figures from the four you have already arrived at, which are known as the Mothers. These further figures are referred to as the Daughters and Nephews, and you generate four of each of these. In the case of the Daughters, the points are produced by putting together the first or top line of each of the four Mothers to form the first Daughter, then the second line of each of the four Mothers to form the second daughter, and so on. So if, for example, you had these figures as your four Mothers:

Fortuna Major	Acquisitio	Puer	Laetitia Minor
*	* *	*	*
*	*	*	* *
* *	* *	* *	* *
* *	*	*	* *

the four Daughters each of their lines in turn produce are as follows:

Puella	Cauda Draconis	Populus	Conjunctio
*	*	* *	* *
* *	*	* *	*
*	*	* *	*
*	* *	* *	* *

You can see that the top line of the four Mothers produced one, two, one, and one point respectively, and these were arranged vertically to give the first Daughter, and so on.

The four Nephews are derived in a different way. The first line of the Nephew is produced by adding the points of the first lines of the first two mothers. If this is an even number, then two points are put down as the first line of the Nephew, if it is odd, then just one point is put down, and so on through the four lines to make up the first Nephew figure. The second Nephew is produced by a similar process using the third and fourth Mothers. The Third Nephew is produced by the same procedure being applied to the first two Daughters, and the fourth Nephew is produced by adding together the respective points of the third and fourth Daughters. So, using the example figures we are employing here, the four Nephews to result would be:

Carcer	Acquisitio	Acquisitio	Conjunctio
*	* *	* *	* *
* *	*	*	*
* *	* *	* *	*
*	*	*	* *

In all, there are now twelve figures involved in the divination – four Mothers, four Daughters, and four Nephews. The next stage is to create two Witnesses. The first of these is produced by adding the respective lines of the first and second Nephews together, and the second by adding together the third and fourth Nephews together. Thus:

Fortuna Major	Fortuna Minor
*	* *
*	* *
* *	*
* *	*

The final figure of this extended form of geomantic divination is the Judge. This is created by adding together the two Witnesses, which in this case would give all odd numbers, thus:

Via
*
*
*
*

This system so works out, apparently, that the Judge can only ever be one of eight figures: Fortuna Major, Fortuna Minor, Acquisitio, Amissio, Via, Populus, Conjunctio, and Carcer.

The reading provided by the Judge figure ought to be moderated by the implications of the two Witnesses. So if a question had been asked that had started off the particular geomantic process we illustrate here, the final outcome would be Via, and the various implications and sense this provides would have to be weighed against the Witnesses and the context of the original question.

Electronic Oracles

In this day and age you can use less traditional methods of divination, and involve basic electronic equipment you probably have in your home. First, see if you have the type of radio which you can set between stations so that all you receive is a steady hiss of static. This type of sound will help to stimulate your alpha brain rhythms, which are optimum for certain forms of divination, meditation, and similar activities. Sit quietly and calmly, mentally posing the question you want to deal with. Listen with eyes closed to the radio hiss, which should be set at a moderate-to-loud volume. See if your mind can make patterns in the sound, and hopefully form the simulacrum of words in it. Note what these seem to be, and associate accordingly as you meditate upon your question, problem, or whatever.

A visual version of this can be carried out with a TV set. The TV receiver is set off channel, so there is a fairly uniform dance of 'snow' on the screen. Sit and gaze at the screen, at whatever is a comfortable distance for you, as long as it is not too far away. Speak your question out loud, then calmly stare into the shimmering dazzle of light on the screen. As you do so, you will notice the dancing points of light coalescing into apparent patterns then dissolving. After some minutes, certain patterns may seem to form that take on more structure. Can you see faces or forms moving around? Can you hear voices? You may find that this becomes the most intriguing 'channel' you can get on your television set!

It is advisable to conduct this type of divination for no longer than about ten minutes at a time, due to possible eyestrain.

Getting Necromancy Taped

In 1959, a Swedish researcher, Friedrich Jurgenson, called attention to apparent voices he could detect in the background hiss of tape-recordings that were not picking up external sound sources via a microphone. Partly through promotion by one of Jurgenson's former colleagues, Dr Konstantin Raudive, 'electronic voice phenomena' (EVP) as it was known had become quite a hot topic in Europe by the 1970s. Further research by leading sound engineers showed these apparent voices could be detected in the background sound of factory-fresh audio tapes run on radio-shielded tape recorders (Bander, 1973). Jurgenson, Raudive, and other EVP researchers came to the belief that the voices were from discarnate spirits. Raudive even went so far as to identify (and tape record) some of them as belonging to certain people, such as Sir Winston Churchill. Jurgenson went on to develop techniques using radio static, and it was reported that he could hold conversations with the voices lodged in the hiss.

I recall that as part of a research project, some colleagues and I left a tape recorder running in the bowels of a Neolithic chambered mound in Ireland – an environment in which portable radios ceased to work, and so was presumably radio-silent. We switched on the machine and left, returning ten minutes later to switch it off. (To hear EVP, one plays back the tape at high volume. If something unexplained is heard, then a 'loop' or multiple repetitions of that passage of sound is made, amplified and replayed.) We played the tape from the Stone Age burial mound, and nearly all of it was just a continuous and very boring hissing noise. But just for a brief moment, a curious sound was heard. We looped this and amplified it, and it did indeed sound like a voice saying, 'Ghost is the listener', a 'message' which, considering the environment in which the taping took place, made a chill run down my spine.

If you want to try using EVP as a means of divination, then set up a tape recorder in as quiet an indoor location as you can manage. If possible, disconnect or muffle the in-built microphone; if that is not possible, then just ensure a silent environment (not an easy thing to do). Put in a new tape, ask your question (perhaps after making some invitation to 'the spirits' to answer your query), switch the machine on, and leave. Come back after whatever period you decide on (though ten minutes seems to be optimum), stop the recording, and at leisure replay the tape at high volume to see if you have caught any unexplained sounds. If you have, then analyse them as suggested above.

Are EVP really the voices of the dead? Personally, I think not. In my opinion, the tape sounds are just some acoustic fragments that get accidentally recorded providing a matrix sound that the mind is able to find patterns within. This is the basis of all acoustic divination. But it doesn't matter even if actual dead people are not involved; the method can work as a divinatory tool just as well. If you can, make yourself believe that you are addressing discarnate entities while you undertake this method. It helps the 'set and setting', and so puts your mental faculties into receptive 'divination mode'. Remember that all we are trying to do in divination is reach Deep Mind, by whatever route we can find that works for us.

The Voices of Nature

In addition to any other methods you try, you might think in any case of finding a place that you can identify with as an oracular site. This could be an anciently established oracle like one of the Greek temples we have discussed, but equally, and in many ways better, it could be a more accessible site that holds power for you. I would urge that you seek one that has not only moody visual properties, but that also produces acoustic effects. So, do you know of an aged tree somewhere whose dense foliage casts a shadow like a soft, green pool of twilight? A venerable arboreal entity that produces 'voices' when the wind blows through its leaves? Or a burbling spring in some dark wood, or a babbling brook cascading down through a rocky, mountain gorge or a shady glen? Or a gloomy cave mouth where the wind whispers its song? If you have found any such place, then visit it when you need to, and absorb its elemental atmosphere before settling to listen to its voice. Choose the best time of day to visit the place – dusk can add an extra dose of that requisite 'betwixt-and-between' or 'liminal' quality that half-light can produce. It is the ideal condition in which to listen to the voice of nature.

Waterfalls make the best oracle locations, in my opinion. Their power as places of divination was recognised by peoples as diverse as Amazonian Indians and Celts. Go out and seek a waterfall to be your oracular site; it can be large or small, as long as its waters make that rushing, roaring noise that provides such a rich matrix of sound and stimulates your brain's alpha rhythms. Take along a good quality tape recorder and make a tape recording of the sound of the water. Ensure that the recording lasts for at least fifteen minutes, and preferably two or three times that length. While you are making the recording, sit or lie down, close your eyes, and listen. You are engaging in a practice conducted by diviners and seers down the ages. After several minutes, you might detect changing tones or 'beats' in the water sound caused by the configuration of rocky walls and how they reverberate the sound of the waterfall. This is the individual signature of the place; think of the sounds as the story this place is telling you about itself. Think of the place as being a living presence as you continue to listen. You may next hear sounds like voices within the noise of the tumbling water. A name is called. Perhaps your name, or that of a relative or friend. (Curiously, it is quite often the name of someone you knew who is now dead.) Think of these voicelike sounds as coming from the spirits that dwell at the place – or that you brought with you. Don't resist what you hear, but let the water speak.

When you are back at home, in your usual routine, play the tape recording at selected times, such as when falling asleep at night. See the waterfall in your mind's eye; imagine that it is calling to you from out there in wild nature. Drift away to the sound of the waters, and have divine dreams.

Dream On

There are many ways to attempt divination by dreams, but first get to know your dream life. The only way to do this is to keep a dream journal. Always have a pen and paper by your bedside, and when you awaken in the morning lie still for a few minutes without opening your eyes – dream memories are fragile, and tend to evaporate when you get up out of bed and launch yourself into your day. Awakening in this manner will help preserve them that important bit longer. Lie still, and think of your dreams. If you can't remember anything at all, don't force it – there will be other opportunities. But often you might find yourself recalling just a single element from a dream. As you calmly think about that, other parts of the dream are likely to come to mind, perhaps in a haphazard fashion. Some researchers suggest that having completed this process in one bodily position, it is helpful to change to other ones, as this may help additional dream recall. When you have the main elements of at least one dream recalled, then you can open your eyes, rise, and write them down in very brief note form in your bedside notebook. Do not elaborate or 'fill in' bits you don't remember. If it is a struggle to remember your dreams to begin with, do not fret or succumb to the fallacy that you don't dream. Everyone dreams; it is just a question of whether you can recall them or not. A bonus of keeping a dream journal or diary is that it improves your capacity to recall dreams and you will find the number of the dream records in your journal increasing.

After a few months of patiently attempting to keep a track of your dreams, you will probably have produced a reasonable collection of dream records. Review them carefully, and see if you can detect any patterns in the imagery your dreaming mind likes to use. Do not rely on 'dream dictionaries' that give set meanings of types of dream – only you can interpret your dreams. Simply get to know their language. You will find that not all dreams are equal. Some will be random rehashes of the day's events, but others will contain pearls of wisdom that cannot be so readily dismissed. You will see creative intelligence at work, and though it may be your own, it is from a part of you that contains a level of wisdom and perception not readily accessible to your waking mind.

There is another value in recording and dating your dreams. Over a long period of time, say a year or two, you may note that you have had a dream that foreshadowed some event in your own life, or that happened in the news. This might be dramatic, but it could also be something relatively trivial. Sometimes, the information might relate to your own state of health. Oliver Sacks, the neurologist famous for his book *The Man Who Mistook His Wife for a Hat*, found that people with multiple sclerosis, strokes, or neurological damage sometimes dream of an improvement in their condition before a medical upturn actually shows itself. One dream researcher, Patricia Garfield, finds that when she dreams of drooping, sickly flowers and plants, it is a reflection of her state of health, but when everything in her dream garden is blooming, so is her physical condition.

The prophetic information in a dream might be direct – an actual imaging of what later occurs – or it might be associative in some way, perhaps using the puns dreams so often produce. If you recognise precognitive dreams occurring occasionally in your dream records, learn everything you can about them: do they occur with regard to particular kinds of happening; do they occur in certain identifiable conditions; do they use a particular vocabulary of imagery – do certain colours predominate, is there a certain mood or aura to such dreams, do you hear dramatic words or phrases, or high-flown language?

When you have become familiar with your dreams to some extent, you can try incubating dreams specifically for divination. Take perhaps two nights per week for incubation purposes. On those nights, change something about your bedroom. Put up an evocative picture or poster, perhaps, or lay out a special bedcover. Light an incense stick or use an essential oil you keep just for incubation. By making the place special, by turning your bedroom into a temple, so to speak, you are sending a signal to your subconscious mind. (This is one of the roles of ritual.) Stand by your bed just before getting into it, breathe deeply, and intone the question you want answering. Repeat this once or twice more. Keep the question in the forefront of your mind as you settle down to sleep. In the morning, or whenever you wake up, remember to lie still with your eyes closed to check if you recall any dreams, then write them down in your journal. Read through these descriptions later to assess whether or not there is any material there that suitably addresses the question you had. It is probable that you will have to repeat this incubation a number of times before you start to get results. In some cases, a divinatory dream can pop up some nights after an incubation.

If you find you are having great difficulty in recalling your dreams, or if they are rarely vivid, you can boost your dream power by using various aids. An important one of these is diet. Certain foods tend to promote strong dreams – cheese being perhaps the best-known example. Nutmeg is also a powerful dream enhancer, so try eating a dish that uses nutmeg an hour or two before going to sleep. Spinach pie is one example, and a search through a recipe book will soon suggest other possibilities. Nutmeg is metabolised in the body to create a hallucinogen that can greatly assist the brain's own mind-altering neurotransmitters in the production of robust dreams. Another dietary dream-enhancing option is vitamin B6. This can increase both the intensity and frequency of dreams. B6 can be taken in tablet form, or you can make an effort to eat foods or supplements rich in B6 such as bananas, broad (fava) beans, avocados, brewer's yeast, raw wheat germ, molasses, pears, salmon, herring, cabbage, green vegetables, and eggs.

Also be aware some foods can inhibit dreaming – alcohol, for instance, reduces dreaming sleep.

Another trick is to use herbs or essential oils that help promote dreams. You could even make up a special incubation pillow stuffed with several ounces of dry mugwort obtainable from any herbal supplier or even some health-food shops. Mugwort can promote vigorous dreaming. (Pregnant women, though, are advised not to use this method.) An essential oil that can help promote dreaming is clary sage. Mix a few drops of this in a carrier oil like grapeseed, and apply it to parts of the body where it will be quickly and effectively absorbed, such as the 'third eye' position in the middle of the forehead, both temples, or the armpits. Apply just a smear of the oil.

BIBLIOGRAPHY

Notes: (i) Each part of the book has its own bibliography, which, while being fairly comprehensive, is nevertheless selective to some extent. (ii) All references in the main text are included. (iii) Dates in parentheses refer to original publication.

Introduction

Bateson, Gregory, *Mind & Nature* (1979), Bantam, New York, 1988.

Turnbull, David, *Maps Are Territories* (1989), University of Chicago Press, Chicago, 1993.

One: World Centres

Bloch, Raymond, *The Etruscans* (1956), Thames & Hudson, London, 1958.

Campbell, Joseph, *Mythologies of the Great Hunt*, Harper & Row, New York, 1988.

Cottrell, Leonard, *The Penguin Book of Lost Worlds*, vol. 2, Penguin Books, Harmondsworth, 1962.

Dames, Michael, *Mythic Ireland*, Thames & Hudson, London, 1992.

Devereux, Paul, and York, Andy, 'Portrait of a Fault Area' Parts I and II, *Fortean Times*, nos. 11 and 12, 1975.

Bibliography

Eliade, Mircea, *Shamanism – Archaic Techniques of Ecstasy* (1951), Princeton University Press Bollingen Edition, Princeton, 1964.

Eliade, Mircea, *The Myth of the Eternal Return* (1954), Arkana, London, 1989.

Freidel, David, Schele, Linda, and Parker, Joy, *Maya Cosmos*, William Morrow, New York, 1993.

Gabriel, Kathryn, *Roads to Center Place*, Johnson Books, Boulder, 1991.

Griffin-Pierce, Trudy, 'The Hooghan and the Stars', in Ray A. Williamson and Claire R. Farrer (eds), *Earth and Sky*, University of New Mexico Press, Albuquerque, 1992.

Hall, Robert L., *An Archaeology of the Soul*, University of Illinois Press, Urbana and Chicago, 1997.

Jones, Gwyn, and Jones, Thomas (translators), *The Mabinogion*, Everyman's Library edition, Dent, London, 1949.

Levy, Robert I., *Mesocosm*, University of California Press, Berkeley, 1990.

Long, Richard, *Walking In Circles*, Thames & Hudson, London, 1991.

Malville, J. McKim, 'Astronomy at Vijayanagara: Sacred Geography Confronts the Cosmos', in Rana P. B. Singh (ed.), *The Spirit and Power of Place*, National Geographic Society of India, Benares Hindu University, Varanasi, 1993.

Michell, John, *At the Centre of the World*, Thames & Hudson, London, 1994.

Parkin, David, 'Ritual as Spatial Direction and Bodily Division', in *Understanding Rituals*, Daniel de Coppet (ed.), Routledge, London, 1992.

Pennick, Nigel, *The Ancient Science of Geomancy*, Thames & Hudson, London, 1979.

Ross, Anne, *The Pagan Celts* (1970), Batsford, London, 1986.

Stirling, William, *The Canon (*1897), Garnstone Press, London, 1974.

Trubshaw, Bob, *The Quest for the Omphalos*, Heart of Albion Press, Wymeswold, 1991.

Tyler, Hamilton A., *Pueblo Gods and Myths*, University of Oklahoma Press, Norman and London, 1964.

Urton, Gary, *At the Crossroads of the Earth and the Sky*, University of Texas Press, Austin, 1981.

Two: Pilgrimage

Appleton, Jay, *The Experience of Landscape*, John Wiley, New York, 1975.

Belloc, Hilaire, *The Old Road* (1904), Constable, London, 1921.

Boulter, B. C., *The Pilgrim Shrines of England*, Philip Allan, London, 1928.

Brenneman, Walter L., 'Croagh Patrick and Lough Derg: Sacred and Loric Space in Two Irish Pilgrimage Sites', in *The Spirit and Power of Place*, in Rana P. B. Singh (ed.), *The Spirit and Power of Place*, National Geographic Society of India, Benares Hindu University, Varanasi, 1993.

Chatwin, Bruce, *The Songlines*, Viking, Ontario, 1987.

Coleman, Simon, and Elsner, John, *Pilgrimage*, Harvard University Press, Cambridge, Mass., 1995.

Cowan, James, *Mysteries of the Dream-Time*, Prism Press, Bridport, 1989.

Dames, Michael, *Mythic Ireland*, Thames & Hudson, London, 1992.

Eck, Diana, L., 'India's *Tirthas*: "Crossings" in Sacred Geography', in *History of Religions*, vol. 20, no. 4, 1981.

Edwards, Nancy, *The Archaeology of Early Medieval Ireland*, Batsford, London, 1990.

Hammond, Norman, and Bobo, Matthew R., 'Pilgrimage's last mile: late Maya monument veneration at La Milpa, Belize', in *World Archaeology: The Archaeology of Pilgrimage*, vol. 26, no. 1, 1994.

Hanna, Span, 'Vast as the Sky: The Terma Tradition in Modern Tibet', in *Tantra and Popular Religion in Tibet*, Geoffrey Samuel, Hamish Gregor, and Elisabeth Stutchbury (eds), International Academy of Indian Culture and Aditya Prakashan, New Delhi, 1994.

Harbison, Peter, 'Early Irish pilgrim archaeology in the Dingle Peninsula', in *World Archaeology: The Archaeology of Pilgrimage*, vol. 26, no. 1, 1994.

Haren, Michael, and Pontfacy, Yolande de (eds), *The Medieval Pilgrimage to St Patrick's Purgatory*, Clogher Historical Society, Enniskillen, 1988.

Huber, Toni, 'Putting the *gnas* Back into *gnas-kor*: Rethinking Tibetan Buddhist Pilgrimage Practice', in *The Tibet Journal*, vol. 19, no. 2, 1994.

Jennett, Sean, *Connacht*, Faber and Faber, London, 1970.

Jones, Bobi, 'Small Paths', in *Selected Poems* (trans. Joseph P. Clancy), Christopher Davies, Swansea, 1987.

Kitagawa, J. M., 'Three Types of Pilgrimage in Japan', in *Experience of the Sacred*, Sumner B. Twiss and Walter H. Conser Jr. (eds), Brown University Press, Providence, 1992.

Kolata, Alan L., *Valley of the Spirits*, John Wiley, New York, 1996.

Kumar, Satish, *No Destination*, Resurgence Books, Devon, 1992.

Loveday, Roy, 'Double Entrance Henges – Routes to the Past?', in *Prehistoric Ritual and Religion*, Alex Gibson and Derek Simpson (eds), Sutton Publishing, Stroud, 1998.

Lovelock, James, 'Gaia – Science or Myth?', in *Resurgence*, May–June 1993.

Marshall, Jenny White, and Walsh, Claire, 'Appendix: Illaunloughan, County Kerry', in Harbison, Peter, 'Early Irish pilgrim archaeology in the Dingle Peninsula', in *World Archaeology: The Archaeology of Pilgrimage*, vol. 26, no. 1, 1994.

Miller, Mary, and Taube, Karl, *The Gods and Symbols of Ancient Mexico and the Maya*, Thames & Hudson, London, 1993.

Morley, Sylvanus G., and Brainerd, George W., revised by Sharer, Robert J., *The Ancient Maya*, Stanford University Press, Stanford, 1983.

Mountford, Charles, *Winbaraku and the Myth of Jarapiri*, Rigby, Adelaide, 1968.

O'Connor, Philip, *Vagrancy*, Penguin, Harmondsworth, 1963.

Patton, Mark, *Statements in Stone*, Routledge, London 1993.

Phillips, Fr. Andrew, *The Hallowing of England*, Anglo-Saxon Books, Pinner, 1994.

Pullan, Wendy, 'Mapping Time and Salvation', in *Mapping Invisible Worlds*, Gavin D. Flood (ed.), Edinburgh University Press, Edinburgh, 1993.

Ray, Himanshu Prabha, 'Kaheri: the archaeology of an early Buddhist pilgrimage centre in western India', in *World Archaeology: The Archaeology of Pilgrimage*, vol. 26, no. 1, 1994.

Singh R. L. and Singh, Rana P. B. (eds), *Environmental Experience and the Value of Place*, the National Geographical Society of India, Varanasi, 1991.

Singh, Rana P. B., 'Panchakroshi Yatra, Varanasi: Sacred Journey, Ecology of Place, and Faithscape', in *The National Geographic Journal of India*, vol. 1, no. 2, 1991.

Singh, Rana P. B. (ed.), *The Spirit and Power of Place*, National Geographic Society of India, Benares Hindu University, Varanasi, 1993.

Singh, Rana P. B., and Malville, John McKim, 'Cosmic Order and Cityscape of Varanasi (Kashi): Sum Images and Cultural Astronomy', in *National Geographic Journal of India*, vol. 41, no. 1, 1995.

Snyder, Gary, *The Practice of the Wild*, North Point Press, San Francisco, 1990.

Stopford, J., 'Some approaches to the archaeology of Christian pilgrimage', in *World Archaeology: The Archaeology of Pilgrimage*, vol. 26, no. 1, 1994.

Taplin, Kim, *The English Path* (1979), Boydell Press, Suffolk, 1984.

Target, George, *The World of Pilgrimage*, AA Publishing, Basingstoke, 1997.

Thompson, Eric, *The Rise and Fall of Maya Civilisation* (1954), University of Oklahoma Press, Norman, 1966.

Turner, Victor W., *The Ritual Process*, Aldine Publishing Company, Chicago, 1969.

von Hagen, Adriana, and Morris, Craig, *The Cities of the Ancient Andes*, Thames & Hudson, London, 1998.

Walter, E. V., *Placeways*, University of North Carolina Press, Chapel Hill, 1988.

Werbner, Richard P., *Ritual Passage, Sacred Journey*, Smithsonian Institution Press and Manchester University Press, Washington, 1989.

Whitley, David, S., *A Guide to Rock Art Sites*, Mountain Press, Missoula, 1996.

Wu, Kingsley K., 'The Road to Saint James – El Camino de Santiago: Power of Place and Environmental Ethics on a Medieval Pilgrimage Route', in *The Spirit and Power of Place*, Rana P. B. Singh (ed.), National Geographic Society of India, Benares Hindu University, Varanasi, 1993.

Yeoman, Peter, *Pilgrimage in Medieval Scotland*, Batsford, London, 1999.

Three: Sacred Geography

Alves, Lara Bacelar, 'Rock Art and "Enchanted Moors": The Significance of Rock Carvings in the Folklore of North-western Iberia', paper read at the 'A Permeability of Boundaries?' conference, University of Southampton, 1999. (B.A.R. Proceedings pending at time of writing.)

Basso, Keith, 'Stalking with Stories: Names, Places, and Moral Narratives Among the Western Apaches', in *On Nature*, Daniel Halpern (ed.), North Point Press, Berkeley, 1987.

Basso, Keith, *Wisdom Sits in Places*, University of New Mexico Press, Albuquerque, 1996.

Bischof, Marco, 'Alpine Lightshows', in *The Ley Hunter*, no. 113, 1990.

Bloom, J. Harvey, *Folk Lore in Shakespeare Land* (1930), EP Publishing, Wakefield, 1976.

Coleman, Simon, and Elsner, John, 'The pilgrim's progress: art, architecture and ritual movement at Sinai', in *World Archaeology: The Archaeology of Pilgrimage*, vol. 26, no. 1, 1994.

Deacon, Janette, 'The power of a place in understanding southern San rock engravings', in *World Archaeology*, vol. 20, no. 1, 1988.

Desjarlais, Robert R., 'Healing through Images: The Magical Flight and Healing Geography of Nepali Shamans', in *Ethos*, vol. 17, no. 3, 1989.

Devereux, Paul, *Symbolic Landscapes*, Gothic Image, Glastonbury, 1992a.

Devereux, Paul, *Shamanism and the Mystery Lines*, Quantum, Slough, 1992b.

Devereux, Paul, 'Acculturated Topographical Effects of Shamanic Trance Consciousness in Archaic and Medieval Sacred Landscapes', in *Journal of Scientific Exploration*, vol. 7, no. 1, 1993.

Devereux, Paul, *The New Ley Hunter's Guide*, Gothic Image, Glastonbury, 1994.

Devereux, Paul, *Re-visioning the Earth*, Simon and Schuster, New York, 1996.

Devereux, Paul, *Places of Power* (1990), Blandford Press, London, 1999.

Devereux, Paul, 'Did Ancient Shamanism Leave a Monumental Record on the Land as well as in Rock Art?', paper read at 'A Permeability of Boundaries?' conference, University of Southampton, 1999. (B.A.R. Proceedings pending at time of writing.)

Devereux, Paul, *The Sacred Place*, Cassell, London, 2000.

Devereux, Paul, *Haunted Land*, Piatkus, London, 2001.

Devereux, Paul, and Thomson, Ian, *The Ley Hunter's Companion*, Thames & Hudson, London, 1979.

Dobkin de Rios, Marlene, 'Plant Hallucinogens, Out-of-Body Experiences and New World Monumental Earthworks', in *Drugs, Rituals and Altered States of Consciousness*, Brian M. Du Toit (ed.), A. A. Balkema, Netherlands, 1977.

Donohue, V. A., 'The Goddess of the Theban Mountain', in *Antiquity*, vol. 66, no. 253, 1992.

Folan, William, 'Sacbes of the Northern Maya', in *Ancient Road Networks and Settlement Hierarchies in the New World*, Charles D. Trombold (ed.), Cambridge University Press, Cambridge, 1991.

Fürer-Haimendorf, Christoph von (ed.), *Contributions to the Anthropology of Nepal*, Aris and Phillips, Warminster, 1974.

Gaenszle, Martin, 'Journey to the Origins: A Root Metaphor in a Mewahang Rai Healing Ritual', in *Anthropology of Nepal: People, Problems, and Processes*, Michael Allen (ed.), Mandala Book Point, Kathmandu, 1994.

Grapard, Allan G., 'Geosophia, Geognosis, and Geopiety: Orders of Significance in Japanese Representations of Space', in *Nowhere: Space, Time and Modernity*, Roger Friedland and Deirdre Boden (eds), University of California Press, Berkeley, 1994.

Herdick, Reinhard, 'Remarks on the Orientation of the Large Stupas in the Kathmandu Valley: A Discussion of Principles of Lunar Ordering', in *Anthropology of Tibet and the Himalaya*, Charles Ramble and Martin Brauern (eds), Ethnological Museum of the University of Zurich, Zurich, 1993.

Huber, Toni, 'When what you see is not what you get', in *Tantra and Popular Religion in Tibet*, Geoffrey Samuel, Hamish Gregor, and Elisabeth Stutchbury (eds), International Academy of Indian Culture and Aditya Prakashan, New Delhi, 1994.

Kolata, Alan L., *Valley of the Spirits*, John Wiley, New York, 1996.

Lévy-Bruhl, Lucien, *Primitive Mythology* (1935), University of Queensland Press, St Lucia, 1983.

Morphy, Howard, 'Landscape and the Reproduction of the Ancestral Past', in *The Anthropology of Landscape*, Eric Hirsch and Michael O'Hanlon (eds), Clarendon Press, London, 1995.

Overing, Gillian R., and Osborn, Marijane, *Landscape of Desire*, University of Minnesota Press, Minneapolis, 1994.

Nebesky-Wojkowitz, René Mario de, *Oracles and Demons of Tibet*, Mouton & Co., 's-Gravenhage, 1956.

Nuttall, Mark, 'Place, Identity and Landscape in NW Greenland', in *Mapping Invisible Worlds*, Gavid D. Flood (ed.), Edinburgh University Press, Edinburgh, 1993.

Peters, Frances, 'The possible use of West Penwith menhirs as boundary markers', in *Cornish Archaeology*, no. 29, 1990.

Reeves, Brian, 'Ninaistakis – the Nitsitappii's sacred mountain: traditional Native religious activities and land use/tourism conflicts', in *Sacred Sites, Sacred Places*, David Carmichael, Jane Hubert, Brian Reeves, and Audhild Schanche (eds), Routledge, London, 1994.

Richards, Colin, 'Monumental Choreography: Architecture and Spatial Representation in Late Neolithic Orkney', in *Interpretative Archaeology*, Christopher Tilley (ed.), Berg, Oxford/Providence, 1993.

Roberts, Anthony, 'The Monk's Ford Ley', in *The Ley Hunter*, no. 20, 1971.

Scully, Vincent, *The Earth, The Temple, and the Gods* (1962), Yale University Press, New Haven, 1979.

Singh, Rana P. B., 'Panchakroshi Yatra, Varanasi: Sacred Journey, Ecology of Place, and Faithscape', in *The National Geographic Journal of India*, vol. 1, no. 2, 1991.

Singh, Rana P. B., 'Towards Deeper Understanding, Sacredscape and Faithscape: An Exploration in Pilgrimage Studies', in *The National Geographic Journal of India*, vol. 41, no. 1, 1995.

Singh, Rana P. B., and Malville, John McKim, 'Cosmic Order and Cityscape of Varanasi (Kashi): Sun Images and Cultural Astronomy', in *National Geographic Journal of India*, vol. 41, no. 1, 1995.

Soekmono, 'Prayer in Stone', in *Borobudur*, Soekmono, J. G. de Casparis, and Jacques Dumarçay, Thames & Hudson, London, 1990.

Stutchbury, Elisabeth, 'Perceptions of Landscape in Karzha: "Sacred" Geography and the Tibetan System of "Geomancy"', in *The Tibet Journal*, vol. 19, no. 4, 1994.

Tilley, Christopher, 'Art, Architecture, Landscape [Neolithic Sweden]', in *Landscape: Politics and Perspectives*, Barbara Bender (ed.), Berg, Oxford/Providence, 1993.

Tilley, Christopher, *A Phenomenology of Landscape*, Berg, Oxford/ Providence, 1994.

Trombold, Charles D., 'An Introduction to the Study of Ancient New World Road Networks', in *Ancient Road Networks and Settlement Hierarchies in the New World*, Charles D. Trombold (ed.), Cambridge University Press, Cambridge, 1991.

Woodward, Alfred, *Memories of Brailes*, Peter Drinkwater, Shipston-on-Stour, 1988.

Yeoman, Peter, *Pilgrimage in Medieval Scotland*, Batsford, London, 1999.

Four: Divination

Bander, Peter, *Voices from the Tapes*, Drake Publishers, New York, 1973.

Bloch, Raymond, *The Etruscans* (1956), Thames & Hudson, London, 1958.

Cavendish, Richard, *The Black Arts*, Putnam, New York, 1967.

Cornelius, Geoffrey, and Devereux, Paul, *The Secret Language of the Stars and Planets*, Pavilion, London, 1996.

Crow, W. B., *A History of Magic, Witchcraft and Occultism*, The Aquarian Press, London, 1968.

Davidson, Hilda Ellis, 'The Seer's Thumb', in Davidson (ed.), *The Seer*, John Donald, Edinburgh 1989.

Davidson, Hilda Ellis (ed.), *The Seer*, John Donald, Edinburgh, 1989.

Davies, Glenys (ed.), *Polytheistic Systems* (*Cosmos*, vol. 5), Edinburgh University Press, Edinburgh, 1989.

Devereux, Paul, *Earth Lights*, Turnstone Press, Wellingborough, 1982.

Devereux, Paul, and Jahn, Robert G., 'Preliminary investigations and cognitive considerations of the acoustical resonances of selected archaeological sites', in *Antiquity*, vol. 70. no. 269, September 1996.

Devereux, Paul, *The Long Trip*, Penguin Arkana, New York, 1997.

Devereux, Paul, *Stone Age Soundtracks*, Vega, London, 2001b.

Eitel, E. J., *Feng Shui* (1873), Cokaygne, Cambridge, 1973.

Eliade, Mircea, *Shamanism – Archaic Techniques of Ecstasy* (1951), Princeton University Press Bollingen Edition, Princeton, 1964.

Emery, W. B., *Archaic Egypt* (1961), Penguin Books, London, 1991.

Evans Wentz, W. Y., *The Fairy Faith in Celtic Countries* (1911), Colin Smythe, Gerrards Cross, 1977.

Fontenrose, Joseph, *The Delphic Oracle*, University of California Press, Berkeley, 1978.

Foreman, Henry James, *The Story of Prophecy*, Tudor Publishing, New York, 1940.

Frazer, James George, *The Golden Bough* (1922), Macmillan, London, 1932.

Freidel, David, Schele, Linda, and Parker, Joy, *Maya Cosmos*, William Morrow, New York, 1993.

Gettings, Fred, *Dictionary of Astrology*, Routledge and Kegan Paul, London, 1985.

Green, Miranda J., *Dictionary of Celtic Myth and Legend*, Thames & Hudson, London, 1992.

Grinsell, Leslie V., *Folklore of Prehistoric Sites in Britain*, David & Charles, Newton Abbott, 1976.

Hand, Wayland D., 'The Mole in Folk Medicine . . . II' in Hand, Wayland D. (ed.), *American Folk Medicine*, University of California Press, Berkeley, 1976.

Hand, Wayland D. (ed.), *American Folk Medicine*, University of California Press, Berkeley, 1976.

Hole, Christina (ed.), Radford, E. and M. A., *Encyclopedia of Superstitions* (1961), Hutchinson, London, 1975.

James, Wendy, 'The Antelope and the Uduk', in *Signifying Animals*, Roy Willis (ed.) (1990), Routledge, London, 1994.

Jaynes, Julian, *The Origin of Consciousness in the Breakdown of the Bicameral Mind*, Houghton Mifflin, Boston, 1976.

Jones, Prudence, 'Shapes in the Stars – Patterns of Western Astrology', in John Matthews (ed.), *The World Atlas of Divination*, Headline, London, 1992.

Keesing, Roger M., *Kwaio Religion*, Columbia University Press, New York, 1982.

Kevlin, Kunderke, 'Oracles in Bone', in John Matthews (ed.), *The World Atlas of Divination*, Headline, London, 1992

Laughlin, Charles D., McManus, John, and D'Aquili, Eugene G., *Brain, Symbol and Experience*, Columbia University Press, New York, 1992.

Lip, Evelyn, *Chinese Geomancy* (1979), Times Books International, Singapore, 1994.

Littleton, C. Scott, 'The Pneuma Enthusiastikon', in *Ethos*, Journal of the Society for Psychological Anthropology, vol. 14, no.1, 1986.

Manas, John H., *Divination Ancient and Modern*, Pythagorean Society, New York, 1947.

Matthews, John (ed.), *The World Atlas of Divination*, Headline, London, 1992.

Menefee, Samuel Pyeatt, 'Dead Reckoning: the Church Porch Watch and British Society', in Davidson, Hilda Ellis (ed.) *The Seer*, John Donald, Edinburgh, 1989.

Miller, Mary, and Taube, Karl, *The Gods and Symbols of Ancient Mexico and the Maya*, Thames & Hudson, London, 1993.

Morinis, E. A., 'Levels of culture in Hinduism: a case study of dream incubation at a Bengali pilgrimage centre', in *Contributions to Indian Sociology*, vol. 16, no. 2, 1982.

Oesterly, W. O. E, and Robinson, Theodore, *Hebrew Religion*, SPCK, London, 1930.

Oxenstierna, Eric, *The Norsemen* (1959), New York Graphic Society, Greenwich, 1965.

Palmer, Martin (ed.), *T'ung Shu*, Rider, London, 1986.

Parke, H. W. (B. C. McGing, ed.). *Sibyls and Sibylline Prophecy in Classical Antiquity*, Routledge, London, 1988.

Pennick, Nigel, 'Ancient Secrets of the Earth', in Matthews, John (ed.), *The World Atlas of Divination*, Headline, London, 1992.

Pennick, Nigel, *Celtic Sacred Landscapes*, Thames & Hudson, London, 1996.

Pennick, Nigel, and Devereux, Paul, *Lines on the Landscape*, Robert Hale, London, 1989.

Pocs, Eva, *Between the Living and the Dead* (1997), Central European University Press, Budapest, 1999.

Porter, J. R., 'The Seer in Ancient Israel', in Davidson, Hilda Ellis (ed.), *The Seer*, John Donald, Edinburgh, 1989.

Puhvel, Jaan, 'The Mole in Folk Medicine. . . I', in Hand, Wayland D. (ed.), *American Folk Medicine*, University of California Press, Berkeley, 1976.

Rakoczi, Basil Ivan, 'Divination', and 'Geomancy', in *Man, Myth and Magic*, vols. 5 and 6, 1970.

Regardie, Israel, *A Practical Guide to Geomantic Divination*, The Aquarian Press, London, 1972.

Rees, Alwyn and Brinley, *Celtic Heritage*, Thames & Hudson, London, 1961.

Robbins, Rossell Hope, *The Encyclopedia of Witchcraft and Demonology* (1959), Crown, New York, 1965.

Roebuck, Valerie J., 'Star Lore in the East – Sidereal Astrology', in John Matthews (ed.), *The World Atlas of Divination*, Headline, London, 1992.

Simpson, Jacqueline, *Icelandic Folktales and Legends*, University of California Press, Berkeley, 1972.

Simpson, Jacqueline, *The Folklore of the Welsh Border*, Batsford, London, 1976.

Skinner, Stephen, *The Living Earth Manual of Feng-Shui*, Routledge & Kegan Paul, London, 1982.

Spence, Lewis, *The Magic Arts in Celtic Britain*, Rider, London, 1945.

Stevens, Keith, *Chinese Gods*, Collins & Brown, London, 1997.

Temple, Robert, 'Consulting the Oracles', in John Matthews (ed.), *The World Atlas of Divination*, Headline, London, 1992.

Townsend, Richard F., *The Aztecs*, Thames & Hudson, London, 1992.

Van Der Meer, L. B., 'The Evolution and Structure of the Etruscan Pantheon', in Davies, Glenys (ed.), *Polytheistic Systems* (*Cosmos*, vol. 5), Edinburgh University Press, Edinburgh, 1989.

Walker, Deward E., and Carrasco, David (eds), *Witchcraft and Sorcery of the American Native Peoples*, University of Idaho Press, Moscow, 1989.

Walters, Derek, *Chinese Geomancy*, Element Books, Shaftesbury, 1989.

Werbner, Richard P., *Ritual Passage, Sacred Journey*, Smithsonian Press, Washington, and Manchester University Press, Manchester, 1989.

INDEX